IN PRAISE OF LITIGATION

IN PRAISE
OF LITIGATION

ALEXANDRA LAHAV

OXFORD
UNIVERSITY PRESS

OXFORD
UNIVERSITY PRESS

Oxford University Press is a department of the University of Oxford. It furthers
the University's objective of excellence in research, scholarship, and education
by publishing worldwide. Oxford is a registered trade mark of Oxford University
Press in the UK and certain other countries.

Published in the United States of America by Oxford University Press
198 Madison Avenue, New York, NY 10016, United States of America.

Library of Congress Cataloging-in-Publication Data
Names: Lahav, Alexandra D., author.
Title: In praise of litigation / Alexandra Lahav.
Description: New York : Oxford University Press, 2017. | Includes
bibliographical references.
Identifiers: LCCN 2016036605 | ISBN 9780199380800 (hardback)
Subjects: LCSH: Civil procedure—United States. | Actions and defenses—
United States. | BISAC: LAW / Litigation. | LAW / Civil Law.
Classification: LCC KF8840 .L255 2017 | DDC 347.73/5—dc23
LC record available at https://lccn.loc.gov/2016036605

1 3 5 7 9 8 6 4 2

Printed by Sheridan Books, Inc., United States of America

CONTENTS

Preface vii

Acknowledgments xiii

INTRODUCTION: A FORCE FOR DEMOCRACY 1

1

ENFORCING THE LAW 31

2

THE POWER OF INFORMATION 56

3

PARTICIPATION IN SELF-GOVERNMENT 84

4

EQUALITY BEFORE THE LAW 112

EPILOGUE 142

Notes 151

Index 201

PREFACE

This book argues that litigation is critical to American democracy. Litigation enables people to protect and promote core democratic values in the course of bringing a lawsuit. Lawsuits *enforce* the law by forcing wrongdoers to answer for their conduct; they increase *transparency* by eliciting information from their adversaries that often benefits the public; and in so doing, they help people *participate* in self-government. All of this is possible when courts treat litigants as *social equals* before the law. The common critique of litigation among people in important positions, including judges and legislators, fails to appreciate how vital litigation is to the successful functioning of American democracy. The aim of this book is to highlight that underappreciated role of litigation.

Critics of litigation focus on costs. In a series of decisions requiring more information from plaintiffs before they can file a lawsuit in federal court, even if that information is solely in the hands of the person they want to sue, the Supreme Court emphasized that litigation "exacts heavy costs in terms of efficiency and the expenditure of valuable time and resources." In other cases, the Supreme Court has underscored businesses' concern with the risk of "in terrorem" settlements—in other words, that fear of liability will cause companies to settle even suits without merit. In Congress laws have been proposed aimed at curbing litigation with names such as the Lawsuit Abuse Reduction Act and Fairness in Class Action Litigation Act, and laws have been passed to limit access to the courts for particular types of claims, such as suits under the securities laws and prisoner suits. These views find support among the general public and popular sentiment critical of lawyers and lawsuits. A book excoriating litigation, *The Death of Common Sense* by Philip K. Howard, was a *New York Times* bestseller. Congress and the courts have reacted to these perceptions by putting up more and more barriers to litigation. If this trend continues, it will ultimately undermine democracy in the United States.[1]

Judge Learned Hand famously wrote that after "some dozen years of experience I must say that as a litigant I should dread a lawsuit beyond almost anything else short of sickness and death." Less often noted is what he wrote just a few lines later in that same essay: "The administration of justice is a good test of civilization of the people where it exists; it shows their interest in equity, their freedom to adapt themselves to new conditions and their courage in protecting the weak and controlling the rapacious."[2] Today the second statement is too often ignored, but it is no less important than the first. This books aims to show why that is the case.

Implicit throughout the book are two strains of political and legal thought that should be made explicit. Both deal with a fundamental problem, which was framed by John Rawls in the beginning of his book *Political Liberalism*: "How is it possible that there may exist over time a stable and just society of free and equal citizens profoundly divided by reasonable though incompatible religious, philosophical, and moral doctrines?" This book does not presume to answer this difficult question, but it suggests that litigation is a way of continually resolving conflicts arising from the deep divisions that inevitably arise in a heterogenous society and avoiding one side or the other resorting to violence. The process of litigation at its best is an exchange of reasoned arguments. In this sense this book is in the tradition of the legal process school, a school of legal thought that emerged in the middle of the twentieth century and focuses on the process of law making and law enforcement as a way to achieve justice. Legal process theory expressed an abiding faith in the power of reasoned argument to bridge disagreements in a pluralist society. I do not mean to imply that substantive principles are not needed—indeed they are the reason people sue and what litigation is about in the deepest sense. Nor do I mean that the process of litigation will inevitably establish a shared sense of *which* substantive principles should govern. Recurring litigation of particularly contentious questions proves that conflict persists. Still, by harnessing the shared language of law and requiring the reasoned presentation of proofs and arguments, litigation provides a good starting point for deliberation. This is the strength of legalism.[3]

The second strain of thought on which this book draws is the work of political philosophers such as Amy Gutmann and Dennis Thompson and their theory of deliberative democracy. These philosophers point out the importance of having a shared process for determining and rethinking justice, a process that expresses individual autonomy and the consent of the governed through some form of reasoned deliberation. In the United States, the courts provide a forum for this type of deliberation, and litigation is the process by which it is performed.[4] By collecting and disclosing information, developing and presenting reasoned arguments in a public setting, litigation not only promotes democratic deliberation—it *is* democratic deliberation. Faith in reasoned argument is the intellectual foundation on which this book sits, but the book itself is a pragmatic look at litigation from the perspective of core democratic values that I hope are widely agreed upon.

The benefit of litigation is not that every lawsuit always reaches the correct outcome. It is not at all clear that reasoned deliberation always leads to results that all of us, individually or collectively, would find to be substantively just. The United States has made a great deal of progress toward inclusion, but often, it seems, developments that move toward a more just society are rolled back in a process of retrenchment as opposing arguments prevail. In truth, it cannot even be said that we have a national consensus on which developments in our society move us closer to justice and which move us further away. As we shall see, litigation is both part of the process of progress and of retrenchment. Still, by forcing reasoned argument, by requiring participants to present proofs and arguments and to challenge the other side's proofs and arguments,

litigation can provide an important forum for realizing deliberative ideals and enable an informed debate, especially when individuals participate on equal footing.

This book praises litigation, but it is not meant to be a starry-eyed
paean for the American court system. Instead, it is an attempt to shed
new light on the ways in which litigation benefits our democracy. The
goal of this book is not to convince you that we live in the best of all possible worlds with respect to litigation, because we do not. There are a lot
of things wrong with litigation in the United States, and these problems
have been pointed out by critics on the right and on the left of the political spectrum. One would think, however, that litigation is *all* cost and
no benefit. Policymakers and judges seem to have forgotten that lawsuits are a social institution with democratic benefits, and, as a result,
have been willing to champion reforms of the legal system that limit
lawsuits without appreciating that these limitations erode our democratic form of government.

The goal of the book is to highlight the underappreciated role of litigation in order to improve it. To understand how litigation really operates
in our society—and as importantly, how it could operate better—we
need to understand its strengths and weaknesses. For most of the book
I consider first the affirmative arguments in favor of litigation, then the
criticisms that enable us to see the fullness of the role litigation plays in
a second-best world, and why democratic values should be our guide
for improving it. The court systems in the United States ought to be
improved, and democratic values are the metric by which to measure
proposed reforms.

When presenting the argument for litigation, one naturally won-
ders how other social institutions compare. This book only considers
other institutions in the context of its discussion of law enforcement,
but otherwise focuses exclusively on the social institution of litigation
and its particular contribution to democracy. The subject of the role and
effectiveness of litigation in achieving democratic values in comparison
to other institutions in the United States and abroad would require an

additional volume, and while that would be a valuable contribution, it is not the subject of this one.

In an effort to streamline the affirmative argument in praise of litigation and to address the key objections, I have placed much of the discussion of the scholarly debates about specific aspects of litigation and some of the more complex counterarguments in the endnotes. The legal scholarship on specific procedural rules—their costs, benefits, and value—could fill many volumes, and while fascinating and important, this extensive field is not the focus of my survey. For readers interested in following these debates, the endnotes point to sources that rigorously develop specific arguments further than this volume can accommodate. My hope is that this book will be accessible to the lay reader, and at the same time will also provide scholars with a new appreciation of litigation as a key part of the democratic enterprise with the end goal of starting a conversation about why litigation matters and what can be done to improve it.

ACKNOWLEDGMENTS

I am especially grateful for the friendship of Peter Siegelman, who is always willing to discuss new ideas over a cup of coffee, and Kaaryn Gustafson, who knows why. I received generous and helpful feedback at different stages from Owen Fiss, Suzanne Goldberg, Amanda Frost, Doug Kysar, Pnina Lahav, Brendan Maher, David Marcus, Martha Minow, Tom Morawetz, Kent Newmeyer, Steve Subrin, and Steven Wilf. I also received crucial advice that made all the difference from Jack Balkin, Lincoln Caplan, James Kwak, and Philip Bobbitt. Two anonymous reviewers provided generous comments that greatly improved the book. Discussions with many generous colleagues at different institutions sharpened my thinking: John Goldberg, Richard Fallon, Pam Karlan, Greg Keating, Bruce Mann, Scott Shapiro, Dan Simon, Reva Siegel, and John Witt. I also benefitted from the comments of participants at faculty workshops at USC Gould School of Law and Roger Williams School of Law, at the Clifford Symposium at DePaul Law School, and a symposium on the civil jury at William & Mary Law School. Over the years I have also learned a lot from Jonathan Abady, Barbara Babcock, Tom Baker, Bob Bone, Matt Brinckerhoff, Jack Coffee, John Cutie, Richard Emery, Tom Grey, Gillian Hadfield, Sam Issacharoff, Jocelyn Larkin, Ilann Maazel, Henry Monaghan, Alan Morrison, Nina Morrison, Jeremy Paul, Judith Resnik, Lee Rosenthal, Bill Rubenstein, Margo Schlanger, Charlie Silver, David Wilkins, and Bill Young. A number of practicing attorneys spoke to me about their work and helped flesh out some of the stories included here; I do not include their names because I promised them anonymity. Laura Kalman gave me sage advice and introduced me to Oxford University Press. I feel very lucky that David McBride agreed to publish the book. I am very grateful to Laura Femino for her help in editing the book and to a number of research assistants at the University of Connecticut, Harvard, and Yale law schools (especially Scott Garosshen, Meghan Houlihan, Joey Kolker, and Cara McClellan). The University of Connecticut School of Law and Deans Jeremy Paul, Willajeanne McLean, and Tim Fisher generously supported my scholarship over the years. Most importantly of all, I feel lucky every day for the love and support of Nick, Oona, and Moshe.

INTRODUCTION
A Force for Democracy

A lawsuit is the result of a tear in the fabric of society. A child dies because the meat in her hamburger was infected with deadly bacteria; a woman is paid less than her male coworkers for doing the same job; a catastrophic oil spill destroys thousands of miles of beaches and the livelihood of fishermen. Often what is broken cannot be repaired, and some say that lawsuits only compound the loss of the original wrongdoing. But litigation has a significant democratic value. Bad things happen and those who believe they have been wronged want and deserve an explanation, a remedy, and a way to prevent the same thing from happening in the future to them or to others. People may bring lawsuits for one or all of these reasons. That they are empowered to do so is an expression of individual autonomy and the fruit of democratic culture. This is why litigation is a social good: it enables people to promote the rule of law and affirms our citizen-centered political system.[1]

Litigation helps democracy function in a number of ways: it helps to *enforce* the law; it fosters *transparency* by revealing information crucial to individual and public decision-making; it promotes *participation* in self-government; and it offers a form of *social equality* by giving litigants equal opportunities to speak and be heard. These four values of litigation—law enforcement, transparency, participation, and social equality—are the key components of a well-functioning democracy. In fact, these four values are so important that vindicating them is worth the transactional costs litigation imposes: the time, money, and effort spent suing and defending suits.[2] This book explains each of these key values and argues that the proper yardstick for measuring the success or failure of our court system—and any potential reform of it—is how well the court system respects and promotes them.

Yet judges, legislators, and many members of the public have lost sight of the value of litigation as a democracy-promoting institution. Instead, arguments that litigation is costly, inefficient, unpredictable, detrimental to social harmony, and hostile to business interests dominate the marketplace of ideas and lead to calls for reform to address these ills— whether real or perceived. We seldom hear how litigation strengthens our society by promoting democratic values. Nor is it often noted how the number of lawsuits is related to the number of disputes in society; the more tears in the social fabric, the more lawsuits there will be. This book stands against the common tide of criticism and explains the value of the right to a day in court in the twenty-first century.[3]

Although enforcement, transparency, participation, and equality are all widely recognized as necessary to democracy, still people can disagree about what these values ought to mean in practice. The need to enforce the law raises questions about the effectiveness of different enforcement mechanisms, including litigation, both in forcing wrongdoers to pay for the injuries they have caused and deterring others from breaking the law. A commitment to transparency raises the question of trade-offs between the public interest in knowing critical information that informs our decisions as citizens and consumers and the countervailing costs of compelling the release of information, both in the sense of the monetary cost of producing that information and because revealing information can damage reputations, disadvantage business interests, or even endanger national security. Recognizing the value of participation in litigation forces us to ask what kind of participation we expect in the litigation process, especially for those who cannot afford a lawyer to represent them so that they can meaningfully participate in their own case. It requires us to question, as well, as how often citizens should adjudicate cases as jurors. The value of equality requires us to face the fact that litigants come to the court without equal resources and may be outmaneuvered by their opponent as a result; we must decide how much the justice system should do to mitigate inequalities outside the court that affect the proceedings inside it.

Take the value of transparency. Ought our commitment to transparency prevent the government from barring the publication of classified information, given a strong countervailing interest in national security? This question demonstrates that most sensitive questions raised by these values cannot be answered in the abstract; rather, the answer always depends on the facts and circumstances at hand. And this is exactly where litigation is particularly adept: it provides a public forum in which discussions of competing values—in the particular factual context giving rise to the conflict—may proceed with input from all interested parties. At its best, litigation both reveals crucial information and provides a forum for reasoned discussion of difficult issues.

In 1971, Daniel Ellsberg famously disclosed to the *New York Times* a multivolume history titled *United States–Vietnam Relations, 1945–1967: A Study Prepared by the Department of Defense,* commonly known as the Pentagon Papers. The United States government sought to stop the *Times,* the *Washington Post,* and other papers from publishing excerpts of this study, eventually seeking the assistance of the federal courts. On an emergency motion to enjoin publication, the government attempted to show that release of the report would irreparably harm national security, while the newspaper made the counterargument that keeping the public informed would *strengthen* American democracy. It was an issue of first impression; no US court had ever articulated a rule on when the government could restrain publication of sensitive governmental information. After two different district courts sided with the newspapers, the cases were appealed—eventually all the way to the Supreme Court, which ruled six to three that the government could not restrain the *Times* and the *Post* from publishing the material as planned.[4]

It is instructive to consider the democratic values affirmed in the litigation of the Pentagon Papers case. The lawsuit helped to *enforce* the law—in this case enforcing the First Amendment's protection of freedom of the press. The litigation also increased transparency by publicizing the government's attempt to block publication. Indeed, it brought about a public debate concerning prior restraint. The government's lawsuit forced the newspapers, as well as the government's own representatives, to articulate arguments for their positions—arguments the lower courts and ultimately the Supreme Court took seriously in adjudicating the case. In so doing, the lawsuit embodied participation in self-government through a public discussion of values in the courtroom and outside it. It also made tangible the values of equality and the rule of law because newspaper editors stood before the court as equals to the government representatives, sending the message that the government is not above the law and reaffirming that the United States is a government of laws and not of men. It is no accident that when the classified information revealed by Edward Snowden was to be published in a number of newspapers, the US government did not bring a lawsuit to enjoin them from publishing.[5]

Not every lawsuit establishes law as fundamental to democracy as the Pentagon Papers case did. Still, the ability of individuals to bring public and private law cases promotes democracy in ways both big and small. This is because the existence of a right to enforce rights is the backdrop of all social interactions. The knowledge that we can rely on our ability to enforce the law if necessary allows us to engage in many exchanges and relationships, and to feel secure in our interactions with others in society.[6]

Permitting litigation does not by itself secure a just society. Litigation, by enforcing the law, simply enforces a given society's values, however just or unjust those may be. But often litigation is also a process of developing arguments about justice and injustice. In a pluralist society such as our own, strongly held values will clash, as did the competing values of national security and freedom of the press in the Pentagon Papers case. The central contribution of litigation is to promote reasoned discussion of competing values through the language of the law by allowing individuals to present their arguments on equal terms and with information that supports those arguments. This process complements other mechanisms within a democratic society for arguing contentious issues, such as elections, legislative debates, and popular protests.[7]

Criticism of the litigiousness of our society and of the role of litigation in our social, economic, and political system has become widespread. Angry calls for reducing lawsuits are commonplace. This movement is pernicious because it prevents important questions from being deliberated. When litigation is not an option, the stronger party can take one side of a nuanced normative question and assert that the law is on its side, without the benefit of deliberation or the requirement of justification. This includes many-faceted questions such as how expansive individual rights should be and what obligations we owe one another in a civilized society. These questions arise in different contexts, from questions about the scope of constitutional rights to be free from unlawful searches and seizures to the private law of accidents and contracts.

Limitations on lawsuits have the practical effect of limiting individual rights, because lawsuits are the central mechanism for enforcing and protecting rights in the United States. When the ability to bring a lawsuit is curtailed, it is rarely replaced with alternative methods of enforcing the law. If the same rights secured by litigation were to be eliminated directly, by legislative or court action, such attempt would meet with great opposition. Yet procedural limitations are little noticed or discussed, even when they profoundly diminish people's ability to enforce rights they rely on and care about. Perhaps this is why instead of explicitly limiting individual rights, legislatures and courts have made changes to procedure that reduce our ability to enforce those rights— a tactic largely invisible to most. These procedural changes happened gradually, often with the justification of reducing the costs of the court system or making that system more beneficial to certain classes of litigants. The fact that the assault on litigation remains largely invisible only heightens the dangers it poses to the core values of democracy.[8]

THE CONTRIBUTION OF LITIGATION TO DEMOCRACY

Democracy implies self-government and participation on the part of the governed under the rule of law. The question has always been: what kind of participation? Litigation offers the opportunity to present reasoned arguments and proofs before an official adjudicator—a judge or jury—and in the process, a chance to debate the values at stake in the lawsuit. A lawsuit is a mechanism for individuals to exercise their autonomy and a form of direct participation in government. Every lawsuit—whether it is a dispute arising out of a contract, the purchase of a defective product, or the conduct of a government official—has the potential to change the rules that govern behavior going forward. We lose this potential when we limit litigation.

Litigation is often understood as an attack by a plaintiff (or plaintiffs) on a defendant or group of defendants. Less often mentioned is that a lawsuit can be brought in self-defense. When citizens turn to the courts to protect them from private or governmental action that they claim will harm the free exercise of their rights, they are defending themselves. For example, when North Carolina passed a law that barred students from using their university identification cards in order to vote, some students sued to defend their right to vote. Whether brought as an attack or as a defense, lawsuits require a branch of government—the courts—to hear people's complaints. In this way, litigation is a vehicle for participation in government and an example of democracy in action, not only for litigants but also for the citizen jurors who adjudicate disputes and for the larger public, whose rights may well be impacted by the proceedings, watching the case unfold.[9]

Participation in self-government requires that people be treated as social equals and that the laws apply equally to all. The most obvious way that the law promotes equality is through the enforcement of rules requiring substantive equality between citizens, such as antidiscrimination laws. But litigation also promotes equality in more subtle ways. By allowing all individuals—regardless of their social standing—access to court to state their claims, litigation promotes equal concern and respect for all and makes sure that the law is applied equally to all. By formally putting everyone on an equal footing, litigation promotes human agency, recognizes the dignity of each individual, and makes participation robust.

This is not to say that there is no real problem in our legal system concerning equality. It is clear that people and institutions with significant resources have an enormous advantage in litigation over those who have few or no resources. For example, consider what the North Carolina students challenging the voter identification laws must do to vindicate their right to vote. How would they pay for a lawyer, court filing fees, and other expenses that will quickly mount? In a society that is characterized by various types of inequality, the court system often reflects that inequality and the legitimacy of the claim that the courts provide equal justice under law is diminished as a result.

Indeed, in some cases winning is an uphill battle for one of the parties not because of the strength of their case but rather because of other disadvantages—that they have fewer resources than their adversary, or are more afraid of litigation for other reasons. An individual of meager resources faces an uphill battle in a lawsuit against a large corporation. In federal court, more often than not this individual will be the plaintiff. Studies show these types of uphill lawsuits are more contested and take longer. But it may not always be the plaintiff who struggles to sustain a lawsuit. Lawsuits where the defendant is an individual end more quickly and are more likely to be resolved in favor of the organizational plaintiff. Whether the impact is on plaintiffs or defendants, there is reason to be concerned about litigation distorting rather than promoting enforcement of the law and other values when the participants in a lawsuit are unevenly matched.[10]

Courts can and should do better than they do now to put litigants on more equal footing. Equality before the law and the idea of a government of laws require that, at least in the courtroom, there be some threshold level of equality between litigants. The fact that the ideal of absolute equality between and among litigants is not realized in practice does not mean that litigation cannot promote democratic values, but it does mean that reforms that move the court system closer to this ideal are needed and reforms that would have the opposite effect should be rejected.

Requiring that alleged wrongdoers publicly defend themselves and answer for their conduct is also crucial to a system of laws. Enforcement of the law includes requiring people to provide justifications for their behavior, holding them accountable (financially and otherwise), and deterring future wrongdoing by clarifying the law and imposing penalties for violating it. Litigation allows individuals to play a direct role in enforcing laws by bringing lawsuits, and allows them to stand up against opposing interests to change unjust applications and interpretations of the law. Litigation can also spur social change, through judicial opinions that revise the law and by inspiring and sustaining social movements. Sometimes these movements are sparked by the perceived injustice of the outcome in the courts. For example, an organization favoring the teaching of intelligent design in schools was able to catapult itself into the national spotlight when it lost a major case. A school district adopted an intelligent design curriculum and was sued because the curriculum was religiously based. The organization that defended the school district touted the loss as a moment of resistance to an oppressive society, a step in a broader campaign to change the law to permit religiously inspired school science curricula.[11]

To adequately self-govern and to enforce the law, people must have access to information that will help them make decisions. Litigation promotes transparency by forcing information out into the open that would otherwise remain hidden. Lawsuits increase citizens' knowledge about the world because discovery in civil cases requires both parties to reveal information related to the subject of their dispute. Sometimes lawsuits even require the creation of information that helps citizens learn more about how government operates.

For example, the New York Police Department created a system for recording stops and frisks and was required to release that data in response to a lawsuit. The information was then analyzed by both the Office of the New York Attorney General and private litigants and confirmed that the New York Police Department had engaged in racial profiling.[12] Litigation also serves as a catalyst for larger public conversations about important issues, since discussions that begin in a courtroom often spill over into the larger public dialogue. Courts provide a forum for people to critique and defend social practices and, of course, an ultimate sense of resolution: knowing why bad things happened or who is to blame provides individual litigants and the public with information that can be used to change the law, as well as begin a process of healing.

Even if one agrees that litigation can promote the core democratic values of enforcement, transparency, participation, and equality before the law, one may still find it troubling that litigation sometimes results in appointed judges overturning the decisions of elected legislators. When judges who do not have to answer to voters in an election strike down laws enacted by democratically elected legislators, is this not *anti*democratic? This is a genuine problem with the system of judicial review because it allows individuals to bring a lawsuit that challenges collective decision-making, creating an irresolvable tension that reemerges every time a court must decide whether to strike down a law—although it is also important to remember that many lawsuits do not ask a court to overrule legislative action. This tension is played out in the *process* of litigation, as parties make arguments not only about the substantive matter at hand but also about the courts' power to decide that matter and the desirability of leaving that question to the other branches of government. This book defends that process, not the particular allocation of power between the executive, legislative, and judicial branches at this historical moment. This defense is particularly important now, because as we shall see, the ability of litigation to promote fundamental values is quickly eroding.[13]

THE LITIGATION LANDSCAPE

To evaluate the importance of litigation to our democracy it is useful to know a few things about litigation in the United States. The picture of litigation that emerges is surprisingly different from the one portrayed in the media. Although Americans are often painted as particularly litigious, most people who suffer an injury do not bring a legal action. Instead, they live with it. Big cases involving millions of dollars make headlines, but most disputes do not turn into lawsuits at all, and the vast majority of disputes that do become lawsuits are simple and involve relatively small amounts of money. Such big cases are important because they capture the imagination and spur public debate and their outcome may help others resolve their disputes outside of litigation or even prevent future harms and claims, but it is still the case that the lion's share of claims are small and many more are never pursued.[14]

A total of about seventeen million lawsuits were filed in the United States in 2012, the most recent year for which data is available, but it is hard to say whether this number is shockingly low or unacceptably high because we do not know how many viable legal claims there were in the same period. A little more than half of the lawsuits filed involve small amounts of money and are filed in special courts that offer simplified procedures. For example, in California a person seeking $10,000 or less can sue in small claims court and they must represent themselves (no lawyers are allowed); a business can sue for no more than $5,000 in small claims court. Not all states have courts of limited jurisdiction, so the number of small cases in state courts is greater than half of the total filings.[15]

The majority of cases in state trial courts are contract cases. A study of seventeen states' courts found that contractual claims made up over 60 percent of the incoming caseload in 2010. Although the numbers differ from state to state, the trend is consistent: there are many more contract cases than any other type of lawsuit. For example, data from 2010 show that in Kansas 81 percent of the civil cases filed were contract cases, in Connecticut that number was 44 percent, and in Hawai'i it was 23 percent. By contrast, tort cases, which are such a big part of the public discussion about litigation, made up only 2 percent of the civil docket in Kansas, 10 percent in Connecticut, and 9 percent in Hawai'i. This means that most people who sue (and are sued) are trying to enforce some business transaction.[16]

Despite the fact that contract disputes usually make up most of the case filings, they take up little air time in the debate about litigation. This inconsistency may be because the real concern of critics is not litigation per se, but the underlying rights people are seeking to enforce by bringing lawsuits, and the enforcement of contractual rights is a more sympathetic cause among those decrying the role of litigation. Or it may simply be self-interest rather than principled opposition. A study finding that the same firms that prefer arbitration clauses in their dealings with consumers do not include arbitration provisions in business-to-business contracts demonstrates that litigants use the available tools to their advantage. This book draws more on the cases that are most often used to support the argument against litigation— torts, civil rights, and consumer law—but contract cases have the same democracy-promoting potential as any other lawsuit and suffer from the same drawbacks. Indeed, it would be a useful exercise for opponents of litigation to test their intuition that litigation is socially harmful by replacing the paradigmatic case they have in mind with a contract suit.[17]

Over time, the mix of cases in the courts has changed, and continues to change in response to developments in the law, technology, society, and the economy. Since Congress enacted many civil rights laws in the 1960s, there has been a marked increase in civil rights cases in the federal courts, as well as other federal statutory claims. But that does not mean that civil rights cases dominate; nonprisoner civil rights cases made up only about 12.5 percent of the federal docket in 2014. Tort filings sometimes increase in response to large-scale developments in manufacturing, technology, or medicine, such as revelations about the harms caused by exposure to toxic substances like asbestos or drugs like Vioxx. These types of events can involve large numbers indeed—there were thousands of Vioxx suits filed in the federal courts—but they are episodic. We will consider the meaning of these large-scale tort suits in later chapters. The important thing is that filing rates are not the result of a growing litigious streak in society but rather of discrete events, be they injuries from a mass-marketed drug, the creation of a new cause of action to address discrimination, or a commercial deal gone wrong.[18]

There are multiple court systems in the United States: a court system for every state and territory and the federal courts. As we have seen, each court system has a different mix of cases, although some general trends emerge. The federal courts have been the most studied because data about federal caseloads is more easily accessible to researchers. What these studies find is that most federal cases involve an imbalance of power between the parties. About 60 percent of the cases involve individuals suing organizations, and only 20 percent involve organizations suing one another. Most of the time, the defendants in federal cases are organizations; organizations are plaintiffs much less often. This means defendants tend to have an advantage over plaintiffs, at least in federal court, because organizations are typically more sophisticated and tend to have more resources than individuals.[19]

Organizations and individuals bring different types of suits. Organizations tend to bring commercial cases such as cases about intellectual property rights, contracts, antitrust, commercial law, and consumer law. By contrast, individual plaintiffs tend to sue for civil rights violations, for torts such as personal injury or products liability, and about government benefits. The arguments against litigation have tended to focus on areas of the law that individuals rely on more than business organizations, although not exclusively. Consistent with the preferences of the antilitigation movement, changes in the procedural rules, such as increased access to motions to dismiss or for summary judgment, are more detrimental to plaintiffs, especially *pro se* plaintiffs, in civil rights and employment cases than in any other area of the law.[20]

Evidence from the development of the market for lawyers supports this conclusion. The market for lawyers representing organizations in sophisticated practices has grown since 1970, but the market for lawyers representing individuals in run-of-the-mill cases, such as those concerning family law or personal injury, has shrunk. Overall this means that individual citizens have less access to legal representation and are at a greater disadvantage before the courts than they were in the past and as compared with organizations. We will revisit this issue of the effect of resource differentials on litigation in chapters 3 and 4, which address participation and equality in the courts.[21]

Litigation can be resolved in a number of different ways, and increasingly cases are resolved earlier in the process. A default judgment occurs when the defendant does not respond to the lawsuit at all and loses by default. One study found that 20 percent of cases brought by organizations against individuals in the federal courts end in default judgments (this study excluded student loan cases, almost all of which end in default). In other words, there is no litigation process to speak of in many cases where individuals are defendants. A case that is litigated is most likely to be resolved by a judge on a pretrial motion, such as a motion to dismiss at the outset of the litigation or a motion for summary judgment as the litigation goes on. A case can settle at any time if the parties agree on some kind of compromise resolution (for example, the plaintiff ending the lawsuit in return for the defendant paying a sum of money). There is a general consensus that a large proportion of cases settle, although the percentage ranges from as low as 36 percent to as high as 70 percent depending on the study. In later chapters, I will discuss the dispute over whether settlement detracts from the democratic potential of litigation and show that settlements can promote democratic values.[22]

The one thing that rarely happens is the thing most associated with litigation: the trial. Studies show that trial rates are very low, and jury trial rates even lower. The most recent data that has been analyzed is from 2002, but court-published data shows that trial rates have held steady since then. The rate of trials was never higher than 20 percent, and the trial rate of federal civil cases had fallen to 1.8 percent by 2002. There has been a 60 percent decrease in the absolute number of trials from the mid-1980s. In the state courts, tort and contract cases make up almost 98 percent of the total trials. By contrast, the largest group of cases that are tried in the federal courts are civil rights cases. In 2002, these represented a third of all trials and 41 percent of jury trials. Tort and contract cases together constituted about 38 percent of federal civil trials that same year.[23]

Not only have the number of trials declined, so has the median award. The median jury award in state courts of general jurisdiction fell from $65,000 in 1992 to $37,000 in 2001. But of course the median award does not describe *all* categories of cases; each type of case has its own trajectory. For example, more than half of tort trials in state courts are motor vehicle cases, which yield a median award of less than $18,000. Products liability trials, by contrast, are a very small proportion of the total trials but have a median award of $543,000. Overall, contract cases have higher median compensatory damage awards and higher punitive damages awards than tort cases (although punitive damages awards are very rare in any type of case). Cases where punitive damages are awarded are a tiny proportion of trials, and there are very few extraordinarily high punitive damages awards. Although the awards have decreased overall, the time it takes to get to trial and the length of trials themselves have grown longer, while the pretrial resolution of cases has speeded up.[24]

What explains the precipitous decline in trials? One theory is that cases are being diverted and resolved in other ways, such as by pretrial motion or mediation. Another is that lawyers perceive trials as more risky, costly, and complex than they did in the past. Thinking economically, parties on opposing sides are more likely to have overlapping settlement ranges when the cost of going to trial increases. This may be true in some cases, but the fact that both awards and trials declined at the same time is inconsistent with this theory. If trials were increasingly expensive across the board, then one would expect to see increased awards overall for cases going to trial, but that is not the case. Marc Galanter, who conducted the definitive study on the decline of trials, suggests that the reason for the decline in trials is not real cost and risk but *perceived* cost as well as perceived risk of trial. The highest verdicts and the most costly, complex cases are reported in the media, whereas defense verdicts, very low awards, and reversals of awards on appeal are rarely reported. This feeds into a general perception that trials are so expensive and juries so unpredictable that trial is something to be avoided if at all possible. On this telling, the decline in trials is attributable less to the actual risks faced by defendants and more to a cognitive error in overestimating the likelihood and magnitude of a large award. A fourth theory is that judges are managing cases to avoid trials because of changes in judicial ideology that favor settlements and early resolution over trials. Perhaps it is a vicious cycle: the less experience judges have with trial, the more likely they are to favor other ways of resolving cases, producing a new generation of lawyers who are even less experienced with trials.[25]

It is important to keep in mind that the numbers reported here do not shed light on the *quality* of the cases being filed, defaulted, settled, decided by judges before trial, or decided with the benefit of a full-blown trial, or the quality of the result. If the most important cases by whatever measure (and this is something upon which reasonable people can disagree) ultimately went to trial and were decided by juries, we would worry less that juries are hearing fewer and fewer cases every year—the important ones would still get the treatment they deserve and citizen adjudicators would still be involved. But if important cases are not being tried, this is a serious problem because this means society loses opportunities to engage in arguments and deliberation over the application of law. The decline in trials also signals a different loss that is equally important: the diminished role of citizen jurors in the court system, a subject I will take up in chapter 3.

Similarly, if all the cases ending in default judgment against the defendant reached the right result (that is, the defendant should have lost) and the decision to default was one consciously and intentionally made, then there is less cause for concern that these cases are not being decided by a judge or that, in many cases, the defendants were not represented by lawyers. But if the defaulted cases have a significant error rate, or are defaulted not by choice but by a lack of wherewithal, there is good reason to be concerned that the legal system is letting people down and reinforcing the inequalities that exist outside the system instead of treating each litigant with equal concern and respect.

All is not well in a system of justice where many people do not participate at all, where some groups have structural advantages in litigation over others, and where the few trials that are conducted end up vilified in the media. The questions raised by the landscape of civil litigation demonstrate what is at stake in having a robust litigation process for individual citizens and for society: the public values of knowing the law and seeing it applied, of participation in our own governance, and of law enforcement.

GOOD VERSUS BAD LITIGATION

This book praises litigation for promoting enforcement of the law, transparency, and participation in self-government.[26] Of course, that is not to say that every case filed promotes democratic values. The cases often cited by critics of litigation indeed appear extreme. There is the case of the man who sued his dry cleaner for millions because his pants were ruined, or reports of schools taking down playground swing sets in fear of lawsuits. Oftentimes these anecdotes are distorted claims that are more compelling than they are portrayed. Other times the anecdotes obscure what is really at stake. For example, the policy question posed by the playground anecdote is who should bear the cost of avoidable injuries: the school district that can put in safer playground surfaces or injured children and their parents? Very often the tear in the social fabric that lawsuits seek to address is real, and much is at stake in the answer of how to repair it, or whether to repair it at all.[27]

This is not to say that there are no instances of the abuse of litigation for any wide range of improper purposes. For example, the editor of an online academic journal was sued for libel because he published a critical book review. He tried to explain to the book's author that although the review was critical, it was not false. She was not satisfied and brought an action against him in France, where she held citizenship but did not reside, hoping that French libel law would give her a better result in her case. The French court found that the review was not libelous, but not before the editor traveled to France to defend his case, found lawyers to assist him, and experienced the emotional strain and distraction from his other work caused by the legal action. Without the support of his academic institution, he might have been unable to defend himself at all and been forced to suffer the consequences, or capitulated and removed the review to avoid the costs associated with his defense. And the author did not benefit either; she only brought international attention to the critical book review by filing the lawsuit.[28]

Anecdotes of worthless or even destructive litigation raise the important question of when and why litigation is good and when and why it is bad. But it is also necessary to remember that while these stories of good and bad lawsuits help test our moral intuitions, they reveal nothing about most cases or the litigation landscape more generally and are not a good basis for making policy decisions affecting all cases. Good lawsuits are brought with the intention of redressing a wrong, forcing defendants to answer for their conduct, enforcing existing law, or improving existing law. Bad lawsuits are brought to harass, annoy, or obtain payment wrongfully, and are without a basis in law. Deciding which is which involves an assessment of the subjective intent of the plaintiff, the wrongfulness of defendant's conduct, and a moral judgment about whether this is the kind of wrong the law should be deployed to address. The problem is that people will differ in their assessment of these criteria and simple formulae prove woefully inadequate.

If we defined bad litigation as litigation with *no* chance of winning, this standard is both under- and overinclusive. It would not include, for example the man who sued his dry cleaner for millions over a pair of pants, which most would agree is "bad" litigation, because, as it turns out, he did have a chance of winning his case. The problem there was not that his lawsuit was entirely without merit, but that he overreached by asking for millions of dollars when the maximum value of what he had lost was a few hundred. And this definition might sweep in valuable lawsuits with only a *small* probability of success. Sometimes plaintiffs bring lawsuits most agree should be brought, but that have little chance of winning. (And miraculously, sometimes these suits do win—*Brown v. Board of Education* is a perfect example and there are many others.) As constitutional theorist Jack Balkin explains, part of the process of legal development is that arguments that were once considered "off the wall" shift to being "on the wall."[29]

When I teach the issue of how to distinguish between different kinds of lawsuits, and why it is so hard to define which lawsuits are frivolous, I assign my students the case of the Confederate employees. In that case, a group of employees who identified as Confederate Southern Americans sued their workplace for discrimination. They claimed that the company discriminated against them by prohibiting them from wearing Confederate flags and symbols at the workplace. The defendant company filed a motion to dismiss the case, sought reimbursement by the plaintiffs for their legal costs in defending against the lawsuit, and asked the court for sanctions, that is, monetary fines imposed on lawyers (or sometimes clients) for bringing lawsuits that are factually baseless or are brought only to harass and annoy. This rule is justified by the idea that in civil society we rely on people to use public institutions fairly, and should only sanction them when they act in bad faith.[30]

The right to wear Confederate gear is not what we usually think about when we think about employment discrimination law, which protects employees from discrimination on the basis of race, gender, religion, and national origin. The question for the court was whether a person identifying as a Confederate American could conceivably fall into one of these legal categories. The court sanctioned the lawyer for that part of the lawsuit that indeed had no basis in fact, but also found that the plaintiffs' attempt to expand the legal category of "national origin" to include Confederate Southern Americans was a valid purpose for a lawsuit and did not merit sanctions. The reason for refraining from sanctioning lawyers who bring new legal theories, even if they lose (as this one did), is to promote the evolution of the law. The law governing frivolous suits today recognizes the need for litigants to pursue novel legal theories, even ones with which many may not agree. This preference is consistent with the democratic value of litigation, which is to allow litigants to participate in a process of presenting reasoned arguments and proofs in support of their case, even if observers find the arguments unconvincing or wrong.[31]

Some lawsuits deserve criticism because they reflect human failings and vices: bad judgment, revenge, anger, and greed. In these cases, the problem is neither the underlying law nor the procedures that permit people to file lawsuits, but the people who choose to file. It would not make sense to construct an entire legal system around a few stories of bad actors without more empirical evidence that the problem is a significant one. Of course the courts should protect litigants from suits brought only to harass or intimidate. Because there is no way to deter frivolous claims without also deterring some meritorious suits, a lot is riding on how courts define frivolous suits.[32]

In other situations, such as the case of the playground equipment, a social problem underlies the litigation. The opposition to litigation in the case of unsafe playgrounds, for example, is really about who should pay for accidents and how much should be invested in preventing them. At bottom the opposition to litigation as a system for resolving disputes is in fact an opposition to regulation, because litigation is a tool that enforces legal rules. For this reason, antilitigation sentiment is often linked to the promotion of deregulation. The debate is framed as being about litigation but it is really about something else, such as, for example, whether playgrounds should be safer and who should pay for those safety measures.[33]

Most of the discussion of good or bad litigation is instead about good or bad social policy. What ought to matter to both opponents and proponents of individual lawsuits is the underlying substance of the law being vindicated. For example, in the early 2000s record companies sued individuals—often students—who downloaded songs in violation of the copyright laws. These lawsuits were reported in the media because the statutory damages the record companies won were so extreme. In one case a record company was awarded over $200,000 from a consumer who downloaded twenty-four songs. The problem there was not with litigation itself, but with the underlying law passed by Congress, which provides for such disproportionate penalties.[34] One reason people were incensed about the copyright cases against students was the disparity between the parties, a problem the substantive law exacerbated.

The debate about litigation can take the form of a debate about the level of regulation and whether courts, rather than other branches of government, are the appropriate institution to make such regulatory decisions. I will explore litigation as a form of regulation in chapter 1, when we discuss enforcement of the law. In that chapter I will explain what we know about litigation's effectiveness as a law enforcement tool and what other options are available. But law enforcement is not the only value litigation promotes, and critics of litigation would do well to consider their stance on the other democratic values that litigation furthers. Many debates over regulation—its forms and its limits—happen in the courts because individuals want the opportunity to assert their rights, participate in self-government, and expose wrongdoing, and they know a courtroom is one space where this exchange can happen.

So far we have talked about litigation as "bad" in the sense that some lawsuits do not fit with normative views of what is an appropriate dispute to elevate to the level of a lawsuit. Litigation can also be bad in another way: it can be bad for the complainant by imposing too many costs, making the pursuit of rights too difficult, emotionally and financially. Filing a lawsuit can impose a stigma on the plaintiff, who is exposed to extreme scrutiny in the course of the lawsuit. Voltaire quipped, "I was never ruined but twice: once when I lost a lawsuit, and once when I won one."[35] There is some truth to this: the process of litigation may add insult to injury. It takes bravery and fortitude to bring and maintain many lawsuits, just as it takes bravery to call out a wrongdoer in other areas of life. This is an unavoidable cost, although it can be mitigated by judicial conduct, especially when judges treat litigants with equal concern and respect. Still, the requirement that both parties prove their case requires that each of them be exposed, answer difficult questions, and reveal information that they prefer to keep hidden.[36]

CONSTRAINTS ON LITIGATION

My decision to write this book was motivated by increasing limitations on the right to sue and by supporting arguments that misunderstand or ignore the democratic purpose of litigation. Restrictions adopted by courts and passed by legislatures have pushed disputes outside the court system to early settlement, arbitration, or, in many cases, nothing at all. These restrictions demonstrate that many policymakers and judges have lost sight of the ways society benefits from litigation. When they see lawsuits, they see only cost. Limitations on the ability to sue fall more on individuals than organizations, and more on cases implicating broad social questions than on cases of only individual concern.[37]

What are these limitations, exactly? To start with, courts have changed the rules of procedure to make it harder to bring lawsuits and to get them to trial. It was once the case that the ideal of procedure was to open the courts and sort out the cases as they came in, with a goal of reaching the merits in most (if not all) cases. Today procedure is restrictive, aiming to keep cases out of court or dismiss them immediately without giving the participants a chance to develop their proofs and arguments. Federal judges have stated explicitly that there are too many cases and have developed doctrines to cull cases early and often.[38]

Jurisdictional doctrines such as standing have been tightened, restricting the ability to bring suit. Consider the suit of Adolph Lyons against the Los Angeles Police Department. Lyons had been stopped on a routine traffic violation when a police officer, without provocation, put him in a chokehold until he lost consciousness. The Supreme Court ruled that Lyons did not have sufficient personal stake to request a court order prohibiting the police's use of chokeholds in the future because there was no evidence that the police would put *him* in a chokehold again. In other words, he did not meet the procedural requirement of standing to seek an injunction to protect others from the same fate. It is not clear that anyone could ever meet this requirement, since such a person would have to demonstrate that he or she is likely to be put in a chokehold in the future. Instead of reaching the merits of the question and addressing the conflict of values posed by the lawsuit (Is the police department putting people in chokeholds? Are chokeholds illegal? If so, what can be done to stop this practice?), the Supreme Court dismissed that portion of the case on procedural grounds.[39]

Standing doctrine requires that in order to have a viable lawsuit in federal court, a person must show (1) that he suffered a real and concrete injury to himself, (2) that this injury was caused by the challenged activity, and (3) that the court is able to redress the injury. In Lyons' case, the Court interpreted the first prong of this test in a very restrictive way. It held that Lyons did not meet the requirement of a concrete injury because he could not show that he was likely to be put in a chokehold again; as a result, he had no personal stake in seeking an injunction to protect others from the same fate. The only way a person like Lyons could maintain a suit, said the Court, was if he could show that police officers in Los Angeles always use chokeholds or are somehow required to use them—a claim the Court called an "incredible assertion"— because only under those facts would he likely be held in a chokehold again. Even if Lyons was likely to be put in a chokehold again because police officers were routinely using this tactic, without access to civil discovery there was no way for him to prove it, and access to civil discovery requires standing. As the use of litigation to enforce civil rights has grown, the Court has narrowed standing doctrine to make it harder for litigants to get in the courthouse door.[40]

There are still more preliminary requirements. Even when a person has standing to sue, he or she has to sue in the right court—a court with power over both the subject matter of the case and over the defendant. In a number of cases the Supreme Court has limited personal jurisdiction over defendants, to the detriment of many plaintiffs and states attempting to discipline foreign defendants who sell defective products in the United States. In one notable case, a New Jersey recycling plant employee was severely injured by the malfunction of a giant shear used for cutting scrap metal. The manufacturer of the shear—a piece of equipment that cost more than $20,000—was based in the United Kingdom. The employee tried to sue the shear manufacturer in his home state of New Jersey, but the Court held that a New Jersey court could not decide the dispute, since the case presented no evidence that the manufacturer's contact with New Jersey extended beyond the malfunctioning shear in question, and because the manufacturer used an American distributor (which could have been sued instead, except that it was bankrupt) rather than selling the product directly. The ruling insulates some foreign manufacturers from American tort law—an important tool for enforcing safety standards and protecting workers and consumers.[41]

It is also harder than ever to move through the process of adjudication, even if a plaintiff can get past jurisdictional hurdles. Decades ago the requirements for filing a suit were relatively easy to satisfy. All the plaintiff needed to do in his pleading was give notice of the lawsuit and its subject matter to the defendant. And the purpose of procedure was understood primarily to help get the case to the merits, which at that time meant to trial. Today in federal court, and in some state courts, the plaintiff must allege facts at the outset of his lawsuit to convince a judge that his claim is plausible. The rationale is that plaintiffs should not have access to court-ordered discovery of information from their opponent until they have demonstrated both a factual basis for their claim and that these facts describe the kind of event that a judge thinks might have happened, because discovery is costly in both money and time. This rationale does not recognize that information, including information obtained through litigation, is crucial to self-government. Requiring parties to state the facts that they know is fair, but this standard takes no account of how information is asymmetrically distributed: one party may have information that the other party needs for his claim (or defense) to succeed. In instituting new requirements for filing suits, the Court considered the cost of revealing information, but not the cost of hiding it. The result demonstrates how narrow the Justices' view of litigation has become. As we shall see, information forced out into the open by litigation is crucial to citizens, consumers, and regulators.[42]

The courts have also made it harder to bring class actions, that is, collective suits in which many plaintiffs sue the same defendant for the same wrongdoing, by tightening the rules that apply to both civil rights class actions and consumer class actions. In particular, people opposing recalcitrant institutions unlikely to change absent collective suit against them have a much steeper hill to climb than ever. For consumers this has meant that people with claims that are valid but too small to bring individually—the kind of claims class actions are uniquely able to address—will never have their rights vindicated.[43]

Probably the most important symbol of equality in the judicial canon, *Brown v. Board of Education*, was brought as a class action. As is well known, that lawsuit was brought to end segregation in public schools, but was it important that the case was brought by a class rather than one individual? If the suit had been brought only by an individual student, the school system could have given that student a seat in a classroom by himself and thereby complied with the court order—the school would have been integrated as a formal matter, although everyone would agree that an isolated black student does not constitute meaningful integration or right the wrong the lawsuit was intended to challenge. Because the suit was brought as a class action, the entire school district was ordered to desegregate.

Recent decisions have made civil rights class actions much more difficult to bring, requiring years of litigation up and down the appellate ladder just to establish that the case can be brought collectively before a court can get to evaluating the merits of the underlying claims. This increases inequality between litigants if one side cannot afford a long legal battle and it makes enforcing the law more difficult. When the barriers to class certification are too high, important cases—perhaps our decade's *Brown v. Board of Education*—never reach the merits or are delayed much too long. For example, a nonprofit organization helped a group of foster care children bring a lawsuit against the State of Texas for failing to adequately care for children who were placed in foster care. The allegations were deeply disturbing, including that the state failed to exercise enough oversight over foster care placements and as a result children were abused, sent to placements far from their families and siblings, moved frequently, and placed in inappropriate settings. This is the type of class action that would have been certified easily in the past.

The case was filed in 2011, but because of increasingly onerous require-ments for proceeding as a class action, the plaintiffs were still litigating the question of whether they could proceed collectively in 2013. The only reason that the case was able to get to the merits is that the defen-dant missed the deadline to file a second appeal. The case did not go to trial until 2015.[44]

Other cases are never filed in court because the parties involved are bound by arbitration contracts agreeing to resolve their differences through a private dispute resolution system. Arbitration differs from in-court litigation in that arbitration proceedings are supposed to be faster, less formal, involve fewer procedural protections, and are private. Arbitrations are paid for entirely by the parties to the dispute, whereas parties who file in court externalize the costs of their dispute because taxes support the courts as a forum of public justice. The fact that arbi-tration outcomes are private is crucial to understanding the prolifera-tion of arbitration agreements, especially in consumer and employment contracts. The arbiters are not required to produce published decisions, and as a result the public is denied the public statement on the law that dispute might have yielded. Sometimes arbitration allows those regu-lated to control how rules are enforced and even to change the rules. For example, one study showed how automobile manufacturers in California changed the meaning of consumer protection laws by cre-ating private venues for resolving warranty complaints that were more favorable to the manufacturers' interests. For this and other reasons, it is of great concern that in recent decades the courts have increasingly privileged private arbitration over litigation. Corporations have begun to include arbitration agreements in nearly every contract consumers sign—especially the kind of contracts that consumers rarely read and have no ability to negotiate, such as the contracts nearly everyone rou-tinely clicks through when opening a new software application.[45]

For a long time now arbitration has looked more and more like litigation in terms of complexity and formality of procedures as well as cost, so that it is not clear anymore that arbitration really does live up to its reputation for providing a more streamlined, shorter, and less adversarial option than the courts do. And arbitration offers little in the way of the democratic benefits of litigation. Arbitrators' decisions need not follow the law, and both the process and the result can be required to be kept confidential—and usually they are. One fact demonstrates arbitration's drawbacks: as we saw earlier, while companies prefer to have arbitration clauses in standard form consumer contracts (the kind that are not negotiated), when they negotiate contracts with their peers they tend to prefer the option of going to court. Why the different treatment? The logical conclusion is that these companies believe they have a structural advantage against consumers in arbitration, but not in court. That is not to say that arbitration or other methods of dispute resolution outside the courts are *always* a bad idea. There may be some cases in which litigants prefer arbitration, such as when the purpose is only to resolve the dispute rather than create a public record. (Indeed, in some cases both disputants may want to avoid precisely the publicity attendant to litigation.) Overall, however, there is increasing evidence that arbitration is being used to hide misconduct and limit access to justice, especially by eliminating potential class actions.[46]

Courts have also jumped onto the arbitration bandwagon, in recent years chipping away at two important legal doctrines that once prevented the use of arbitration as a weapon to strip procedural protections from individuals. The first is the state contract law doctrine of unconscionability, which allows a court to void a contract that is too unreasonably one-sided in favor of the party with superior bargaining power. This doctrine is intended to protect unwitting consumers who "agree" to unfair terms they likely did not understand (and in many cases did not read). The second is a federally created doctrine called "vindication of rights," which required that if an arbitration provision prevented people from being able to enforce their rights, it would be struck down. In recent cases the Supreme Court rejected attempts to void arbitration agreements under each of these doctrines, eliminating important avenues for the preservation of litigation and its contributions to civil society.[47]

Arbitration agreements can also constitute another barrier to class actions which, as we saw above, are key to preserving individual rights. If an arbitration agreement forbids collective litigation—as is fairly common today in consumer contracts—then individuals are forced to sue individually, a prospect too expensive for the average person. As a result of these ever-proliferating provisions, fewer wrongdoers are held to account. Worse yet, the public may not even be aware of the wrong, because there is no public filing in a court to tell the story.[48]

The courts have also made it more difficult to bring a case to trial by using procedures that encourage settlement and making it easier for judges to resolve cases without a live hearing through tools such as early settlement conferences. Federal judges, for example, are evaluated by how quickly they decide motions and close cases, not by how much time they spend on the bench, how many trials they preside over, or the quality of their decisions. Prominent federal judges have complained about this, arguing that this measurement incentivizes judges to decide cases through motions or push them toward settlement rather than allow them to proceed to trial. Litigation today is dominated by settlement, which is not made public and as a result limits the public's knowledge of the development of the law (or even distorts its development) and can lead to inequality among settling parties. Settlement can be useful, but overemphasis on settlement can threaten the public values litigation ought to promote, especially transparency about facts crucial to regulators, and clarity about what the law is and how it is applied. In some courts litigation is also dominated by summary judgment, which has the benefit of being transparent in the sense that the judge's grounds for decision are articulated in an opinion, but it can also be used, as we will see later, to take decisions away from a jury.[49]

A final way courts have curbed litigation is by limiting the attorneys' fees that a winning party can recover from a losing party in certain cases, especially civil rights cases. In the United States, each party usually pays for its own fees and costs of litigation. However, in a small subset of cases that Congress has decided are particularly important, such as civil rights cases, the defendant must pay the plaintiff's attorneys' fees if the plaintiff wins. The idea behind this one-way fee shifting rule is to encourage lawyers to take on lawsuits that assert a violation of civil rights even if the client cannot afford their services, because if the client wins, the lawyers are guaranteed payment. When courts and legislatures limit the fees that can be awarded, however, fewer attorneys are willing to bring these important cases. Further, courts have held that plaintiffs who settle may be asked to give up their right to such compensation as part of the settlement agreement. This issue will come up again when I discuss the effect of litigation on equality later in the book.[50]

Lawsuits for civil wrongs such as those arising from accidents, the use of faulty products, and medical malpractice are also under attack. The emphasis on these areas of the law is somewhat surprising when one considers the fact that tort suits make up only 6 percent of cases brought in the United States every year and the evidence shows that most people who are injured do not sue. Nevertheless, legislators have passed a number of laws that make bringing tort suits more difficult. For example, laws now limit statutes of limitations, especially for medical malpractice claims, to shorter and shorter periods of time, meaning that many may lose their claims before they have even been able to retain a lawyer. Additional requirements for filing a lawsuit, such as the submission of expert reports with the complaint, increase the costs of litigation so that only cases where the likely damages are very high can proceed. What this means is that procedural barriers keep even those who are genuinely injured by wrongdoing from vindicating their rights.[51]

On the back end, damages caps limit the plaintiff's recovery in cases that are able to proceed, and these caps discourage other suits from being brought in the first place. Since many personal injury cases are brought on a contingency fee basis—that is, the lawyers are paid little up front but will receive a percentage of their clients' recovery if they win—damage caps reduce the incentives for lawyers to take cases on behalf of people who cannot afford to pay up front, or in other words, most Americans. Such caps disproportionately affect people who are not able to claim significant damages for lost wages, including low wage earners, the elderly, and stay-at-home parents. As we shall see later in the book, when lawsuits are not brought to reveal—and stop—wrong-doing, this can have grave consequences for the family of the person injured and for society generally.[52]

THE KEY TO REFORM IS UNDERSTANDING THE STAKES

Observing the debates about litigation, it became clear to me that a fundamental assumption in these debates is incorrect. That assumption is that litigation is only about resolving disputes. Of course litigation is about dispute resolution; when people sue it means that they were not able to resolve their problem on their own, and they need a neutral third party to help them. But litigation is also about much more than this. It is a political process that affects both the individual involved in the lawsuit and society as a whole. The legal theorist Roscoe Pound wrote in the beginning of the twentieth century that the common law system so elevates the individual that it "tries questions of the highest social import as mere private controversies between John Doe and Richard Roe."[53] Today individual and collective lawsuits can and should be understood as controversies of the highest social import that should be brought to public attention and debated.

Lawsuits serve multiple functions that are necessary for civil society to flourish and are a fundamental component of Americans' political identity. In some cases, the courts are the only place a person can turn to obtain redress and protection. In others litigation is but one part of the broader political conversation, a way to reveal critical information, sharpen reasoned arguments, and apply the language of the law to divisive problems. This is not to deny that litigation can be a drain on resources, that lawsuits are an imperfect method for resolving disputes, and that sometimes the expense and effort of pursuing a lawsuit perhaps could be better redirected. But the democratic benefits of litigation, too often ignored by critics, must also be taken into account. For this reason we should be concerned that as criticisms of litigation gain traction, they threaten to change the character of this important social institution, irrevocably and for the worse, by limiting the capacity of the legal system to provide funda-mental social goods.

What is needed is to restore some balance to the discussion and pro-vide guiding principles for reform by showing the benefits litigation provides for civil society. Lawsuits can enforce rights, they can hold people and organizations accountable, and they can open the flow of information to the public and equalize the playing field in a way that reaffirms our collective commitment to mutual respect. Reforms ought to be aimed at making the courts a better place for individuals and groups to realize these democratic values.

ENFORCING THE LAW

In 2002, if you were wheelchair-bound and wanted to go to a Taco Bell in California, you were out of luck. Many Taco Bell parking lots lacked accessible parking for the disabled. Once inside the restaurant, the line to the register was too narrow for a wheelchair to navigate, so you could not approach the register. Even if a friend had parked and ordered the food for you, you could not sit and eat because the tables were not wheelchair-accessible. This was the status quo until four disabled people sued Taco Bell in a 2002 class action lawsuit that sought changes to the construction and design of 220 California restaurants owned by the chain. The lawsuit was brought under the Americans with Disabilities Act (ADA) of 1990, which provides that restaurants of a certain size must accommodate disabled consumers by providing parking, accessible seating, and the like. Taco Bell settled the lawsuit by agreeing to satisfy, and even to exceed, the ADA requirements. While the ADA had for twenty-four years required Taco Bell to accommodate disabled patrons, it was not until that lawsuit was settled in 2014 that the restaurant fully complied with the law.[1]

Lawsuits can enable ordinary citizens to insist that the law be enforced, as in the Taco Bell case, when legal rules might otherwise be ignored for decades or longer. There are three ways litigation helps society to enforce the law: forcing people to *answer* for their wrongdoing, holding them *accountable* for that wrongdoing, and *deterring* them (and others) from violating the law in the future. Answerability allows a person to call someone they think has done them wrong into court to answer for what they did. It fills a need that people have for answers. But demanding an answer is only the first step. If that person indeed harmed another, the accountability principle requires that the wrongdoer pay for that harm and in some cases that they be ordered to stop engaging in the harmful act. Finally, lawsuits can also have a deterrent effect; they can prevent the wrongdoer in a particular case from transgressing again and, because the consequence of the wrongdoing is publicized, also deter other people or institutions from engaging in the same unlawful conduct.[2]

The process of litigation acknowledges that people who are harmed are entitled to receive direct recognition from the person who caused them harm and from the court, and to be made whole in some way. In so doing, litigation affirms the values of autonomy and human dignity. Both answerability and accountability are backward looking in that they respond to and correct an alleged *past* wrong. Deterrence, by contrast, looks *forward* to prevent similar harms in the future. A single lawsuit can promote all three goals. The lawsuit against Taco Bell, for example, required the restaurant's representatives to appear in court to answer for the fact that Taco Bell restaurants were still not accessible to people in wheelchairs. The suit sought a statement from the court that the restaurant chain's conduct was wrong (a form of accountability) and concrete changes to existing restaurants. It also sought an injunction to make sure that Taco Bell altered its restaurant architecture going forward so that new construction would be accessible to disabled patrons. At the same time, as the lawsuit was highly publicized, it encouraged other fast food restaurants to make architectural changes to their establishments to comply with the ADA. Notably these goals were achieved even absent a trial—in other words, litigation may achieve all three enforcement goals even when a lawsuit ends in settlement.

Plenty of anecdotes describe lawsuits that forced wrongdoers to answer for their conduct or lawsuits that changed the way companies do business. But there are also stories of recalcitrant defendants who have simply paid lip service to the law without changing their ways, perhaps because they do not want to obey the law, or because settlement is cheaper, or because they are not sued often enough to make change worthwhile. Critics on the left argue that lawsuits are not effective enough because most people do not sue, and even when they do, defendants pay less than they ought to. Critics on the right argue that lawsuits are *too* effective, leading companies and individuals to avoid useful activities or stifle innovation because they are afraid of being sued. Although there is anecdotal support for both these positions, the weight of the empirical evidence shows that enforcement through litigation is weak rather than punitive, and recent changes to the litigation landscape will make enforcement through litigation even more difficult and less effective than before. People may perceive the threat of litigation to loom large, but in fact the trend is toward less enforcement, or even in the case of some consumer protection laws, no enforcement at all. Because private litigation is a crucial component of the American system for enforcing law in multiple areas of social and economic life, the erosion of enforcement raises a serious concern for the future of the rule of law in the United States.[3]

The battle over enforcement of the law through litigation is really a disagreement over whether certain conduct should be regulated and how much regulation is appropriate, although the debate is often presented as being about lawyer overreach or frivolous lawsuits. Litigation over civil rights, antitrust, tort law, patents, and environmental disasters is controversial because the underlying legal intervention is controversial, whereas litigation over contracts is less controversial, although contracts suits make up many more of the lawsuits brought in the United States.

Litigation, however, is just one means for regulating conduct. The first part of this chapter will compare litigation to two other forms of regulating conduct: agency regulation and government suits. Litigation is symbiotic with these other forms of regulation, as well as with activism of social movements or nongovernmental organizations. Although the point seems obvious once articulated, the idea that litigation is a complement to other forms of regulation and should be harnessed to that end is often ignored in the debates about its merit.

After exploring different ways wrongful conduct is regulated in the United States to gain a better understanding of the role of private litigation among the choices available for this purpose, the bulk of this chapter will investigate how well lawsuits achieve answerability, accountability, and deterrence, particularly in the concrete contexts that have been among the most controversial and under attack: civil rights and tort litigation. Lawsuits have an important role to play in regulating conduct within a complicated landscape of direct government regulation and market forces, and although it is sometimes difficult to tease out the specific effects of litigation on social problems, there is evidence that litigation is an important component of law enforcement.[4]

THREE TYPES OF REGULATION

Different mechanisms exist to enforce the law, including enforcement by administrative agency, government lawsuits, and private litigation. Government inspectors, for example, check that food manufacturers have taken proper precautions to keep their product safe and can impose fines or even shut down a plant if safety standards are not met. This is an administrative enforcement regime and it provides deterrence and some level of answerability and accountability, although only to the government regulator, not to consumers except indirectly through publicity. Some laws can only be enforced in suits brought by government lawyers, such as claims that a state government policy has a disparate impact on protected groups in violation of Title VI of the Civil Rights Act. Finally, private lawsuits enforce the law for the party who brought the suit and sometimes for everyone else as well, as happened in the Taco Bell case.[5]

The United States has adopted an amalgam of all three of these approaches, which sometimes work in tandem and sometimes compete. The question of which enforcement mechanism should be given primacy is often hotly contested. In order to understand the nuances of the enforcement dimension of litigation, we need to look more closely at each type of regulation.

REGULATION BY AGENCY

The first way of regulating conduct is to empower administrative agencies to enforce the law. Federal agencies are given their authority by Congress, which delegates limited rulemaking power to an agency in areas that require specialized or technical expertise. State-level agencies operate similarly. Agencies fall under the supervision of the executive branch. Because agency staff answers to the executive branch, the staff is ultimately accountable to the elected branches of government (at least in theory). An agency is typically staffed by experts in the field it regulates. Such expertise is a key ingredient to making good policy because, in an ideal world, experts apply specialized knowledge in a neutral and objective way to their specific subject area and can determine the optimal regulatory approach. A particular benefit of agency regulation is that regulators can act preventatively, such as for example when the Consumer Finance Protection Bureau ordered a bank to stop collecting undocumented debts before consumers were harmed by the practice. By contrast, litigation, whether private or public, ordinarily addresses problems after they have already surfaced and caused harm.[6]

The Food and Drug Administration (FDA) is a good example of the many benefits of agency regulation and its drawbacks as well. Among other things, the FDA regulates access to pharmaceutical drugs, and is responsible for determining which drugs may be sold and which may not. As one would expect, the FDA is peopled with experts, scientists who are specialists in their field and tasked with such duties as reviewing clinical trial data and speaking with drug manufacturers about their progress in bringing new drugs to market. They also oversee the safety of existing drugs and can move quickly if needed to recall drugs that are dangerous, fast-track drugs that are beneficial, and prevent dangerous drugs from entering the market. Because the FDA sometimes requires follow-up studies, it can also catch dangerous drugs that were erroneously approved. For example, when the painkiller Vioxx was discovered to increase incidents of heart attacks and strokes in studies conducted after the drug was approved, the company voluntarily pulled the drug from the market, but if it had not done so, the FDA could have ordered the drug recalled.[7]

But agency regulation also has drawbacks and chief among them is the propensity of agencies and their staff to be subject to political or interest group influence, in other words, regulatory capture. When experts within an agency have close ties to the companies they regulate, when they stand to benefit from the success of those companies, or plan to work there in the future, their opinion about the safety of drugs is suspect. It is well known that experts and agency staff move from positions in government to private industry (and back again) and can capitalize on the knowledge developed in each position. This revolving door from government to private industry for people working on the regulation of everything from food and drugs to securities is worrisome. Even absent a revolving door, shared ideology or shared factual assumptions among government experts and industry may also result in bias. If the experts are not objective in their analysis, or do not have the best interests of the general public in mind, then we cannot trust that the regulations they propose are the best ones for society as a whole.[8]

Here the history of Vioxx provides another useful example. After Merck, the pharmaceutical company that manufactured the drug, voluntarily pulled Vioxx from the market, people started to wonder whether similar products manufactured by other pharmaceutical companies presented the same dangers and should also be pulled. The FDA convened an expert advisory panel to weigh the risks and the benefits of this particular type of drug (called a COX-2 inhibitor) and to determine the appropriate course of action. Ultimately, the panel recommended against banning the sale of COX-2 inhibitors, indeed even of Vioxx itself, but also recommended that because of their dangers these drugs should not be advertised directly to the public. Sometime after that decision became public it was revealed that the panel included scientists with financial ties to the drug companies that manufactured the drugs being investigated. Perhaps in light of these revelations, the FDA decided not to take the panel's advice and pulled many COX-2 inhibitors off the market. This mitigating result aside, the Vioxx panel remains a well-publicized example of the problem of regulatory capture.[9]

REGULATION BY GOVERNMENT LAWSUITS

A second mechanism of regulation is government lawsuits. Some agencies enforce the law through litigation rather than through inspection and review. Because government lawyers answer to the executive branch, government-driven litigation shares the benefits of political legitimacy and expertise that is the hallmark of agency regulation and some of the drawbacks as well. For example, the Securities and Exchange Commission, tasked with enforcing the securities laws through litigation if necessary, is staffed by government experts who are overseen by the president. In theory, these lawyers are responsive to the elected branches and the lawsuits they bring are consistent with the legislative purpose of any particular law. We might trust the Department of Justice, for example, to bring antitrust suits that are more consistent with social welfare and the legislative intent of the antitrust laws than private attorneys with private incentives. Government attorneys also have no immediate financial stake in the outcome of a lawsuit in the sense that they are salaried employees, although they may have a professional stake in the success of lawsuits they prosecute. Finally, governmental lawsuits do not require the creation of a complex bureaucracy in order to enforce the law, and in that way may be less expensive and wasteful than some types of direct agency regulation.[10]

Government-driven litigation also involves costs and, accordingly, practical limitations. Government lawyers may decide to wait or not to pursue a lawsuit at all even when members of the community believe wrongdoing has occurred. Government lawyers may choose not to pursue a case for lack of funding, may not be aware of the violation, or may decide to pursue wrongdoing incrementally either to give potential defendants the chance to cure or for other reasons. For example, in 2012 the New York Legal Aid Society and private law firms filed a lawsuit alleging a policy and practice of using unlawful excessive force against inmates at the Riker's Island jail. Perhaps because of lack of awareness of the severity of the problem at Rikers, it was not until December 2014 that the Manhattan US Attorney's Office joined that class action and helped negotiate a settlement with New York City. In the aftermath of protests in Ferguson, Missouri, the Department of Justice initially decided to give that city's police department an opportunity to reform before bringing civil rights charges. This type of forbearance has been the subject of withering criticism, such as the admonitions of a prominent federal judge, Jed Rakoff, who criticized the government for failing to prosecute those responsible for the 2009 financial crisis.[11]

REGULATION BY PRIVATE LAWSUITS

A final form of regulation is litigation brought by private individuals, institutions, or groups. The benefit of regulation through private litigation is that it does not depend on funding agencies or lawyers employed by the government. Instead, private actors, pursuing their own self-interest, confer the collateral benefit of enforcing the law for the public good. Unlike other forms of regulation, in a private lawsuit the parties participate directly in calling one another to answer and account for wrongdoing, rather than through a government intermediary. Private litigants are also not subject to regulatory capture, as government employees looking toward their next job in the private sector might be. To the contrary, the interests of the lawyers bringing these cases are well-aligned with the merits of the legal action. Many private lawyers are paid only if they win, either because of fee shifting or a contingency fee arrangement. And when private lawyers are paid by their clients directly, those clients must believe in their cases enough to be willing to invest large sums in vindicating their rights.

American society values decentralization and individualized enforcement of the law as opposed to enforcement through a bureaucracy engaged in centralized decision-making. Private litigation reflects these values. The American preference for regulation through litigation reflects individualistic attitudes because litigation allows individuals and groups to sue rather than giving large-scale governmental institutions the exclusive power to enforce the law. Many lawsuits in the federal courts are part of this private regime for enforcing federal statutes, and as a result the American legal system depends on private lawyers to bring cases for many substantive laws to be enforced.

Why do American legislators choose private over public enforcement? One intriguing answer comes from political scientist Sean Farhang. Farhang studied enforcement regimes that enabled private litigation, such as the Civil Rights Act of 1964, which provides that plaintiffs may recoup their attorney's fees from defendants when they prevail in a lawsuit brought under the act. It is undisputed and unremarkable that this legislation encouraged private litigation on civil rights matters such as employment discrimination. The result of these and similar laws was a steep rise in filings in the federal courts in the last forty years. Over 165,000 lawsuits are filed in the federal courts every year to enforce federal statutes, and 97 percent of these are filed by private litigants.[12]

What *is* surprising is that the legislation that enabled these lawsuits was sponsored by Republicans. Farhang shows that Congress' decision to enable private litigation instead of empowering administrative agencies to do the same work was a strategic choice. Private enforcement regimes insulate Congressional decisions from executive power. Instead of strengthening or building administrative agencies, Congress chose to create private rights of action allowing individuals to vindicate statutory rights on their own. In doing so, Congress took power out of the hands of the president, who controls administrative agencies, and insulated its decisions from future leaders who might defund those agencies. It is much easier to defang an agency than to roll back civil rights legislation. Accordingly, the American preference for private enforcement of public rights does not only evidence disdain for bureaucracy or preference for individualism, though it fits into these tropes. It is also a legislative strategy in a divided government.[13]

The fact that Americans regulate through private lawsuits in addition to public administration is described as the negative side of American individualism when critics claim that litigation prevents government agencies from doing their job efficiently. This is certainly sometimes the case, although other times lawsuits may spur government regulation that otherwise might have been hampered by regulatory capture. In addition, private lawyers may prefer cases with high damages over cases with low or nominal damages, even if the low-value cases have merit and bringing them would be important for the public interest. At least theoretically, government lawyers bring suits without regard to their personal benefit and are more likely to represent those whose chances of winning or damages are too low to merit a private suit. Private attorneys, driven by a profit motive, may also bring suits that try to expand the law in directions not intended by the legislature, whereas government lawyers are likely to hew more closely to the legislative intent in the arguments they make. And as is the case with government-driven lawsuits, private litigation can be slow and clumsy as compared to agency action. The Taco Bell lawsuit, for example, went on for ten years even though objective evidence of ADA violations was available by the third year of that suit. Finally, some argue that private litigation has not had much effect on institutional conduct at all, or, at the other extreme, that winning lawsuits causes a backlash, inhibiting the very legal progress plaintiffs sought. We will evaluate these arguments later in this chapter.[14]

Litigation is indeed an imperfect form of regulation, as critics point out, but it is important to remember that the alternatives—the free market or agency regulation—are also flawed. When the government fails to regulate, private litigation fills the breach. This means that where private litigation is a replacement for agency regulation or government suits, limiting access to the courts can result in no regulation at all. Furthermore, litigation does not operate in isolation from these other forms of regulation. As we shall see, litigation works as a complement to other types of enforcement.[15]

HOW EFFECTIVE IS LITIGATION?

At the end of the day, each form of regulation has its costs and benefits, and although they have so far been presented as alternatives, they are in fact complements. The remainder of this chapter looks more closely at the arguments about the effect of litigation, focusing on the debates over the efficacy of civil rights actions and tort suits in achieving answerability, accountability, and deterrence. I focus on these areas of the law as examples of the different ways the debate over the benefits of litigation has played out because they have been very controversial. The choice of these two particular case studies does not mean that litigation is exclusively useful in civil rights and tort law; in fact, litigation has also played an important role in antitrust enforcement, where it has been controversial, and in enforcing contract law, to name just two examples. As this analysis illustrates, litigation has played a crucial role in spurring change in combination with legislation and direct citizen action. These case studies show that society needs litigation to establish rights, bring attention to problems, and, frankly, frighten wrongdoers. Institutions such as the legislature, administrative agencies, executive branch officials, and community activists are more likely to take action following a lawsuit and sometimes will not act without that catalyst.

LITIGATION, ACTIVISM, AND THE CASE OF CIVIL RIGHTS

When institutions are not recalcitrant but in fact want to change, litigation can help spur needed changes in internal regulations. For example, the Portland, Oregon, police department learned from monitoring lawsuits that officers on the night shift in one station were repeatedly sued for excessive force because they hit prisoners on the head and in response invested in additional training and supervision in that station. The incidents declined.[16]

When the government or municipality is recalcitrant, litigation is equally important. One of the most powerful criticisms of civil rights litigation, however, is that it is ineffective as compared with community activism and legislation. Critics have suggested that legal rulings have little independent effect on rights and that instead it is broad social movements that spur social change. Somewhat corollary to that view, critics have also suggested that activists would do better to invest their resources in direct action rather than litigation. *Brown v. Board of Education* is for many the strongest case for the proposition that the courts can spur social change. Yet *Brown* and its legacy have come under attack from scholars who argue that it not only did little to promote equality, but in fact caused a violent backlash.[17]

The basic facts that give rise to competing interpretations are these. *Brown* was decided in 1954 and in that case the Supreme Court held that legal rules segregating schools on the basis of race violated the equal protection clause of the Fourteenth Amendment. The following year, the Supreme Court issued an opinion mandating that the states desegregate schools, as the Court put it, "with all deliberate speed." That language signaled to segregated states that they could proceed slowly. Southern states resisted school integration in the courts and in the legislature; Virginia shut down its public schools altogether for a period of time rather than integrate them. As a result of that resistance, the process of integration took many years. Lawyers continued to litigate desegregation cases, and in the meantime, the civil rights movement grew. Ultimately, in response to that movement and the violent resistance of segregationists, Congress enacted the Civil Rights Act of 1964 codifying antidiscrimination principles into federal law and providing private rights of action for their enforcement. That is the basis of the argument that it was protest followed by legislation, not the Court ruling, that made the genuine impact.[18]

Despite all this litigation, schools today are still not fully integrated, not because of legal segregation but because of facts on the ground: neighborhoods are segregated by race and for that reason so are neighborhood schools. In other words, today the problem is a structural one that persists despite efforts to combat it. In the 1990s, the federal courts turned away from their previous calls to enforce integration and allowed school desegregation orders to expire. And in 2007 in *Parents Involved in Community Schools v. Seattle District No. 1,* the Supreme Court (in a plurality opinion) struck down a system of race-conscious school assignments in Washington State intended to integrate public schools by addressing the racial disparities in neighborhood populations.[19]

In light of the foregoing, some scholars have argued that the decision in *Brown* led to a backlash against equal rights for African Americans and may have even set back their cause. In a thoughtful examination of this issue, Michael Klarman has argued that the effect of *Brown* was ultimately not to desegregate schools, but rather to turn southern whites toward violent resistance and away from an emerging moderate compromise with respect to segregation. Klarman demonstrates that white resistance to integration, in turn, sparked opportunities to confront segregationists, resulting in violence that was projected into millions of living rooms. That violence led to Congressional action and turned the tide of public opinion in favor of civil rights legislation. This backlash thesis suggests that the while the Court's ruling inspired white resistance to black equality, the decision did little standing alone. It was ultimately the civil rights movement and Congressional legislation that led to real change. Other scholars argue that *Brown* did not even do that much, but instead that the decision was largely ignored and that the sole responsibility for forward movement on racial equality lies with the civil rights activists who laid their bodies on the line.[20] These criticisms lead to the twin observations that legal rulings have little effect and activists would be better off investing in other forms of protest. After all, it was direct action in the face of violence that ultimately resulted in antidiscrimination legislation.

But these are the wrong lessons to take from the history of desegregation. The Court's assertion of equal rights in *Brown* indeed had a mixed history in terms of its effect—much more action was needed inside and outside the courts to eliminate legal segregation and geographic segregation persists—but the *Brown* decision and those that followed had a real world impact. When activists faced violence, when they engaged in civil disobedience, they could assert that they were doing so to vindicate the law of the land already validated by the Supreme Court. *Brown* gave activists a powerful language for asserting their rights and inspiration that grounded their hopes in the legitimacy of law.[21]

One impact of *Brown*, notwithstanding the pace of practical change it prompted, is that it established that society could be made to answer for legally enforced inequality. The next steps were accountability and deterrence. As Martin Luther King Jr., rallying people to support the Montgomery bus boycott in the winter of 1955, said: "[I]f we are wrong, the Supreme Court of this nation is wrong. If we are wrong, the Constitution of the United States is wrong. If we are wrong, God Almighty is wrong."[22] Note the progression of authority here: the Supreme Court, the Constitution, and ultimately God. The position against segregation was always *morally* right, but it became *legally* right and *politically* feasible because of *Brown*. The contribution of litigation to activism is more complex than an inspiring statement, however, as a more detailed look at the relationship between litigation and activism in the context of the Montgomery bus boycott shows.[23]

Black citizens of Montgomery, Alabama, boycotted segregation on the public buses for nearly a year starting in December 1955. The Court in *Brown* had held only that schools could not be segregated, but had purposefully been silent about other aspects of Jim Crow laws such as segregation in public transport. Although the Court would soon extend the logic of equality to many other areas of social life, it had not done so when the bus boycott began. Because there were limits to the inspiration *Brown* provided, the boycotters did not ask for full integration at first. Instead, in the beginning of the boycott, the leaders of the black community in Montgomery sought courtesy from bus drivers, reorganization of the seating arrangement, and the ability to board at the front of the bus (rather than paying in the front and boarding at the back door). Despite the boycotters' attempt at compromise, however, the lawyer for the bus company took a hard line, saying that the state and municipal law was not flexible enough to grant their requests. So the boycotters demanded integration under the logic of *Brown* and as a result, two legal visions—of segregation and integration—clashed directly.[24]

The movement to integrate the buses involved both direct activism and litigation. Most of the African American community in Montgomery was involved in the boycott and it was extremely effective. Not only did most of the community avoid the buses, crippling the local bus company economically, but the community showed discipline and fortitude by creating their own volunteer transportation system, called the Montgomery Improvement Association, to make the boycott possible. In addition, two civil lawsuits were filed by opposite sides of the boycott. Several boycotters filed a class action in federal court on behalf of all African Americans in Montgomery, seeking a ruling that the segregation of public transportation was unconstitutional. While they initially hesitated to file suit, these boycotters were ultimately spurred to do so by the bus company's uncompromising stance. On November 13, 1956, the Supreme Court affirmed that segregation in public transportation violates the equal protection clause of the Constitution. On December 20, Montgomery city officials received notice of the Supreme Court's ruling, and the next morning boycott leaders rode the buses, sitting in seats formerly reserved for whites only.[25]

Litigation provided a decisive victory, but activism remained a central tool in the ongoing battle for civil rights. Violent incidents on buses intimidated African American passengers, and many reverted to sitting at the back of the bus. As Randall Kennedy pointed out in his history of the boycott, it was easier for black residents to retreat from the color line by boycotting than to cross it by sitting in the front of the bus.[26] The rest of Montgomery remained practically segregated for many years to come, and the fight to enforce civil rights continued in the courts, in the legislature, and on the ground.

In this story, litigation functioned as a form of political activity that, in combination with direct action, brought about real change. For this reason, it would have been a mistake for the citizens of Montgomery to choose between grassroots action and litigation. There is no either/or here; political action within and outside of the courts work together. In the case of the Montgomery bus boycott and the Supreme Court's decision to strike down segregation in public transportation, litigation established rights that were realized on the ground with the help of direct action.[27]

It is important to remember, however, that litigation is not a one-way ratchet to expand individual rights or equality. Courts can move the needle in both directions. During the Montgomery bus boycott, for example, the City of Montgomery responded to the boycotters' federal suit with a lawsuit of its own in state court, seeking and ultimately obtaining an injunction to prevent the Montgomery Improvement Association from continuing to provide boycotters with that informal but very effective alternative transportation network that allowed the boycott to go on for as long as it did. In fact, the state court issued its injunction on the very same day that the Supreme Court ruled segregation in public transportation unconstitutional.[28] Of course, the state court's injunction was superseded by the Supreme Court's decision, but the point still holds.

As a result of the capacity of courts to curb rights as well as expand them, some scholars have argued in favor of doctrines that keep the courts from definitively deciding the scope of rights. This is a mistaken approach for several reasons, most importantly that we should not want litigants in the future, when the judiciary is more rights friendly, to be barred from court. It is indisputable that courts make mistakes and also that courts issue decisions that many disagree with; the first is a natural consequence of a human institution and the second is the product of living in a pluralist society. Indeed, all institutions produce decisions that are mistaken or controversial some of the time. When the courts are wrong, people sometimes turn to other institutions to cure those errors or they return to the courts with new arguments in a new case. This does not mean that litigation should be the only strategy for social movements or that it is a strategy for every situation, but it does mean that the doors to the courthouse should remain open.[29]

THE ENFORCEMENT POWER OF TORT LAW

A second set of controversial arguments about enforcement through litigation concerns tort suits, particularly those involving medical malpractice or products liability. Although tort litigation makes up only 6 percent of case filings, it is the subject of so much lobbying, legislation, and press coverage one would think most lawsuits are tort cases. The general trend in the media is to depict these cases as overblown, outrageous, or a lottery for undeserving plaintiffs, but the facts reveal a different picture. Evidence indicates that most people who are harmed do not sue, many who do sue receive relatively small recoveries, and the number of cases where there have been large punitive damages awards are in the single digits. Looking at the numbers, some scholars have argued that the tort crisis in America is not too much litigation, but too little. Yet every year more laws are passed to put caps on compensatory damages, limit punitive damages, and adopt onerous procedural requirements in order to make lawsuits harder to pursue.[30]

Given that most people do not sue, one might respond that litigation largely fails to achieve the enforcement goals of answerability, accountability, and deterrence. But the minority of cases that are brought can alert institutions to problems, spur regulatory change, and deter future wrongdoing for parties not involved in the litigation. We will consider two cases, one about faulty cars and the other about a devastating outbreak of foodborne illness, to illustrate the benefits of litigation and the costs of limiting it, before turning to an analysis of the empirical evidence regarding litigation as an enforcement tool in the most studied area of tort litigation: medical malpractice.

GENERAL MOTORS AND THE COST OF DAMAGE CAPS

For tort law to deter wrongdoing, the law needs to provide clear incentives for compliance and penalties for noncompliance. But that is not the end of the story because manufacturers also need to pay attention to those incentives. The case of General Motors' faulty ignition switches in Cobalt cars provides an example of how limitations on recovery have diminished the ability to regulate through private litigation, and what happens when agency regulation does not step into the breach.

In 2006 Natasha Weigel was killed when her Cobalt swerved off the road and plowed into some trees. A police investigation showed that her ignition switch had turned off moments before the crash, and as a result the airbags did not deploy upon impact. That same investigation also revealed that several similar incidents had been reported to the car's manufacturer, without response. It seemed likely that Natasha's death, which may well have been prevented had the airbags functioned properly, was attributable to a defect in the design of the Cobalt car.

When Natasha's family asked a reputable law firm to represent them in a suit against the car's manufacturer, the firm declined because limits on pain and suffering damages and on punitive damages, combined with the expense of proving fault, meant that the lawsuit did not make economic sense. A lawyer at that firm told the *New York Times*, "I've told many people that the value of your dead child doesn't warrant a case. It's a terrible thing to have to do."[31] As a result of laws restricting litigation, Natasha's family was not able to force GM to answer for its conduct or hold it accountable.

Because cases like Natasha's were not brought at all, and because GM was able to settle inexpensively those that were, Cobalt cars were not recalled for many years and in the meantime other drivers suffered accidents as a result. Without the pressure of litigation, GM did not have the incentive to fully investigate why its Cobalt cars were malfunctioning. In the end, it was only a 2010 lawsuit brought in Georgia—a state without punitive damages caps—that brought the problem to the forefront. And it was a 2012 lawsuit in West Virginia—another state without punitive damages caps—which resulted in a diagnosis of the problem by an expert. Most surprisingly, it was the *plaintiffs'* expert in that suit—not GM—who identified the cause of the problem.[32]

The GM story shows the costs of limiting enforcement by curtailing private litigation. Litigation can alert companies to information, and the process of discovery can assemble information that employees might otherwise overlook, such as the expert report showing the cause of the defect in Cobalt cars. But that warning will not surface if the ability to sue is limited by damages caps or other restrictions. Although litigation cannot make up for management dysfunction of the type that was prevalent at GM, the situation would have been worse if there were no litigation threat at all. Without punitive damages in West Virginia or Georgia, those cases would never have been brought, the plaintiffs' expert who diagnosed the design flaw never hired, and the truth might have taken longer to surface (if it surfaced at all). While the automobile industry is regulated, mistakes still happen, and the law needs to create incentives to cure defects as soon as possible. The threat of litigation—and high awards—provides one such incentive.

E. COLI AND LAX GOVERNMENT REGULATION

A 1993 *E. coli* outbreak, and the litigation that followed, changed the way we regulate meat in the United States. Before then, a few doctors and scientists knew of the dangers of *E. coli* and that there was a crisis waiting to happen, but the pathogen was not on the radar of the food producers, restaurants, and supermarkets that sell ground meat and the relevant government regulators did not specifically monitor for it or regulate to prevent *E. coli* contamination. Worse yet, the practices in slaughtering facilities were not designed to prevent contamination, and plants were shut down for unsanitary practices too rarely, if at all. Even when inspectors reported problems, including previous, small-scale *E. coli* outbreaks, nothing happened. The change came only when a lawsuit following the death of four children and infection of many hundreds revealed the depth of the problems.[33]

No restaurant wants to serve dangerous food, but that does not mean that they always follow best practices. Because *E. coli* in meat was not regulated at all, meat processers and restaurants did not take adequate precautions to prevent contamination. When the outbreak resulting from contaminated and undercooked meat at the fast food chain Jack in the Box first surfaced, the company, advised by lawyers for its insurers (who were responsible for up to $100 million in damages and costs), tried to settle cases quietly, offering to pay medical costs and small sums in exchange for victims' promises not to sue. If they had succeeded in resolving the outstanding liability while incurring only minor costs, it is not clear that the restaurant would have had the incentive to put into place the far-reaching reforms necessary to prevent future outbreaks. Fortunately, the negative publicity from these attempts to settle resulted in a change of course. As the lawsuits proceeded, discovery revealed the source of the contamination and the fact that the company's burgers were undercooked due to using older grills.[34] Although local regulations in Washington State, the locus of the outbreak, required hamburgers to be cooked to a higher internal temperature than national regulations, the company had disregarded these rules. At least one employee had communicated customer complaints about undercooked hamburgers, but that complaint was ignored because the management was not attuned to the risk.[35]

Under pressure from the lawsuits, the publicity from these suits, and a falling stock price, Jack in the Box not only changed its cooking practices but also overhauled its chain of distribution—from farm to table. The lawsuits were not the sole driver of these changes—after all, no restaurant wants to make its patrons sick—but they were a major impetus.

Like GM, Jack in the Box had failed its customers, but the truth is that the federal government had done no better in its failure to regulate the meat supply. Federal regulations in the early 1990s, at the time of that *E. coli* outbreak, had set minimum cooking standards too low to effectively kill the bacterium. It was only in the wake of this litigation and the accompanying public outcry that federal regulations were changed to better prevent future outbreaks. All of this shows that litigation is an important, albeit imperfect, regulator and that litigation is especially necessary when government and self-regulation fail. Sadly, such failures are much too common yet still unpredictable.[36]

THE CASE OF MEDICAL MALPRACTICE LITIGATION

So far this analysis of tort law has presented stories that demonstrate how litigation creates incentives to ensure consumer safety and how it can spur both internal corporate changes as well as government regulation. This next section will discuss enforcement in the context of one of the most studied and controversial areas of tort law: medical malpractice litigation.

Medical malpractice suits deter misconduct in a number of ways. First, hospitals and practitioners make use of data cataloguing medical malpractice claims, including lawsuits, in order to improve practices and to protect themselves from future liability. Indeed, as we will see in chapter 2, much of the power of litigation to enforce the law lies in its ability to elicit information. While data cataloguing medical errors might be obtained through self-reporting, underreporting of errors and the complacency of medical personnel mean that evidence of what actually went wrong only surfaces when a lawsuit has focused attention on the incident and created an incentive for the hospital to fund experts to investigate and evaluate what happened. Lawsuits can be powerful on their own, but the collection and study of prior suits are necessary complements to litigation. Such studies are needed because medical malpractice litigation, by its nature, focuses on what went wrong in the individual case, but often the problems within an institution are systemic.[37]

Studies of claim patterns have provided useful information that has changed concrete practices in hospitals and among specialists, even though most patients who are injured do not file claims. One study looked at hospital records from patients discharged in New York State in 1984 and estimated that a claim was filed in only 1.53 percent of the cases where there was negligence. That means that most people were not claiming at all, even under a legal regime (as was true of New York in 1984) that was not very hostile to medical malpractice claims. If too few people are compensated, then the institutions that are supposed to keep them safe do not have incentives to improve quality of care. Indeed, in light of the evidence that claiming rates are less than 2 percent, it is surprising that medical malpractice is such a hot political issue and that it has a significant effect on doctor behavior. Perhaps this is because medical malpractice suits tend to involve claims of severe injury, which in turn leads to memorably high awards. In any event, the low claiming rate in medical malpractice makes the case for *more* litigation, not less.[38]

A second source of evidence on whether medical malpractice litigation deters misconduct is whether legislation that curbs litigation has an effect on patient safety. If tort reforms do decrease litigation, and litigation has a deterrent effect, one would expect that as tort reforms took effect the rates of injury would rise. One study has shown this to be the case. Researchers who compared preventable injuries to patients in states with damages caps to patients in states without such caps and found that adverse outcomes short of death increased gradually in the years after a cap was put into place. After ruling out most other explanations for the decline in patient safety, the conclusion they drew is that the quality of care likely decreased because the threat of liability was diminished. There is some contrary evidence. For example, studies have found that damages caps have no effect on death rates, indicating that medical malpractice reforms do not affect the most catastrophic cases. Perhaps this is because damages caps and other barriers to suit are not a factor in the decision to bring a lawsuit when the patient has died, or perhaps it is because (one would hope) doctors take care to prevent patient death regardless of the threat of liability. More empirical work remains to be done before drawing a definitive conclusion on the overall deterrent effect of medical malpractice litigation.[39]

The main argument against medical malpractice litigation has been the contention that there are too many frivolous claims. But the evidence does not support this assertion. The most reliable studies show that patients make claims against doctors and hospitals when they are genuinely injured and that most of the time (but not all the time) patients who are entitled to compensation receive it. For example, a Harvard study asked doctors to evaluate 1,452 closed claims from five insurance companies. The study found that almost all of the claims these physicians reviewed involved a treatment-related injury, and many of these injuries were severe. This means that patients were claiming with a good reason: they suffered an injury caused by their treatment. That does not mean, however, that they were all entitled to a remedy—sometimes patients suffer bad outcomes although the doctor did not act negligently. In 63 percent of the claims they studied, the independent reviewing physicians thought the case involved doctor error. In about 20 percent of the claims there was no evidence of doctor error at all, in about 10 percent there was slight to moderate evidence of doctor error, and the remaining 7 percent were a close call, meaning that there was some evidence of error, but ultimately the reviewers thought the injury was not the result of doctor error. Every indication was that filing a claim was part of the process of finding out what happened after things went wrong—in other words, to get answers.[40]

Another allegation has been that medical malpractice suits are paid even when the doctor was not negligent, in other words, that the results are unfair. The Harvard study showed that the claiming system worked pretty well about three-quarters of the time. However, they also found that in 16 percent of the cases where an independent physician evaluating the case thought that there *was* medical error and the patient was injured, the patient was not compensated (and recall that most of these cases involve serious injuries), and in 10 percent of the cases where there was no medical error, the patient was compensated anyway. In sum, the study showed that too many patients who should have been compensated were not, some patients who should not have been compensated were, and that in a supermajority of the cases the system worked well.

Finally, prosecuting a claim was expensive for patients and providers, which is not surprising given the expertise needed to litigate a medical malpractice claim. The Harvard study found that 54 percent of the total cost of the system went to fees and administrative costs. It is likely that most patients paid the usual contingency fee, about 30 percent, to their lawyers. But importantly, only 13 percent of the expenses were for claims that the researchers were fairly certain involved no doctor error (even though there was an injury)—that is, most of the costs incurred were for valid claims. That is a good thing if the expense of the system causes hospitals to alter their conduct and improve patient safety, but if hospitals fight claims that have merit rather than settling, they simply harm injured patients.[41]

THE ROLE OF ENFORCEMENT IN CIVIL SOCIETY

Litigation is a way to spur social and institutional change, in combination with other methods of regulation such as agency oversight, public lawsuits, legislative action, and community activism. It requires alleged wrongdoers to answer for their conduct and provides a process for them to be held accountable. In many cases, litigation is the only way to achieve answerability and accountability, and in other cases litigation is one among a number of regulatory options. Where regulation by agency or government lawyers is weakest is where private litigation can do the most good.

Even the wrongs wrought by litigation itself can be repaired through litigation. Recently the practice of banks selling debts that were poorly documented—meaning that the debtor may not have owed the money—has come to light. A law firm adopted the dubious practice of using the court system to collect these debts by filing lawsuits by the thousands and asserting that the lawyers had verified the validity of the debt when they had not in fact done so. Most of the people who were sued did not respond to the suit (the allegation was that they never received notice of it), so they suffered default judgments. This practice meant that thousands of people were subject to having their wages garnished and the erroneous debt collected in other ways. The practice was not regulated by any administrative agency at that time. When the practice was discovered, the people who had been sued brought a class action against the debt collectors. Although the battle over whether the case could go forward was fierce, it was ultimately allowed to proceed as a class action and settled to the benefit of the debtors.

One prominent federal judge's reaction to the case illustrates the extent to which antilitigation sentiment and the idea that litigation is only about resolving disputes, rather than answerability, accountability, and deterrence, have overtaken common sense. That federal appellate judge railed against the "hungry" lawyers who brought the class action, but had no similarly harsh words for those lawyers who had taken advantage of the legal system to collect on bad debts. He suggested that an administrative process for vacating the judgments would be enough, even though such a process would not require the law firm to answer for its conduct, would not have held it accountable, would not have compensated the plaintiff class, and would not deter unscrupulous debt collectors from doing the same thing in the future.[42]

Enforcement is crucial to the rule of law. In order for civil society to exist, people and institutions need to know that they can enforce their rights and that they will be held to account when they do wrong. But in order for the courts (or any other institution that attempts to enforce the law) to work, litigants need access to information. The next chapter addresses the role of information in litigation and how litigation can contribute to the democratic value of transparency.

THE POWER OF INFORMATION

In the fall of 1996, an unpasteurized apple juice manufactured by the popular Odwalla company was linked to twenty-five serious *E. coli* infections—including one death—in a number of states. Through a series of public apologies, the company offered to pay all the children's medical expenses while labeling the infections an accident, probably the result of feces from deer grazing in the apple orchards that supplied fruit for their product. Despite these apologies, the victims decided to pursue lawsuits against Odwalla. In the process of court-ordered discovery these plaintiffs received some, but not all, of the company's inspection reports for its juice manufacturing facility. Acting on an anonymous voicemail tip, the lawyer for the families filed a Freedom of Information Act request with the US government. That search recovered a letter from the US Army to Odwalla, revealing that army inspectors had found that the juice manufacturer's "plant sanitation program does not adequately assure product wholesomeness" and rejecting the company's application to provide juice for US soldiers. The letter proved that the company had known about sanitary problems at its plant at least as early as August of 1996, months before the *E. coli* outbreak, yet they continued to market their juice through the fall. Had the plaintiffs in this case been satisfied with the company's apology and taken the fast settlement, Odwalla would never have been called to account for its actions. Only though litigation was the real story uncovered.[1]

The Odwalla story demonstrates how litigation can increase transparency by bringing to light vital information that would otherwise remain hidden. The lawyer received the anonymous tip because of the publicity of litigation and was able to obtain additional information about the company's safety practices through court-ordered discovery. Litigation can also produce narratives that help us understand a complicated world, providing insights into whether the contamination was purely accidental or caused by carelessness. While the Odwalla story began with a narrative of purely accidental contamination, additional facts discovered in the course of the litigation showed that in fact this was a case of fault: Odwalla had been warned that its sanitation program was inadequate and did nothing. The case did not reach a trial and final judgment because the families settled, but the information was still publicized and the story told. This demonstrates that while a trial is the paradigmatic forum for getting to the truth in litigation, even cases that settle can produce socially valuable information and narratives.

Transparency is a social good, necessary not only for individual well-being but also for the successful functioning of a democratic society. People need information to make choices as consumers and voters. For example, information revealed about unpasteurized juice may alter buying habits or spur voters to choose candidates based on their position on regulation of the food industry. Manufacturers need information to make better products. We saw in chapter 1 how automobile manufacturers were alerted to problems with their cars through litigation. And institutions need information to optimize their services and comply with the law, such as hospitals using patterns of claims to track problems with their provision of medical care.

Litigation can reveal different kinds of information that individuals and society need. The first type of information litigation produces are facts about the world. Litigation can reveal and draw attention to social or regulatory problems that might otherwise go unnoticed, such as when a car manufacturer begins investigating a design flaw in response to a lawsuit. It can police the government by forcing governmental entities to release information that would otherwise be kept secret and, in so doing, promote individual liberty by placing an additional check on governmental authority. On an individual level, a lawsuit can reveal information important to the litigants involved. For example, recall the parents of Natasha Weigel, a young woman killed in a car crash, who wanted to know why the airbags in their daughter's car did not deploy. For individuals and the broader public, the process of litigation can combine the facts and the law to produce narratives and provide explanations for why past events occurred, frameworks for addressing hurtful incidents, and opportunities for healing as a result. Even when these narratives are not fully satisfactory, as every story forecloses some other narrative path, they help participants come to terms with the past.[2]

A second type of information litigation produces is information about the law itself. Often underestimated is how important it is for people to understand how a law will be interpreted by judges and applied in fact situations that are likely to repeat themselves. Where the law is unclear, a lawsuit can clarify what people's obligations are to one another or, alternately, can lead to the development of new law that addresses an emerging set of problems. In the Odwalla case the legal rules were clear so the fact that the lawsuit settled did not impede the development of the law, but in other situations settlement may limit or obscure access to information about the law. Clarity about legal rules makes law more predictable and understandable, and hopefully more just and fair, and, at a minimum, litigation can reveal legal rules that are unfair. In some cases this information can lead to social change through other governmental institutions or citizen action.

GETTING INFORMATION

Any discussion of transparency through litigation must begin with discovery—the process by which civil litigants can compel one another to produce the factual information needed to press their case. Discovery is governed by a number of technical rules that permit parties to force information from one another that is relevant to their claims and defenses in the lawsuit and proportional to the needs of the case. In discovery both sides of the litigation have an opportunity to ask questions, obtain documents, and seek evidence that they might use to prove their case at trial or to negotiate a settlement. The lawyer for the plaintiffs who became sick from Odwalla's juice, for example, could question the company's executives about the army inspection and what they knew about the sanitary conditions in their plant. By the same token, the lawyer for Odwalla could obtain the medical records of the victims who sued, question them under oath, and even require them to submit to a medical examination.[3]

Discovery in the United States is lawyer-driven. This means that the parties seek information from one another independent of the court. Only when there is a dispute between them about how much information must be released or in what form it will be produced will the judge become involved. As a result, much of the information produced in discovery is not public unless the litigants choose to publicize it, as the lawyer for the plaintiffs did in the Odwalla case, or unless they file the documents with the court as part of a motion or other court proceeding. Some information needs protection, such as trade secrets, business plans, and medical or employment records, and courts are empowered to issue orders that prevent this type of private information from being publicized. Protection of other information is more controversial. For example, should a manufacturer be allowed to obtain a protective order for information relating to a potentially dangerous defect in its cars?[4]

Because discovery is lawyer-driven, parties who do not ask for information in discovery will not get that information. Having a good lawyer who knows what to ask for matters. In this way transparency through litigation is dependent on some modicum of equality between the parties and can exacerbate inequalities because if one party does not have the capacity to ask for what she needs to pursue her case, she will be at a significant disadvantage. As a corollary, for the most part, parties pay for the costs of producing discovery and the costs of seeking it themselves. Producing a lot of documents can be expensive, and this can create incentives for litigants to increase the costs of discovery—that is, to ask for more information than they really need—in order to encourage their opponent to settle. But it is also important to remember that sometimes crucial information is in the exclusive possession of one side, and that although there is a cost to producing that information, there is also a cost to keeping it obscure. This cost asymmetry, as well as the information asymmetry in civil litigation, is at the core of the controversy over court-ordered discovery. Thus transparency requires a balance; policymakers must think carefully about the trade-offs between cost and access to information in litigation.[5]

Information obtained from litigation provides one of the clearest benefits of transparency for individuals: learning what happened to them and why. In fact, sometimes people bring lawsuits primarily for this reason. An extraordinary example that illustrates the point is the lawsuit brought in 2002 by the family of a Kuwaiti citizen whose parents suspected he was being held in the Guantánamo Bay prison. In 2002 the names of persons detained at Guantánamo were not made public; even the fact that anyone was being detained there at all was kept secret. After making some inquiries with the State Department and other agencies and being rebuffed, the family's lawyers decided to file a lawsuit in federal court. This was a difficult decision because it was an intense period in American politics and society. The terrorist attacks of 9/11 loomed large; Anthrax scares rocked the capital. The lawyers were worried about the public perception of seeking to free terrorists, so they sought to work on behalf of their clients in light of these political constraints. Their claims were based on Department of Defense regulations and what the lawyers asked for was very limited. One lawyer who was involved characterized the strategy as purely information-seeking in the beginning: "[N]umber one, do you have these guys? Number two, if you do, have they been charged with anything and if so, what charges? And number three, we want to contact them. That's it. Nothing about release, nothing about habeas corpus, that's it."[6]

Even in more ordinary, everyday cases, information can provide satisfaction. For example, surveys of patients who brought medical malpractice suits found that many patients just wanted to find out why their injury occurred. Once injured patients got information about what caused their medical injury, they often dropped their lawsuits. Perversely, the reason they had to file lawsuits to obtain the information was that doctors withheld it in fear of a medical malpractice suit. Once these studies were published and the effect of the doctors' refusal to communicate was understood, some hospitals responded by requiring disclosure of medical errors to patients. One Michigan hospital that instituted such a policy and further offered compensation in cases where there was negligence reduced its overall costs associated with medical malpractice claims.[7]

The process of legal argument and the presentation of proofs also helps people form information into narratives in order to understand the world and create social meaning. These narratives provide frameworks for understanding the past and the present, a process that can be satisfying for those who have suffered injury and can assist in finding closure and resolution. These narratives can coalesce at a trial, where lawyers for each side present competing narratives for the judge or jury to choose between, but the trial is not the exclusive forum for creating such narratives, as I will explain later in this chapter.

Litigation not only helps individual plaintiffs, but also assists defendants and especially institutional defendants who are repeat players in particular kinds of disputes to identify and fix problems in their practices or policies. A second example from medicine illustrates this well. In response to a high volume of medical malpractice suits against its members in the late 1990s, the American Society of Anesthesiologists (ASA) collected and studied over four thousand claims against anesthesiologists. They found that more than one-third of these claims resulted from "adverse respiratory events" that led to some of the most severe injuries but, importantly, were also largely preventable. The ASA supported the development of improved anesthesia equipment and drafted better practice guidelines for their members. The result was a marked increase in patient safety and fewer claims. This success story is no exception; hospitals today have risk management departments tasked with similar work.[8]

A series of lawsuits about the same subject can alert an institution to problems that might otherwise go undetected. The GM story from chapter 1 illustrates the point. In late 2013, information surfaced that certain GM cars suffered from a fatal design flaw: the weight of a keychain pulling down the key in the ignition could cause the car to shut down without warning—a design defect that led to a number of serious and sometimes fatal accidents particularly where, because the car had been turned off, airbags did not deploy upon impact as they should have. Later investigations revealed that GM employees possessed information that could have prevented these injuries and deaths, but the company failed to investigate the design flaw quickly and effectively. Ultimately, the internal investigation was revived when the family of a woman who was killed as a result of the defect brought a lawsuit against the manufacturer. In part because it waited so long to act, GM was forced to pay billions of dollars in compensation and product recalls.[9]

People also use litigation to force the government to reveal information to which the public is entitled, often to the benefit of many. The controversy surrounding distracted driving offers a useful example. In 2003, National Highway Traffic Safety Administration officials conducted a long-term study to assess the safety of cell phone use while driving. This study found that traffic accidents could be caused by distraction from any cell phone conversation, whether or not the phone was hand-held. Many states that regulate cell phone use while driving nevertheless permit hands-free devices for talking on the phone. Hearing reports of this research in the press, two nonprofit organizations, the Center for Auto Safety and Public Citizen, filed requests for the study results with the US government. The Freedom of Information Act enables people to obtain information from the government upon request, but in this case the government refused.

The organizations responded by filing a lawsuit, and as a result the agency revealed that officials had drafted a letter to state governors to tell them about this research and warn of the risks, but ultimately the letter and the research were shelved. In interviews, agency officials said the agency leadership had decided not to release the information for fear of angering Congress because it might be seen as trying to influence state policy. In other words, the information was buried for political reasons and it would have remained buried but for the lawsuit bringing it to light. Now that it is available, voters and state legislatures can make better informed decisions about how best to ensure safety on the roads.[10]

In addition to revealing information, litigation can also create it. Consider *Floyd v. City of New York*, a lawsuit brought against the City of New York about a controversial policy adopted by the city's police force in the early 2000s, under which officers were permitted to stop and pat down—that is, stop and frisk—citizens on city streets. The police department admitted that they made use of this policy most frequently in certain neighborhoods, and that a vast majority of the people they stopped were black and Latino men. As the litigation would so well publicize, tens of thousands of men were stopped and frisked by the city's police force, with many of those stopped asserting that there was no basis whatsoever for the stop.[11]

Experts hired by the plaintiffs in the *Floyd* case analyzed all the stops and frisks documented by New York City police officers, and their analysis found racial disparities in these stops, which particularly affected black and Latino New Yorkers. This data only existed for them to analyze because the police department required officers to document stops, among other reasons, in order to "protect the officer and the Department from allegations of police misconduct which may sometimes arise from the proper performance of police duty."[12] In other words, the threat of litigation was a catalyst for requiring that the officers fill out forms when they stopped people. These forms provided the data that enabled plaintiffs alleging racial disparities in police practices to test and prove their case, and ultimately put an end to the discriminatory practices, at least for the time being.

So far the discussion has been about factual information revealed through litigation, but as noted earlier information about the law itself is also a valuable form of transparency produced by litigation. Often the answer to the question "Can they do that?" is arrived at through litigation. For example, for many years Warner/Chappell Music has asserted that it owns the copyright of the song "Happy Birthday to You." When filmmakers wanted to use the popular song in television shows or movies, they would have to pay Warner/Chappell or not use the song. A law professor researched the history of the song and concluded that it was not legally under copyright. He published his findings in 2009 with little impact; Warner/Chappell continued to assert its copyright. Finally, a lawsuit was brought in 2013 challenging Warner/Chappell's claims of copyright ownership. In 2015 a federal district judge ruled in favor of the plaintiffs against Warner/Chappell, leading the parties to settle the lawsuit under terms that will likely mean the song can finally be performed without paying royalties.[13]

Litigation also leads to new interpretations of the law or new understandings about how old principles apply to new situations. When the Supreme Court was called on to decide whether a state can refuse to recognize adoption by a same-sex parent (it cannot), or whether a public employee can be fired for testifying before a grand jury regarding corruption in the workplace (he cannot), the Court addressed for the first time how existing law applies to novel situations. These rulings are only possible because someone brought a lawsuit. This does not mean, however, that new interpretations always expand individual rights. Whether that happens depends on the direction of the substantive law. Whatever one's political preferences, litigation is one means of challenging the present legal order that has the added benefit of producing and testing proofs and arguments and promoting public deliberation.[14]

Sometimes the outcome of a legal challenge to the existing legal order is widely perceived as incorrect, in which case recourse is to the legislature to change the law. In 2007 the Supreme Court was asked to interpret the statute of limitations provision of Title VII of the Civil Rights Act, which prohibits sex discrimination in pay. Lilly Ledbetter, who had worked for Goodyear Tire for over twenty years, learned only after the fact that she had been paid less than her male counter-parts in identical positions during the long course of her employment. She tried to sue but the Supreme Court held that the statute of limitations ran 180 days after each pay period, so that she could only sue about salary disparities in the last 180 days. The *Ledbetter* decision led to a public outcry and gave Congress the impetus to act: in the Lilly Ledbetter Fair Pay Act of 2009, Congress amended the statute of limitations so that going forward plaintiffs like Lilly Ledbetter can seek vindication for unequal pay claims for the entire period of their employment.[15]

The process of litigation requires participants to combine facts and law, forming this information into narratives that help litigants and the public understand events. Trials are the quintessential moment for the framing of such narratives. "The basic purpose of a trial is the determination of truth." So says the Supreme Court. But this does not mean that the truth is easy to find. Sometimes the facts are complicated and contradictory; they are formed into narratives by the parties, and these stories fit the facts into a broader framework of social life. The adjudicator must decide between these competing narratives.

In the *Floyd* trial, for example, the plaintiffs constructed a narrative of racial discrimination through policing that targeted minority neighborhoods (or simply targeted minorities). The city's counternarrative was that the case was not about discrimination but about public safety, and that the police engaged in stops and frisks to reduce crime. These narratives framed the debate about policing in New York City, which continued beyond the courtroom and into a broader public discussion. Without the information produced in the lawsuit and the framing provided by the lawyers, that dialogue would not have received the same attention. The critical contribution of the trial was that the proofs and arguments of each side were rigorously tested as witnesses were cross-examined and each side was forced to justify their arguments with both facts and legal analysis. The rigor of this process was reflected in the long and thorough opinion that the judge issued at the end of the case.[16]

Litigation can sometimes produce new narratives that change the way we understand institutions. Consider how a trial in California to overturn a referendum barring same-sex marriage changed the perception of marriage equality. That trial did two things. First, it publicized the existence of stable families headed by same-sex couples, contributing to a popular change in understanding about how a more inclusive right to marry that included same-sex couples could promote stable family life rather than erode it. It also tested the best arguments *against* permitting same-sex marriage. As Kenji Yoshino points out in his book about that trial, in political discourse people can rely on misrepresentations, speculation, and hyperbole, but a trial is exacting and challenges such assertions. That trial "forced an unusually direct, disciplined, and comprehensive confrontation between opposing sides." While these same arguments had been articulated and parsed in litigation leading up to that California trial, at the same time they had not been required to withstand cross examination, and it was that process which produced a new understanding of their force. David Boies, who tried the case for the plaintiffs, explained of opponents to marriage equality: "When they come into court and they have to support those opinions and defend those opinions under oath and cross-examination, those opinions just melt away. That's what happened here. There simply wasn't any evidence."[17]

One of the criticisms of litigation is that it requires that individuals fit their stories into the categories mandated by law. Although there is some truth to this observation, especially when it comes to trials with their exacting rules of evidence, a trial can also provide the impetus for the creation and dissemination of stories that might not otherwise be heard, as well as testing narratives that cannot withstand scrutiny. By fitting facts into legal standards, by laying blame and freeing from blame, a trial produces narratives about our society. The competing narratives presented by defendants and plaintiffs sharpen understanding of existing disagreements and help participants and observers to clarify what is at stake for society. Individuals and groups can then debate those narratives and dispute them, so that although the legal process ends with the trial and appeal, the democratic conversation can continue.

Cases need not go to trial to contribute to transparency; sometimes even a preliminary step in the litigation process forces information into the open. The litigation against some Swiss banks for retaining funds of Holocaust victims never went to trial, but the plaintiffs succeeded in forcing information from the banks that would otherwise never have seen the light of day. The lawyers prosecuting the lawsuits against the banks sought records that would reveal the names of Jewish account holders immediately preceding and during the Second World War. Without these records, plaintiffs—the victims' heirs—had no way of proving their claims because they had no evidence of the deposit of the funds. The Swiss banks resisted on the grounds that their business depended in large part on a promise of secrecy. Ultimately, the banks struck a deal that was short of full discovery but required the banks to open their records to a limited committee. In the absence of that agreement the banks might have faced the much harsher and more significant effects of discovery, because evidence came to light during the course of the litigation that the banks had intentionally and systematically destroyed records. An out-of-court compromise resulted in the release of some of the information needed for plaintiffs to understand what happened to their accounts.[18]

In addition to forcing information out into the open, the Swiss banks litigation created a forum for the victims to tell their stories even though there was no trial. In this way litigation provided the impetus for the formulation and dissemination of narratives that would not have been heard otherwise. When the case settled, the judge held a hearing to determine whether the settlement was fair, as required by the class action rule. At that hearing, victims came forward with their personal narratives. One of these victims was Estelle Sapir, whose father was deported to the Majdanek concentration camp and killed there. Before he was deported, Estelle's father told her of the money he had deposited in Credit Suisse. When she reached out to the bank after the war, however, the bank's representatives said they needed a death certificate in order to look for her father's account. Needless to say, she did not have one. Her story, which was retold in the national and international media, only came to light as a result of the litigation.[19]

The Swiss banks litigation was also a catalyst in the creation of broader historical narratives about the role of corporations in the Third Reich, beyond the individual litigants. Twenty-four European countries commissioned historical investigations of the claims of Holocaust victims and their families in the restoration movement. One of those commissions' reports was used in the Swiss banks litigation to determine how money should be allocated to victims and their descendants. In response to other lawsuits against private companies that profited under the Third Reich, private corporations like Daimler Benz, Volkswagen, and Hugo Boss opened up their archives to a greater extent than that required by law to prominent historians and hired them to write histories of the companies' involvement in atrocities. The commissioning of these histories was driven by the threat of the litigation, by the promise of a settlement without a trial, and by the immunity from liability that the companies ultimately obtained. Without the lawsuits brought as part of the broader restitution movement, these companies' archives would likely have remained closed.[20]

Today a lawsuit such as that against the Swiss banks would be impossible to bring for three reasons. First, the case was brought under the Alien Tort Claims Act, but that statute has since been interpreted so narrowly (in response to human rights class actions like the Swiss banks litigation) that it no longer permits cases like this one to proceed. Second, subsequent Supreme Court opinions have also limited the power of American courts over multinational companies doing business in the United States so that the federal court in New York would likely not have had jurisdiction over the Swiss corporate defendants in the case. Finally, the class action doctrine has also been narrowed so that it would be hard for the Holocaust victims to proceed as a class, leverage that was crucial to making the litigation possible. On every front the courts have closed the doors to these types of cases, losing the possibility of revealing important hidden stories in the process.[21]

THE CRITIQUE OF CIVIL DISCOVERY

The primary way that litigation forces information into the open is through civil discovery. In some cases, mostly big complex cases where the stakes are high, discovery can be a very costly and complicated process. For this reason, discovery is a core target of critics of litigation. The idea that discovery is disproportionately expensive in relation to the value of underlying claims is not supported by empirical evidence, as we shall see, nor is there any consensus about how much discovery ought to cost as an absolute matter. In many situations, because information is a prerequisite to winning a suit, an individual's ability to protect his or her rights is dependent on the outcome of these debates.

One criticism is that the expense of the discovery process is not justified by the value of the underlying case and therefore not efficient from a societal point of view. Furthermore, critics argue, discovery can be abused in cases where the burden of discovery falls more on one party than the other as a result of information asymmetry. For example, in some lawsuits most of the information is in the defendant's possession, in which case discovery will cost the defendant more than it will cost the plaintiff because the cost of producing information is higher than the cost of requesting it. If discovery raises the cost of the suit to more than that suit is worth, then rational defendants will choose to settle even if they could prevail at trial. Critics, including prominent federal judges, have expressed concern that this dynamic gives plaintiffs the incentive to abuse the litigation process by needlessly increasing discovery costs in meritless cases so that defendants may feel forced to settle suits that they think they can win at trial because they calculate that discovery is so expensive it is not worth the cost of defending themselves. These critics tend to lack empirical evidence for their claims and they consider only the monetary costs of producing information as compared with the plaintiff's likely recovery in their analysis of the potential problems, but they neglect the benefits of revealing information to the individual, others similarly situated, and society at large.[22]

Even focusing only on the monetary costs and benefits of discovery, the criticism that discovery is disproportionate to the value of most lawsuits, or that it is very costly in most cases, is not borne out by the facts. Every study of discovery has found that discovery in civil litigation is generally proportional to the stakes of the case. One recent study was conducted by independent researchers at the Federal Judicial Center (FJC), an arm of the federal courts. Researchers surveyed lawyers about discovery costs in their most recent federal cases. They found not only that the cost of discovery was proportional to the value of the case but that very expensive discovery is rare. For example, plaintiffs' discovery costs in the study were about 1.6 percent of the stakes of the case, and defendants' costs were about 3.3 percent. These numbers included the cost of attorney's fees, the most significant cost in prosecuting a lawsuit.[23]

Not only is discovery on average proportional to the monetary value of the litigation, the dollar amounts of discovery in most cases are not that high, nor are costs significantly higher for defendants than for plaintiffs. The FJC study found that the median cost of discovery was $15,000 for plaintiffs and $20,000 for defendants, which is not such a big difference in dollar terms. In the 95th percentile—the highest cost cases—plaintiffs paid $280,000 in discovery costs and defendants $300,000. In sum, plaintiffs and defendants pay similar amounts in discovery, and defendants are not especially disadvantaged. When lawyers were asked about the amount of discovery in their particular case, most of them thought that the amount was just right, and indicated that they did not feel pressure to settle due to discovery abuse by the other side. The study also showed that, when adjusted for inflation, discovery costs had not increased in the previous ten years.

Although the FJC study gives reasons to be sanguine about discovery, there is cause for concern that discovery actually reveals *too little* information. In a disturbing study from 1980, when the discovery rules provided litigants more leeway than they do today, 96 percent of law-yers reported that they settled cases without disclosing "arguably sig-nificant" information. Without more information, it is hard to know how this fact impacts the outcome of cases because it depends on who is holding on to the significant information and why. But settlements produced without the benefit of significant information are likely not as fair as they should be to the person who is not informed.[24]

There is no evidence that, in the run of cases, discovery is dispropor-tionate to the value of the case, or that its costs exceed its benefits either in human or monetary terms. Those few cases in which the cost of discov-ery is very high tend to be lawsuits where a lot is at stake, fought by equal adversaries. The most shocking case of high discovery costs is proba-bly the litigation between Apple and Samsung over whether Samsung infringed on Apple's patents relating to the iPhone. This was scorched-earth litigation. Discovery was massive: in this one lawsuit, two hun-dred people were deposed and there were over a thousand requests for documents. The total cost was estimated at $60 million for Apple alone and as much as $1 billion total. These are appalling figures, but to put them into perspective, at that time $1 billion represented roughly two weeks of iPhone sales. This case raises some important questions, such as whether this litigation was socially beneficial and whether with more judicial control or tweaks to the discovery rules this information could have been exchanged more cheaply. To really evaluate these questions would require a rigorous evaluation of our patent system and its costs and benefits. For present purposes, it is important to remember that this was a case of two equal adversaries choosing to engage in a very costly process in which no stone was left unturned in order to vindicate their rights. Discovery in high-value cases can benefit from judicial control, but outlier cases like this one should not be considered emblematic of the discovery process in most lawsuits, where evidence indicates too little information is revealed rather than too much.[25]

Critics also attack the nonmonetary costs of discovery, such as the time spent distracted from other, more productive pursuits. For exam-ple, Supreme Court justices have expressed concerns that the human cost of discovery—especially the cost in time and effort to high-ranking government officials and corporate leaders—is too high. In *Ashcroft v. Iqbal*, Muslim immigrants alleged that they were arrested shortly after September 11, 2001, because of their religion or national origin, not because they posed a terrorist threat. The Supreme Court held that their suit against high-ranking government officials should be dismissed unless they alleged specific facts concerning the involvement of those officials. The problem was that the specific information required of the plaintiffs (such as what former Attorney General John Ashcroft did and said) was solely in the possession of the government, inaccessible to the plaintiffs without court-ordered discovery. One of the Supreme Court's main concerns in that case was that civil discovery would distract high-ranking government officials from their important work in protecting the country (although as it happened one named defendant, John Ashcroft, was no longer in government service when the lawsuit was adjudicated). There is a trade-off between protecting government officials from distracting litigation on the one hand and transparency on the other, but there are better ways to balance those interests than dismissing cases just because they involve high-ranking government officials. For example, courts can limit discovery to lower-level officials at first, or to documents, and require that plaintiffs use discovery to provide some support for their allegations before a high-ranking official need be deposed.[26]

THREATS TO TRANSPARENCY

We have seen how information obtained through litigation is important to good government and to individual well-being and how litigation is one critical way to force information into the open that would otherwise remain hidden. In recent years, however, courts have curbed people's ability to obtain information through litigation. These limitations include reduced access to courts altogether, presumptive limitations on discovery, and rules that permit and enforce secret settlements. All of these share the common thread of reducing access to information and thereby reducing transparency, which is not only beneficial in its own right, but is also crucial to participation in self-government and to enforcing the law.

Limitations on access to the courts reduce transparency because they limit access to information through court-ordered discovery and cut short the process of producing narratives about the events in dispute in the litigation. One example is recent court rulings on arbitration. We learned in the introduction that arbitration has been expanded at the expense of litigation in recent years. In 2011 the Supreme Court upheld forced arbitration agreements in consumer contracts and in 2013 upheld similar arbitration agreements between businesses, even when those agreements effectively prevent individuals and small businesses from being able to vindicate their rights. The Justices reasoned that arbitration is both more streamlined and less costly than litigation, albeit without empirical support for that claim. But arbitration is also private. This may be good for individuals or businesses who want to keep disputes confidential, but it has negative consequences for society because arbitrated disputes do not produce a public record and cannot advance the development of the law or bring wrongdoing to light.[27]

Cases have been blocked at the courthouse door precisely because they seek transparency. A legal doctrine called the state secrets privilege allows the government to refuse to release information that it claims could endanger national security. Revealing this information is claimed to be so risky to national security that even the judge is not allowed to review it behind closed doors. Because the information is kept from the court as well as the opposing side, nobody is able to check that the government is being honest about the importance of keeping that particular information secret. And because many times the plaintiff cannot pursue the case without the confidential information, the government's assertion of the privilege effectively ends the lawsuit before it even starts.

The Supreme Court case that created this privilege illustrates the problems this doctrine can create. *United States v. Reynolds* concerned the deaths of three civilian observers aboard a military flight for the purpose of testing secret electronic equipment who were killed (along with military personnel) when the B-29 in which they were flying crashed. The widows of these three civilians sued the United States for wrongful death. In the course of discovery, the plaintiffs asked to see the findings of the Air Force's investigation into the crash. The government responded by asserting the state secrets privilege, that is, it asserted that the report contained sensitive information and that releasing it would jeopardize national security. It was an issue of first impression for the Supreme Court, which established in that case that there was a state secrets privilege. The widows settled the case without ever finding out what caused the crash.[28]

The *Reynolds* case was decided at the height of the cold war, a context that surely influenced the Court's decision. "[W]e cannot escape judicial notice," the Court stated, "that this is a time of vigorous preparation for national defense." But many years later, when the documents relating to the B-29 crash were declassified, it was revealed that they in fact contained no sensitive national security information. Instead, the documents showed that the B-29 was not fit to fly and that the Air Force knew this before the flight's departure. Had this information been revealed at the time of the widow's lawsuit, it would have meant a likely win and potentially a public rebuke of the Air Force. The subsequent history of the *Reynolds* case reveals the danger inherent in permitting the government to claim a privilege with no check on its assertion. This danger has only increased in the wake of 9/11 as the government claims the privilege ever more frequently.[29]

There are cases where national security requires secrecy, but other options exist for protecting sensitive information that do not involve such serious threats to transparency. Recognizing that citizens need to have access to information about government conduct that affects their lives, some courts have refused to allow blanket assertions of the state secrets privilege. A good example involves allegations surfacing in 2005 that the National Security Agency (NSA) had been intercepting email and telephone communications inside the United States without a warrant since 2001. Two statutes exclusively control the government's ability to engage in electronic surveillance: the Electronic Communications

Privacy Act and the Foreign Intelligence Surveillance Act. Both of these laws recognize Americans' right to privacy in their calls and emails and both require that the government obtain a court order before collecting such communications. After news sources published a whistleblower account that the government was using an electronic surveillance dragnet without court approval, a number of people filed lawsuits alleging that their communications had been illegally intercepted in violation of surveillance statutes as well as the Fourth and Fourteenth Amendments of the Constitution. These plaintiffs sought to bar the government from intercepting communications without a warrant.

The government responded with a number of arguments, including assertion of the state secrets privilege. It argued that the very subject of the lawsuit—that is, the existence of the surveillance—was a state secret and for that reason the suit should be dismissed. This was a strange position for the government to take because by the time government lawyers asserted the privilege the government had already acknowledged its surveillance program, in part as a result of the disclosure of a trove of documents by Edward Snowden. The trial court ruled that the state secrets privilege did not shield the government from inquiry into the surveillance program, but may protect some of the particular documents sought by the plaintiffs. Of course, that raised the issue of how to determine which documents were protected and which were not—a problem that the judge noted could be solved by private, in chambers review of the sensitive documents by a federal judge, a procedure which indeed was built into the Foreign Intelligence Surveillance Act.[30] A similar procedure could have benefitted the widows in *U.S. v. Reynolds*.

Another way that information can be suppressed in litigation is through protective orders in discovery and secret settlements. Defendants can also keep information hidden by settling before they are required to reveal it. Even after information is revealed, sometimes a defendant will ask the plaintiff to sign a confidentiality clause; such contracts can require that anything from the amount of the settlement to information about the underlying allegations be kept confidential. Again and again defendants have agreed to settle cases, sometimes for very large amounts, in order to keep information out of the public eye. By buying secrecy, these defendants have allowed harms to proliferate that could have been avoided with the threat of public censure or regulatory intervention had the information been public. Consider, for example, the scandal of sexual abuse involving the Catholic Church. For many years, Church leaders covered up misconduct, obtaining protective orders from the courts to prevent discovery from becoming public, settling lawsuits on condition of confidentiality and then moving accused priests to new parishes where they might be dangerous to children. After Cardinal Bernard Law of the Boston Archdiocese admitted that he had given a serial abuser a plum job although that priest was accused of sexually molesting a child, further investigation revealed a pattern of using confidentiality agreements in settlements to protect the Church from public censure. This pattern was eventually publicized, but without the use of secret settlements the scandal would likely have broken earlier and involved fewer victims.[31]

Secret settlements and protective orders can be damaging in a number of ways. Hiding misconduct can permit it to continue and deny others, who are also victims, the information they need to pursue their own claims, such as when witnesses are subject to confidentiality agreements agreed to in prior lawsuits. The traditional view has been that lawyers should help clients obtain the best possible settlement for that person, even if this means that the client agrees to a confidentiality provision which prevents the release of important information and is damaging to society or to other victims. But lawyers have a competing duty to the legal system as a whole, because when they agree to confidentiality they prevent third parties (especially other victims) from obtaining crucial information to pursue their cases and, as a result, allow systemic injustice to continue.[32]

A good example is the case of the Firestone tires litigation. A series of lawsuits was brought against Firestone due to an alleged defect that caused the treads to separate on long hot drives. Lawyers who had brought early cases agreed to confidentiality clauses and so could not speak with would-be plaintiffs about the information they had uncovered. In one case that settled on the eve of trial, lawyers for the company asked the plaintiff's lawyer to return all the evidence gathered in preparation for trial so that it could not be revealed to other plaintiffs. The result was that while the defects in the tires were known as early as 1996, Firestone did not recall the tires or warn consumers until the press exposed the story in 2000. Although the crucial information had been obtained through litigation, secret settlements delayed these revelations with the consequence of additional injuries that could have been avoided.[33]

To keep plaintiffs from revealing critical information, institutions enforce confidentiality provisions with the threat of litigation or demanding return of the settlement money. In one case relating to sexual abuse by priests in New York, the settlement agreement provided that if the confidentiality of the settlement were broken, the victim would have to pay the Diocese $400,000 (the settlement itself was for nearly $1 million). It is hardly surprising that the victim did not come forward to share his story until the pattern of abuse was well known and the Church unlikely to enforce the agreement.

In another case, this one involving medical malpractice, a hospital was accused of causing bacterial infections as a result of their unsanitary operating rooms. The family of one patient who died of an infection contracted during surgery and another patient who was severely disabled after a similar infection sued the hospital. Documents obtained through discovery showed that the hospital had hired a respected nursing organization to investigate the link between patient infections and unsanitary conditions, but then declined to follow the report's recommendations to save money. Discovery also revealed that a hidden camera installed in the operating room had recorded some doctors failing to wash their hands before surgery, that both doctors and nurses entered the operating room to make personal calls on a telephone located in the room although it was supposed to be a sterile environment, and that doctors wore street clothes—laden with germs—to surgery. The hospital settled the lawsuit and vowed to improve sanitary conditions in its operating rooms, but it also negotiated to have the settlement terms and the information revealed in the course of the litigation remain confidential. Despite the agreement, the patients who had sued spoke to the *Chicago Tribune* about their experience and what they learned from their lawsuit. When the resulting article was published, the hospital sued the patients for breaching their confidentiality agreement. Understandably, there was a public outcry, criticizing the hospital for its retaliation. After all, the plaintiffs could claim credit for forcing improvements to operating room conditions and the result of these changes was that infection rates were down to almost zero. In response to the public reaction, the hospital withdrew its lawsuit, demonstrating that transparency not only benefits citizens but also empowers them to harness the force of public opinion against wrongful behavior. In that case, the wrongful behavior was a retaliatory lawsuit, one intended to suppress the truth rather than reveal it.[34] And this is a point that is important to note: although it is not common, lawsuits can be used to silence useful speech and it is crucial for judges to be alert to the risk of intimidation as well as to the risk of suppressing information obtained in litigation.

To address concerns about confidentiality agreements, secret settlements, and especially the threat of public safety that results from concealing ongoing risks, some states have passed laws prohibiting secrecy in matters that relate to public safety, such as the problems with Firestone tires. A similar law has been periodically considered at the national level as well. Publicity requirements can have their own limitations and drawbacks, however. For example, litigants truly committed to confidentiality can settle cases before they are filed to avoid revealing information. And of course some information is genuinely worthy of protection, such as trade secrets, business strategies, and personal employment or medical records. While some of these categories are already protected by law, others will require a case-by-case review by a judge. The guiding principle ought to be that secrecy requires a compelling justification; this standard should apply not only to information appended to court filings but to any other information produced by litigation where the information at issue threatens public safety. The competing interests of privacy on the one hand and transparency on the other will always have to be balanced by a judge, but it must be done with the recognition of what hangs in that balance: not only the interests of the parties to the lawsuit, but the societal interest in transparency.[35]

Even where settlements do not contain confidentiality clauses prohibiting the participants from discussing their contents, many are functionally secret because their terms are not made open to the public. Settlements need not be filed in court; when a case settles, the plaintiff dismisses the lawsuit and the settlement becomes a contract between the parties. No public database exists to collect and disseminate settlement information. There is a private database that contains some of this information, compiled by insurers who use it to calculate settlement offers in the many thousands of cases they resolve each year. The result is that settlement terms are not accessible to most individuals, and most lawyers are only likely to know the outcomes of cases they settled or ones that they have heard about through professional networks.[36]

There is no good reason that access to systematic settlement information should only be in the hands of insurance companies. All settlements of filed lawsuits could be publicly available in a database that has been redacted to ensure privacy of litigants. First, such a database would help people know what a fair settlement is, to determine a going rate and promote consistency in results across cases. Plaintiffs could compare what they were being offered to what other, similarly situated persons received in order to determine whether their offer was fair. A settlement database would correct some of the information asymmetry between repeat players in litigation, such as insurers, who have access to information about many cases, and individual plaintiffs, for whom this is the only lawsuit they will ever bring and who may not have a good basis for evaluating whether their offer is fair. Second, litigation is a public process paid for in part with tax dollars; when a case is adjudicated, the public (not just the litigants) benefits for all the reasons discussed in this book, including the development, refinement, and explanation of the law. When a case ends with a settlement, by contrast, the public is deprived of these benefits and of the return on its investment in the legal system. A public database of settlement outcomes would ensure that the benefits of that lawsuit accrue to the public, rather than only to the particular litigants who settled. As Professor Stephen Yeazell, who first proposed this idea, points out, when home buyers are trying to price a house, they can look at comparable properties, and when consumers want to buy a used car, they can use online or print services such as the *Kelly Blue Book* or Edmonds. Even when people are in the market for unique objects, they can price them on online marketplaces such as eBay. Not so with respect to civil settlements. The only entities that come close to having a broad view of what a lawsuit is worth based on comparable data are insurance companies, and their data is proprietary.[37]

Some people might object to this idea because they would prefer that people not know either how much they paid out, in the case of defendants, or how much they received, in the case of plaintiffs. Plaintiffs might worry that revealing how much they received in a settlement will affect their relationships. Defendants might worry that publication of settlement amounts could encourage other litigants to pop out of the woodwork. In large-scale settlements, transparency about terms may result in longer litigation and holdouts. As Kenneth Feinberg, who oversaw the 9/11 Victims Compensation Fund and countless large-scale settlements, recently explained: "Most lawyers prefer remaining under the radar screen. First of all, we don't want anybody mucking up the deal; if too many people opt out, people will come into the fairness hearing and object. Too much sunshine gives you sunburn. It's a dangerous thing." Revealing settlements, in other words, may infringe on plaintiffs' privacy interests and have a negative effect on the lawyer's ability to reach closure for both sides, which are also important values. Still, these interests must be balanced against the interests of plaintiffs and the legal system in providing consistent and fair outcomes to all litigants. A settlement database system could be designed to accommodate both these sets of interests.[38]

A final threat to transparency through litigation appears when courts refuse to decide legal questions properly presented in the cases before them. In *Wood v. Moss*, for example, the Supreme Court was asked to rule on the question of how the First Amendment applies to the actions of the Secret Service when protecting the president. That case arose out of a campaign stop during George W. Bush's 2004 presidential run. While securing the premises of a restaurant where the president intended to dine, the Secret Service moved demonstrators who were protesting the president's policies out of sight of the restaurant. These demonstrators alleged that they were treated differently than demonstrators who were supporters of the president, as the president's supporters were permitted to remain within eyeshot of the restaurant. If it were the case that the Secret Service treated speech by opponents of the president differently than that of supporters for no reason other than their political point of view, the Secret Service might have violated the First Amendment's prohibition on viewpoint discrimination, except that this prohibition has never been applied to the decisions of Secret Service agents protecting the president in the field. There are reasonable arguments on both sides of the case, as it pits important interests in political expression against equally important interests in protecting the safety of the president. Yet although the case has clear import, the Supreme Court refused to decide it. Instead, it held that the Secret Service was immune from suit under the doctrine of qualified immunity and dismissed the case.

Qualified immunity is a doctrine that protects government officials from suit when the law that governs their actions is not clearly established. The purpose behind this doctrine is to immunize government officials from liability when the law that the official was accused of violating was not clear at the time the official acted. The catch-22 in *Wood v. Moss* and similar cases is that if the court dismisses the case on qualified immunity grounds and does not decide the underlying question of substantive law, the next time the same thing happens, the officer will once again be immune from suit because a court has never established the governing law. In *Moss*, the Court had the power and opportunity to settle the law. Had the Court decided the legal question presented in this case, that holding would not only have clarified the application of freedom of speech to Secret Service actions, but potentially fueled a national conversation about the appropriate limits of freedom of speech. Without such a ruling, the impact of the case was to insulate the Secret Service from future liability, given that the law remains unsettled and therefore qualified immunity still applies.[39]

There was a brief period when the Supreme Court recognized the value of developing the law and held that even when a governmental officer is entitled to qualified immunity, the court must still decide and clarify the underlying legal standard that gave rise to the lawsuit. But the Supreme Court quickly reversed itself, holding that while courts may clarify the legal standard, they are not obligated to do so, and increasingly the Court has required that the established law be more and more specific to defeat the qualified immunity defense.[40] Qualified immunity is but one doctrine that allows judges to avoid the merits of a decision. There are also doctrines that do the opposite and allow judges to force a decision on the merits. The principle at stake in the application of these doctrines is the law declaration function of the courts, a crucial aspect of transparency and the rule of law. One core purpose of litigation is to provide the vehicle for courts to declare, develop, and refine the law so that judicial decisions can govern conduct going forward and so that citizens and legislators can know what the law is in order to evaluate whether they think it is fair and just or needs revision. This contribution needs to be taken into account when courts decide whether to address substantive questions raised in lawsuits.[41]

THE PUBLIC VALUE OF TRANSPARENCY

Litigation helps provide the transparency that democracy needs to thrive and that people need in order to make good decisions. Litigation reveals information about risks and wrongdoing, and sometimes the threat of litigation can even spur valuable information gathering.

Finally, the process of litigation can frame narratives about events in the world that help people understand what happened and why through a trial or a public settlement hearing. Transparency through litigation serves not only the individual participants but also the broader public by producing shared informational goods.[42]

The power of litigation to reveal information that would otherwise be inaccessible is crucial to law enforcement both in the courts and outside of them. The role of litigation in promoting public safety and welfare by allowing individuals to obtain and publicize important information that would otherwise remain hidden is too often ignored. But access to information is not just about enforcement; it is also critical to litigants' ability to participate in the process of litigation, and through that process, in self-government. We turn to litigation's contribution to self-government in the next chapter.

PARTICIPATION
IN SELF-GOVERNMENT

Litigation serves the democratic value of participation by enabling individuals to engage directly in the process of lawmaking and law enforcement. Whenever a person files a lawsuit, that act calls the attention of a government officer—the judge—to her problem. This is easiest to see when a citizen sues the government itself. By bringing a lawsuit, ordinary individuals, even those without many resources or political connections, can call government representatives into court to explain and be held accountable for unjust practices. In lawsuits between private parties, as well, the process of litigating forces a reasoned dialogue between the two sides as they present their evidence and arguments to the court—a form of reasoned deliberation. The court's ruling will decide the parties' case, but it will also affect many other, similar cases. Even a case that seems entirely private, such as a dispute about how the provision of an insurance contract should be interpreted, has the potential to set legal rules that will govern others. Every type of lawsuit involves participation in self-government.[1]

Citizens also participate in government by serving on a jury. In deciding both criminal and civil cases, juries help shape the direction of social change—sometimes by asserting long-standing norms, other times by signaling a shift in course. As Justice Scalia wrote of the right to a jury trial in criminal cases, "Just as suffrage ensures the people's ultimate control in the legislative and executive branches, jury trial is meant to ensure their control in the judiciary."[2]

In the last century, the courts were opened up to citizen participation in a variety of ways. The Supreme Court held that citizens could not be excluded from jury service based solely on their race or gender. State legislatures required that court fees be waived for indigent persons. Some state legislatures and state courts also required that indigent people be given access to a lawyer in important civil matters such as the termination of parental rights. But many questions remain unresolved, and many barriers to participation in the courts persist. What should courts do about people who cannot advocate for themselves? How should courts manage individual participation when lawsuits involve thousands of injured people, such as those that follow natural disasters? Given that jury trials have declined to as few as 2 percent of cases filed, what should be done to preserve the institution of the civil jury?[3]

For those who believe that litigation is only a particularly expensive form of dispute resolution, it may not matter when citizens' opportunities to serve as jurors are curtailed or when people are unable to participate fully in lawsuits. But litigation does more than resolve disputes. It is a form of participation in government, complementary to voting or running for office. It requires that participants produce reasons for their positions in the form of proofs and arguments. These reasons are then tested against one another in an adversarial process. Arguments made during the litigation process are not only for the benefit of the parties and the judge but also the public at large.[4]

PARTICIPATION AS A LITIGANT

One way litigation enables participation in government is when people sue the government itself for wrongdoing. Consider, for example, a New York statute that made loitering for the purpose of begging a criminal offense. The law was used by the New York City Police Department

(NYPD) to arrest homeless people and clear them off the streets. In 1993, a group of homeless people sued New York City in a case called *Casale v. Kelly*, arguing that the law violated their First Amendment right to freedom of speech. The US Court of Appeals for the Second Circuit held that the law was indeed unconstitutional. Nevertheless, the NYPD continued to enforce this unconstitutional law for the following eighteen years. As late as 2010, police officers in New York City carried with them "cheat sheets" listing loitering as a basis for an arrest under the old, invalid law. Homeless people continued to challenge the NYPD practice. Ultimately, a federal judge held the City of New York in contempt of court, and the police stopped the arrests.[5]

This is a story of members of one of the least powerful groups in society—the homeless—bringing a municipal government to account in the courts. Those harmed by police actions in this case were largely powerless and lacking in the resources required to mount a political campaign. They were a minority group, disliked and ignored, and unable to vindicate their rights through the political process. For these reasons, and probably from convenience and habit as well, the NYPD persisted in enforcing an unconstitutional statute for far longer than anyone would care to contemplate. The elected branches turned a blind eye to these violations. But this homeless population still had access to the courts, and it was through that access that they presented their case and obtained relief. By filing lawsuits, homeless plaintiffs were able to have their complaint heard by an impartial government official—a judge—who was required to listen to their arguments and issue a reasoned decision with respect to their claims. The *Casale* case illustrates how the ability to bring suit in order to enforce one's rights against the government is the foundation of judicial review.

Cases that do not involve suing the government are also a form of participation in self-government because they can have broad social impact beyond the individual litigants participating. An ordinary tort suit is a form of social ordering, for example. As we saw in chapter 2, a severe *E. coli* outbreak at Jack in the Box fast food restaurants in the 1990s killed four children and sickened many others. Parents of the victims sued and through their lawsuit obtained evidence that the restaurant chain had overlooked out-of-date grills that undercooked hamburgers. They learned that when one employee complained of the restaurant's regulations leaving meat undercooked, the restaurant responded that burgers cooked longer were too tough. In other words, the company had been informed of the risks but did nothing about them.[6]

Jack in the Box settled the lawsuits for millions of dollars and became a model citizen for observing food safety regulations. But the impact of the suits was even greater. The tragedy, along with the documents revealed through the lawsuit, spurred a national conversation about meat safety and let to federal regulation of *E. coli* in meat for the first time. As one state food safety regulator said at the time: "No one wants to be the 'next' Jack in the Box."[7] The Jack in the Box story is about participation of injured individuals in changing the status quo as well as about enforcement and transparency.

Litigation is beneficial to society because individuals and corporations make decisions with the background knowledge that rights can be enforced in court and that they may be held to account for any wrongdoing. The background rules that smooth day-to-day interactions are effective because we know they are enforceable. Businesses, for example, know that contracts are enforceable; the mere threat of legal remedies often suffices to police their enforcement. Society functions well only when people can rely on the knowledge that while it is cheaper to resolve their disputes without resorting to a lawsuit, they can enforce their rights in court when needed. For the most part, as we saw in chapter 1, people do not resort to litigation, but access to litigation as a backstop means that people can enter into trust relationships with one another. The ability to participate in maintaining the rule of law by bringing suit is part of the foundation of civil society.[8]

In the background of everyday dealings, from contracts in business to the regulation of family life, lies the faith that rights and obligations are enforceable. When a municipality fails to follow the law, its residents can sue for redress. When a restaurant sells unsafe food, customers can call it to account in court. All civil cases involve the ordering of social life—whether they concern civil rights or commercial transactions. The process of bringing these cases to the court, making arguments, and presenting evidence in support of those arguments constitutes self-government through litigation.[9]

Although our legal system promises participation—that each person will have his or her day in court—in the twenty-first century it has become increasingly difficult for the courts to deliver on this promise. Two main problems currently present challenges to participation through litigation, though each also presents an opportunity to promote, rather than impede, this important democratic value. The first problem is that many people do not have the resources to hire good lawyers to represent them, and thus may be forced to represent themselves although incapable of doing so adequately, to skip bringing a lawsuit altogether, or to fail to defend themselves if sued. The second is the advent of mass litigation, a phenomenon where hundreds or even thousands of lawsuits are litigated together, often with all the plaintiffs represented by only a small group of lawyers. While the practice is obviously efficient, and indeed may be the only avenue to be heard for some individuals, plaintiffs in mass litigation may find themselves relegated to the sidelines and denied a real voice in their own case.

THE CHALLENGE OF SELF-REPRESENTATION

Because hiring a lawyer is out of reach for ordinary people, one of the biggest problems facing state courts in America is self-represented or pro se litigants. Chief justices of a number of state courts have used their influence to call attention to this issue. The problem is that the American legal system relies on each side presenting its arguments and evidence to a neutral arbiter—a judge or a jury. The court system is not equipped to help litigants make their case; that is generally considered the litigants' own responsibility. While judges want to help litigants who are not represented by a lawyer to make their case, this is difficult because judges do not want to be perceived to be favoring one side over the other. For example, in a recent case a prominent federal judge, Jack

Weinstein, asked leading questions in order to determine whether the plaintiff—who was appearing on his own behalf—had a case for discrimination that could survive a motion to dismiss. The judge was able to determine that the plaintiff had a claim as a result of this direct questioning, but worried that his neutrality was compromised in the process of conducting this inquiry and therefore recused himself. Explaining his conundrum, the judge wrote: "If the plaintiff were to continue pro se, the court would probably be forced to intervene and, in effect, advocate on his behalf, possibly prejudicing the defendant's case." When someone comes to court unable to represent himself adequately, there is often little help available. The judge explained: "In many cases, pro se justice is an oxymoron. Without representation by counsel, it is probable, to some degree, that adequate justice cannot be served in this case."[10]

This matters because a self-represented plaintiff may get her day in court, but be unable to speak a language those in power can comprehend. For many vulnerable people, meaningful participation in litigation requires representation by a lawyer. Consider the case of Abby Gail Lassiter. Abby was a flawed mother, convicted of second-degree murder and serving time in jail in North Carolina. The state, concerned about the youngest of her five children, William, removed him to a foster home. Because she was in jail, Abby was unable to visit William in the foster home. She hoped that he would be placed with her mother, who was then caring for Abby's other children, but the state insisted on keeping him in foster care, and three years later filed a suit to terminate Abby's parental rights. The state was represented by a lawyer, but Abby came to the courthouse alone, straight from her jail cell. She was uneducated and inarticulate. Abby tried her best to question the witnesses, but she did not know how. She tried to make arguments, but her arguments did not make sense to the judge, who quickly became exasperated. If she had had a lawyer, or if she were better educated and more articulate, she might have argued that the state had little evidence of her lack of fitness to be a parent. Under the law, a criminal conviction was not a sufficient reason to terminate parental rights. If she had had a lawyer, the judge might have been convinced that most of the evidence the state presented was not admissible in court. Most of all, a lawyer might have underscored that there was no permanent home for William to go to except his grandmother's—his foster family did not want to adopt him.[11]

In the end, Abby Gail Lassiter's case went all the way to the Supreme Court. The Court held that the appointment of a lawyer in parental termination proceedings ought to be decided on a case-by-case basis, but that a lawyer would not have helped Abby's case, and thus she was not entitled to one. Yet the idea that Abby would have benefited from a lawyer—indeed that her case might have turned out differently had she had one—was vindicated by legislative action. After the Supreme Court decision, the North Carolina legislature enacted a law mandating the appointment of a lawyer for indigent parents like Abby in parental termination proceedings. Since the 1970s, most state legislatures have passed similar laws. Some state Supreme Courts have also rejected the case-by-case approach and required counsel for indigent parents. Abby did not receive a right to counsel, but her case was a catalyst for legislative change that gave other parents that right. One need not always win the case to obtain a victory for the principle at stake, and although the result is indirect, this too is a meaningful form of participation in self-government.[12]

Abby's participation was mediated in another way. Not only was her victory indirect because she lost her case, but it was only possible through the intermediary of a lawyer presenting arguments on her behalf at the appellate level. Lawyers are essential to the functioning of the legal system because they serve this role, but the need for lawyers to mediate people's interaction with the courts limits people's ability to fully participate when lawyers are not available or when the available lawyers are not very good.[13]

THE CHALLENGE OF COLLECTIVE LITIGATION

"I never saw a single plaintiff appear before me." Those were the words, in sum and substance, of a judge presiding over a large-scale pharmaceutical litigation involving the drug Zyprexa. Large lawsuits such as class actions and other mass litigation can involve tens of thousands of cases consolidated before one court. This can sometimes result in "factory justice" where individuals cannot meaningfully participate, but there are many innovative ways that judges can promote robust participation even in a litigation involving thousands. Participation in these cases can be more effective than critics think, but it takes judicial commitment.[14]

The biggest lawsuits brought today happen when thousands or even millions of people are injured by large institutions or corporations. In these situations, thousands of lawsuits are joined together through the class action, or formally separate lawsuits may be transferred to one court and consolidated into a single proceeding, retaining their individual status only as a formal matter. Sometimes these suits are mass torts, such as the tens of thousands of lawsuits brought against the oil company BP in the aftermath of the Deepwater Horizon oil spill in the Gulf of Mexico, or the tens of thousands of suits brought against the pharmaceutical company Merck in connection with heart attacks and strokes that patients alleged were caused by the pain-relief drug Vioxx. Other times these suits are class actions involving amounts of money that are too small to justify filing an individual lawsuit, but affect millions of customers and collectively add up to damages in the many millions of dollars.[15]

There is no denying that when large numbers of plaintiffs are lumped together through a variety of procedures, individuals can be lost in the shuffle, without a voice in their own lawsuit, much like self-represented litigants who cannot meaningfully participate in their suit. It is a mistake, however, to assume that the only form of participation that is truly meaningful is an individual hearing. It would obviously be best in terms of participation if each plaintiff was afforded an individual hearing, but enabling participation does not require that the legal system jettison the efficiency gains of collective litigation altogether, because the individual hearing is not the only democratically valuable form of participation in litigation. Indeed, courts can develop mechanisms that provide opportunities for participation *within* large-scale litigation. The way to do this is to adopt a broader understanding of what it means to participate in litigation and to develop alternative forms of participation that are consistent with democratic values.

The important form of participation that must be preserved, even in collective litigation, is reasoned dialogue. In many disputed cases this will require trials and public hearings, but it does not mean that each plaintiff in a massive lawsuit involving thousands is automatically entitled to a full-blown trial. The crucial ingredient is that plaintiffs have an opportunity to engage in the form of participation distinctive to litigation, that is, participation characterized by the presentation of proofs and reasoned arguments. Such procedures already exist; they just need to be harnessed by willing judges. For example, in a class action where there is a trial, individuals can participate as witnesses, as observers, or simply by following it in the media, participating in broader social discussion of the case, or taking on an activist role by using the trial to draw attention to their point of view.[16]

Indeed, citizens did just that in *Floyd v. City of New York*, introduced in chapter 2. Some community members applauded the stop-and-frisk policy at issue in that case as a crime reduction measure. Others saw it as an illegal method of singling out people of color for intimidation. This debate took place in the press and among politicians, but also in the courtroom when four men filed a class action lawsuit—on behalf of all similarly situated persons—against the City of New York for violating their Fourth Amendment right to be free from unlawful search and seizure.[17]

As the lawsuit progressed from filing through fact gathering, trial, and appeal, the underlying issues were discussed in the press, among political representatives, and in the various communities around New York City. At trial both sides presented evidence about the rates of stops and frisks, the racial composition of those frisked, and underlying crime rates. The plaintiffs successfully argued that police officers disproportionately targeted minorities even when there was no evidence that the stops were preventing crime. The judge issued a decision over one hundred pages long explaining the legal framework, the facts, and her conclusion.[18] In sum, the lawsuit gave New Yorkers a structure and a language for debating and deliberating together about neighborhood crime and the way police treat minority men. It spurred political participation outside the courtroom, even while the litigants were inside it making their arguments and presenting their proofs. Without the lawsuit, this rigorous debate might never have taken place.

Another way judges have promoted participation in mass cases is through sample or "bellwether" trials. About 70,000 lawsuits were brought against Merck arising out of the injuries caused by the drug Vioxx. If each person was entitled to a trial of four days (which is a short trial), it would take a judge 1,120 years to try all the cases. Insistence on individual participation in a situation like this would mean that almost nobody would get a day in court. So the judge chose a small number of cases to go to trial in the hope that the results of those cases would spur the lawyers to arrive at a mutually agreeable settlement. Ultimately, the approach worked. In the process, evidence was presented in public trials about whether the drug actually caused individual heart attacks or strokes, what Merck knew or did not know about the drug while it was selling it, what the company told the Food and Drug Administration, and why the drug was ultimately taken off the market. This not only helped litigants evaluate how their case would come out, but also made possible a kind of vicarious participation in the process of revealing what happened and why.[19]

Even when there are no trials, judges have encouraged participation in large-scale litigation through public hearings, which can facilitate the same kind of debate and deliberation as a trial might. For example, in the 1980s Vietnam veterans sued chemical manufacturers for sicknesses resulting from their exposure to the defoliant chemical Agent Orange. The case settled as a class action in the late 1980s, with the judge, Jack Weinstein, holding town hall forums for veterans all over the country to learn their reaction to the settlement and also to hear their stories. In this way, individual veterans still participated in the litigation, even though that participation did not involve them getting their own day in court. Public hearings have been held in other mass tort cases as well and in school desegregation and other civil rights suits.[20]

Community observers, sample trials, and public hearings are all ways that the court system can accommodate mass litigation while still promoting the distinctive benefits of participation in reasoned dialogue through litigation. Notably, they all have one thing in common: they require the presentation of proofs and arguments and in so doing promote the use of reason in public life. The law provides a shared language for talking about what we owe each other, and promoting reasoned argument is one of the special contributions of litigation to democracy.[21]

Contrast the value of participation through reasoned argument with a proposal recently put forward to have mass cases settled by plaintiff vote instead of by a process of reasoned exchange of proofs and argument. Although voting is a form of participation, introducing this form of decision-making is corrosive to the democratic value of litigation because it stifles reasoned deliberation and the presentation of proofs and arguments. The impetus for the voting proposal was to increase fairness and legitimacy of outcomes in aggregate litigation. In a class action, a settlement is approved after a hearing before the judge, but in mass tort cases plaintiffs settle individually without a hearing. The proposal put forth by the American Law Institute would permit plaintiffs in a mass tort case to approve a collective settlement by voting. Each plaintiff would agree when they retained their lawyer to abide by a supermajority vote (such as 75 percent) of all the plaintiffs, even if they individually opposed the settlement. (Dissatisfied plaintiffs could still ask for a judge to hold a hearing, but only if they had a reason to dispute the settlement.) The rule today is that each plaintiff must individually agree to any collective settlement, so a switch to a voting system would require a major change in the law, but it would not improve participation very much. The argument in favor of this proposal is that voting leads to results that are both efficient and fair, and that it grants each plaintiff agency in the resolution of the litigation. But voting is a weak form of participation precisely because it does not require the public exchange of reasoned arguments. Instead, this voting proposal brings to litigation the type of decision-making we usually see in the political sphere. Voting, unlike litigation, does not require presentation of proofs, arguments, and deliberation. Every person may vote their conscience without needing to justify their decision to anyone. Only if the voting process spurred discussion and deliberation among plaintiffs would this system promote the participation value in litigation. Requiring a public hearing on the fairness and equity of mass settlements would better promote participation in mass litigation.[22]

Collective hearings and sample trials can turn what could be factory justice into a process involving reasoned deliberation for plaintiffs who might otherwise get sidelined in the name of efficiency. Indeed, studies show that people want some type of participation, and that desire is particularly important in the context of mass litigation, where the risk of an individual's interest being subordinated unfairly to that of the group is greatest. Psychological studies have found that people find participation through adversarial hearings to be fundamentally fair, even if those procedures do not yield the desired outcome. Reasonably, plaintiffs expect to be heard in the justice system and are disappointed when the financial and other realities of life make it difficult to insist on a public trial or hearing. When there is some public airing of the arguments and proofs, even if it is in a small sample of cases rather than every case, this is more satisfactory than a resolution to the litigation that provides no such public deliberation. Participation, in other words, provides sociological legitimacy to the judicial process. While people's preferences are not the only consideration in deciding whether a process is fair, they provide one useful data point in favor of innovative procedures that facilitate participation.[23]

The litigation surrounding the terror attacks of 9/11 illustrates the desire for participation in addition to resolution. The judge who oversaw the litigation arising out of the attacks, Alvin Hellerstein, told me a story of the firefighters who sued. They lost their case early on in a motion to dismiss, but came to the judge anyway to ask for a public hearing so they could tell their stories. Judge Hellerstein agreed. Although no rule of procedure required it, he held a hearing for the sole purpose of allowing the firefighters to explain in open court what had happened to them. Permission to tell the court their story was the irreducible minimum of just procedure for these firefighters, even if doing so did not change the outcome of their lawsuit.

Judge Hellerstein provided similar opportunities for other first responders to participate collectively. More than 9,000 cases were filed by people who claimed that they experienced illnesses as a result of working at the World Trade Center site in the aftermath of the 9/11 terrorist attack. As is often the case in these types of lawsuits, a few lawyers represented hundreds of individuals. After extensive negotiation, the lawyers for both sides came to the court asking for approval of a global settlement agreement for all these cases. The judge did not feel comfortable approving that agreement because, in his view, the terms of the settlement were too vague and did not adequately inform plaintiffs of their award. To remedy this deficiency, the judge scheduled a hearing where all the plaintiffs could come and ask questions. The lawyers were surprised and unhappy at this development, and questioned whether the judge had the power to hold such a hearing. In the end, however, they improved the settlement agreement by offering more money and clarifying how the funds would be distributed. The threat of a hearing was effective in producing a better outcome; just as important, however, was the judge's public commitment to provide a way for litigants to participate and voice their concerns. The prospect of a hearing turned what would have been factory justice into the possibility of a participatory proceeding. Ultimately, the judge did not hold a hearing because he was satisfied with the outcome of the settlement negotiations, but to realize the value of participation, he should have.[24]

The special importance of participating in a hearing before a judge came to the fore in the most high-profile 9/11 cases, those concerning compensation for injuries and deaths of victims of the attacks. The victims of 9/11 and their families were entitled to receive money tax-free from a Victim Compensation Fund (VCF) set up by Congress. The condition of participating in the VCF was that participants would waive their right to file a lawsuit against the airlines and the federal government; victims who participated agreed to resolve their case exclusively through the fund. One researcher interviewing victims and their families who chose to participate in the VCF rather than sue reported that these victims regretted missing out on the public dialogue that accompanies a lawsuit. Reflecting on their choice to receive a settlement from the VCF, many lamented not participating in a formal public proceeding in which they might call the airlines to answer for what happened, present their proofs, and make their arguments. Even though the 9/11 Commission had issued a thorough report, a number of victims' families wanted further opportunity to find out what had happened and to confront the airlines in court.[25]

Some might argue that the families who chose to sue could not expect more proofs and arguments from a trial than had already been aired before the 9/11 Commission. In most situations where there is a mass wrong, however, there is no congressional commission to investigate, and litigation may be the only way for people to ask questions about what occurred and to demand answers. The insistence of many 9/11 victims on participation in a legal process, and their regret in not choosing that path despite the Commission report, illustrates how central participation in court proceedings is to many people's ideas about justice.

The discussion so far reveals how opportunities to participate can overcome factory justice, whether that participation comes in group form, as in a hearing following a class action settlement, or individual form through a bellwether trial that then serves as the basis for settlement negotiations. These judicial innovations to promote participation should be encouraged. But today the judiciary lacks incentives to promote participation because administrators of the court system are primarily concerned with how many cases a judge has closed (or, as judges revealingly call it, how many cases they have "disposed"). A judge is not measured, as she should be, by how carefully she listened to litigants, how many hearings she held, how many self-represented litigants she treated with respect, or how many trials she adjudicated. It is little surprise, then—if what is measured is how many cases judges close—that most cases are settled or decided by motion before trial. As we shall see next, these techniques not only reduce the ability of litigants to participate in their own suits, but also reduce the opportunities for citizens to participate in the justice system by adjudicating lawsuits as jurors.[26]

SELF-GOVERNMENT THROUGH JURY SERVICE

The second way citizens participate in litigation is by serving on a jury. The jury is a constitutional office, like the presidency, Senate, or the federal judiciary. Article III of the Constitution mandates a jury for the trial of all crimes, and the Seventh Amendment mandates a jury for civil cases in suits at common law, that is, lawsuits that were traditionally decided by a jury in England around the time the Seventh Amendment was ratified. There is good reason for this constitutional protection. The jury allows ordinary citizens to participate in adjudication, it expresses a societal belief that citizens are sufficiently educated and thoughtful to decide the fate of their fellow citizens, and it relies on the precept that law can be accessible to ordinary people. The Supreme Court, quoting Alexis de Tocqueville, affirmed this idea: "[T]he institution of the jury raises the people itself, or at least a class of citizens, to the bench of judicial authority [and] invests the people, or that class of citizens, with the direction of society."[27]

People often speak of jury service and voting in one breath. But in a crucial way jury service offers a more robust form of participation in self-government than voting: it requires deliberation. Unlike voters, who do not have to explain why they picked a particular candidate, jurors hear evidence and arguments from both sides, must consider the evidence presented in light of the applicable law, and must justify their conclusions to their fellow jurors.[28] When a jury of one's fellow citizens decides important questions, they are participating in social ordering. In cases determining the limits of governmental power over people, the jury's decision is a direct exercise in self-government by the people themselves. A case of how far the police should go to stop a speeding motorist and whether police officers can use lethal force in doing so helps illustrate the jury's participatory role in self-government.

Imagine a man speeding late at night on a rural road in Georgia. The police try to pull him over. He accelerates. Sirens blaring, the police chase him down the road through several intersections and the quiet parking lot of a mall closed for the night. A few other cars are on the road. At several points the driver crosses a double yellow line. Finally, one of the police cars giving chase bumps the back bumper of the speeding car to run it off the road. As a result, the car careens off the road and crashes. The driver is severely injured, paralyzed from the neck down. He sues, arguing that when the officer bumped his car, this was excessive force under the Fourth Amendment. The question in the case is straightforward, but hardly easy: Was the officer's conduct reasonable?

This case should be decided by a jury, and in particular by members of the community who interact with this police department, fund it with their taxes, and expect protection from it. Who better to determine what constitutes "reasonable conduct" by the officers? But no jury had a chance to hear *Scott v. Harris*, the case on which this story is based, before the Supreme Court weighed in. Police officers had videotaped the entire incident with cameras mounted on their cars. The Supreme Court watched the video and eight of the nine Justices agreed: Officer Scott's decision to ram the back of Mr. Harris's car was reasonable because the high-speed chase was extremely dangerous to the officers and potential innocent bystanders. The Justices believed that the video showed them everything they needed to know. They did not see how any reasonable person could interpret the video differently than they did, even though their colleague on the bench, Justice Stevens, dissented.[29]

This is precisely what makes juries so valuable. In cases that do not concern technical legal questions, but rather people's values and sense of reasonableness, people are going to differ. Indeed, a study of reactions to the *Scott v. Harris* video confirmed as much, with some viewers taking the majority's view and others strongly disagreeing. The jury right recognizes that reasonable minds can interpret facts differently from one another and asks for consensus from a group intended to be representative of the local population, the same people who will also be subject to police action in the future, and who are in a better position to evaluate the roads in rural Georgia than Supreme Court Justices sitting in Washington, DC.[30]

There is nothing so technical about the reasonableness standard of the Fourth Amendment that it requires a legal expert, and federal judges have no monopoly on determining the appropriate police response to a speeding car on rural roads in Georgia. In fact, as the federal judge is only one person and the jury consists of between six and twelve, it is likely that the range of experience of the jurors will lead to a better result. The jurors will reach their decision not only by reflecting on their own experience but by deliberating with others and coming to a consensus. This is the essence of participation in a deliberative democracy.[31]

Serving on a jury involves serious deliberation and engagement with self-government like no other experience except, perhaps, serving in public office. Yet many criticize the jury and seek to limit its power or even abolish it altogether. Their justifications are numerous: that cases are too complex for jurors to understand; that jurors are too unpredictable and do not loyally enforce the law but instead indulge their personal preferences, emotions, or prejudices; and that trials are too expensive to be left to such unpredictable decision-makers.[32]

Perhaps as a result of this increasing criticism, jury trials have been declining in both state and federal courts in the last fifty years. Since the mid-1980s, the absolute number of trials has declined by 60 percent. These include both trials by jury and those presided over by judges. Today more and more cases are being decided by judges at earlier and earlier stages, depriving litigants in cases such as *Scott v. Harris* of the chance to tell their stories (whether to a judge or a jury), and depriving juries of the chance to deliberate and determine the standards of reasonable conduct.[33]

Critics of the jury system often compare juries to judges, and rightly so—judicial decision-making is an obvious alternative to jury trials. And, as I explain in the arguments examined next, this judge-versus-jury debate implicates many of the touchstone issues in modern democracy, such as the wisdom of entrusting sophisticated decisions to the general population, the difficulty of reaching consensus in a pluralist society, and the legitimacy of popular sovereignty when important decisions are made by the people instead of by a small group of virtuous elites. This discussion will show that the correct response to critiques of the jury system is to make improvements to that system, not to do away with it altogether. Only in this way can the critical contribution of juries to citizen participation in the judicial branch of government be preserved, while ensuring that decision-making in litigation is both well-informed and fair.

One easy critique is that juries, because they are less educated about and less specialized in the law than judges, are more unpredictable and less consistent in their decision-making. Jurors are perceived as unpredictable in part because we know that points of view differ across our nation and even within particular populations. Recall the research eliciting varying reactions to the car-chase video in *Scott v. Harris* and finding observers split on what the video showed.

This critique raises one of the key touchstones in the conception of modern democracy: how to reach a fair consensus in a pluralist society and how to respect the very different views of the individuals governed while recognizing that ultimately we must all be governed by certain uniform standards. This is precisely where juries are so useful. The *Scott v. Harris* study was an accurate reflection of the variety of views held throughout our society; it reiterated the importance of using juries to acknowledge the possibility of heterogenous responses before reaching consensus on value-laden questions. Some find troubling the thought of many different, yet equally valid, interpretations of the same facts—particularly because it disrupts the much more comforting (if less accurate) perception that we live in a homogenous society where people agree on both facts and basic values. These critics are far more comfortable with leaving value judgments to judges, who with their similar training and a unified professional outlook are expected to resolve cases more consistently.[34]

The unpredictability claim is particularly easy to dismiss outright because there is little evidence that juries are more unpredictable than legal professionals. Judges and juries agree on liability about 80 percent of the time. When they disagree, there is no reason to think that juries are necessarily the decision-maker more likely to be mistaken. Studies comparing the ways that juries and legal professionals determine compensation, for example, have found that jury-awarded compensation varies less than that of judges.[35] And where jury responses *do* differ significantly from those of judges, or from those of other juries, that inconsistency reflects reality; it is an expression of pluralism and recognition of the uncertainty inherent in fact-finding. As Justice Sotomayor wrote for a unanimous Supreme Court in 2015: "[D]ecisionmaking in fact-intensive disputes necessarily requires judgment calls. Regardless of whether those judgment calls are made by juries or judges, they necessarily involve some degree of uncertainty[.]"[36]

One core difference between judges and juries, even if they agree much of the time, is that juries may usefully mitigate judicial bias or callousness toward parties in those cases where the jury does not agree with the judges' determination. When the Founders debated the civil jury right, one concern they had was with the possibility of judicial corruption or bias against certain types of litigants. Virtuous elites can lose touch with the lives of ordinary people. Even if judges are clear-eyed and open-minded, the strain of seeing the same type of litigant over and over may jaundice them in their view of that type of litigant. Consider the case of *Turner v. Rogers* as an illustration of the principle that familiarity breeds contempt. Like Abby Gail Lassiter, whose case was described earlier, Michael Turner was a flawed parent. He was out of work and unable to pay child support, and for this he had been held in contempt and jailed five times. He had admitted to the court his drug addiction as well as his inability to work due to a back injury. Although South Carolina law required the judge to determine whether Michael had the ability to pay child support, the judge did not. Instead, he neglected to fill out the required form documenting whether Michael had the ability to pay and sentenced him to twelve months in prison. When Michael asked why he could not obtain "good time or work credits" to reduce his term of imprisonment, the judge responded with the opposite of a rational explanation: "Because that's my ruling."[37]

The case was appealed to the Supreme Court, where it was presented as raising the question of whether an indigent person was entitled to a lawyer in a civil contempt proceeding. Just as in the *Lassiter* case, the Court refused to set a bright-line rule requiring a lawyer for every indigent person facing potential jail time. But the case was not really about access to a lawyer; it was about judicial callousness. There was no pretense of presentation of proofs and arguments in Michael's case because the judge did not want to hear them. The judge did not apply the law; he never made the required factual finding that Michael could not pay child support, nor was he willing to show Michael the minimal respect and recognition of giving him a reason for the decision. Michael could not hope for any semblance of participation in the process that determined his fate because it was decided by judicial fiat. The *Turner* case illustrates why it is so important to the rule of law and to democracy that judges show equal concern and respect for the litigants before them, a subject I take up in the next chapter. The alternative is decisions based on whim or bias. The judge's disdain for Michael Turner was a bigger problem than Michael's lack of legal representation.[38]

One role of a jury is to serve as witness to judicial action. Although juries are not empaneled in civil contempt proceedings, a jury might have caused that judge to think more carefully about his actions before ruling without explanation or adequate consideration of Michael's situation because a group of citizens was watching him. Alexander Hamilton, who was not a great proponent of the jury right, wrote that the judge and jury together offer a "double security," because a jury made up of multiple people is more difficult to corrupt, and because the jury's presence in the courtroom disciplines the judge. Perhaps a jury in the *Turner* case would have been such a double security—not because the jury would have disagreed with the judge that Michael Turner deserved no more chances, but rather because the jury's presence might have disciplined the judge into following the formal legal processes required in the case. Unlike clerks, bailiffs, judges, and lawyers, juries do not answer to judges, nor do their futures depend on being in the judge's good graces. The disapproval of the citizenry may spur judges to behave better, especially in the workaday types of cases that are important to individual participants but hold no glory for the judge. In other words, the jury can function as a much needed check on the judicial branch.[39]

Another objection to juries is that cases are just too complex today for ordinary people to decide. People often trust experts more than they trust laypeople, and the preference for judges over juries is consistent with this view, particularly when it comes to important societal decisions. The idea underlying this view is that experts' technical knowledge prevents them from making decisions based on emotion or bias so that they are more likely to reach the objectively correct result, in contrast to jurors who, lacking access to expertise, will decide based on passion. This view further assumes that there is objective knowledge that will lead to the correct result and that only experts can access this knowledge.[40]

Indeed, modern litigation, like modern life, is increasingly complex, and this is true for both juries and judges. Judges are legal professionals, but they are also generalists. A judge presiding over a technical case may be untrained in the relevant field, such as science or economics. As one might expect, judges who lack training are more likely to make mistakes. For example, one study of antitrust cases found that trial judges with economic training were reversed less often than those without such training.[41]

The solution to the complexity problem is not to take cases away from juries and give them to similarly generalist judges, but to educate both judges and juries in such cases. In a technical case, we expect that the judge will learn enough in the course of the litigation to decide matters fairly. We should expect the same, and encourage the same, of juries. Instead of being a threat to expertise, virtuous elites, and professional homogeneity, the jury can be understood as a welcome complement. Even in technical cases, reasonable minds will differ about what happened and, importantly, about the *significance* of what happened—and, as discussed above, this is where the jury can be utilized to improve the quality of justice.

The next criticism to confront is the assertion that jurors do not take their jobs as decision-makers as seriously as do judges. The claim is that jurors, unlike judges, are not committed to enforcing the law, and indeed the image of recalcitrant would-be jurors scheming to escape jury duty is pervasive. And yet, studies show that once a jury is empaneled, this is not at all the case. One innovative study in Arizona observed real juries deliberating and found that jurors take their obligation to follow the law very seriously. In their deliberations these jurors sometimes asked questions of one another about issues that were supposed to be outside of the scope of their deliberation, but they did not use impermissible considerations in their decisions and were careful to consider only the evidence offered. Often when one of their number made a mistake, other jurors would correct that person. The study found that overall, jurors do a good job of following the law, taking care in their evaluation of the facts, and making reasoned decisions.[42]

It matters who decides cases. *Scott v. Harris* made law in the sense that going forward, police and citizens will know a little more about what is appropriate in the context of a high-speed chase. In deciding that case, the Supreme Court determined the scope of a constitutional right that informs everyday interactions between individuals and the state; it regulated primary conduct in society between citizens and the police. The parameters of those interactions affect all citizens, and for that reason it has been our tradition that they be set by the community. Still, it is important to remember that there is no guarantee that any adjudicator, judge or jury, will always produce a just result. Both types of adjudicators have made decisions in the past that today are universally viewed as unfair or even prejudiced. Good laws and thoughtful deliberation are what protects litigants from injustice.[43]

HELPING JURIES DO THEIR JOB

The most surprising and disappointing thing about the jury as an institution is how little instruction jurors receive on the key questions they must decide and how few tools they are given to answer them. In many jurisdictions jurors are still not given instructions on the law in writing to consult while deliberating. Often jurors are not allowed to take notes or ask questions. They are not informed that damages caps may apply to the plaintiff's award, so they may end up setting a damages amount they think is reasonable only to have that award reduced by a statutory cap. They are not instructed on doctrines of comparative negligence or joint and several liability that may be used by judges to reduce the jury's compensatory damages verdict. Jurors are not told that when issuing special verdicts, they must be consistent in their answers to each special verdict question or the entire verdict may be overturned. They are not allowed to know whether the defendant or the plaintiff has insurance, even though many jurors speculate about this question. Nor are jurors informed of any indemnity or subrogation claims, or the taxability of the award. They are not given information regarding attorney's fees, although they often want to consider this question as well. Jurors are also not instructed that if the judge finds their award in a civil case to be excessive, the judge can remit that award or order a new trial. Nor are jurors told how other, similar cases have come out so that they can determine whether their contemplated damages award is an outlier. In criminal trials, jurors are not informed of minimum or maximum sentences. The Arizona study of jurors' actual deliberations showed that most of these topics are of interest to jurors, and that jurors discuss them in deliberations even though they are not instructed about them. In fact, they likely discuss these forbidden issues *because* they are not instructed about them.[44]

Juries' lack of information may partly explain any inconsistency they display in their decisions as compared to judges, although as we have seen, such inconsistency is the exception rather than the rule. Judges see a lot of cases tried and settled; as a result, they develop a sense of the value usually accorded a particular type of case. Jurors only participate in one case, and they cannot compare it to others. They have no way of knowing if their determination happens to be an outlier. Given all of these gaps in juror knowledge, it is unfair to criticize juries for being unpredictable compared with judges when they are asked to decide cases with much less information than judges have. It is impressive that jurors do as good a job as they do working under conditions of limited knowledge and information.

Courts should give juries the information they need to do their job well. To correct the problem of a lack of context, for example, judges could provide juries with the outcomes of similar cases. One criticism of this idea is that providing comparable cases will constrain jurors into thinking they must accommodate their award to the norm, even if they do not find the norm fair in the case before them. This is a real concern, yet if we believe judges can separate their knowledge about how similar cases come out from the case before them, there is no reason jurors cannot do the same. Concerns about anchoring could be cured by specifically instructing the jury that the information is not a mandate. This would be better than keeping jurors in the dark. At a minimum, the effects of providing jurors with this type of information should be studied before being rejected.[45]

The threshold for withholding information from a jury should be much higher than it is today. More serious study of juror reactions to different types of evidence is in order. We should not rely on unreflective assumptions about human behavior in deciding what information is revealed to jurors. If, notwithstanding instruction to the contrary, jurors still reach decisions based on their guesses about the parties' insurance coverage, the taxation system, attorney's fees, or any other fact, the justice system can fix this. A better approach is to give to jurors access to the same information as judges, both providing them with the restricted information and explaining why the law asks that they not consider it. This more transparent approach comports with evidence that jurors are serious about applying the law. It also demonstrates respect for jurors as adjudicators who are capable of setting aside their personal preferences, just as judges are asked to do.

Consider damage caps as an example of what *not* to do. Many states have legislatively mandated limits on noneconomic damages (such as pain and suffering). Jurors are never told that a cap exists, and so will sometimes award an amount that exceeds it. Courts have explained that concealing the existence of a cap from jurors is intended to prevent them from moving damages around from one category to another to reach the result they favor. For example, if a plaintiff was disfigured by an accident, a jury can award compensation for the suffering of being disfigured (noneconomic damages) and compensation for the loss of income that the disfigurement caused (economic damages). If a jury knew that noneconomic damages were capped but wanted to give the plaintiff more than that amount, they could just characterize the excess as economic damages. There is evidence that lawyers, who are well aware of caps, do exactly this at trial. Lawyers try to characterize damages so that the bulk of the award lies in the uncapped category. Rather than hiding caps from jurors, it is more respectful, and potentially more effective, to explain the cap and its purpose. At the very least, it is worth studying how jurors react to this type of information and how it affects their verdicts.[46]

One of the most encouraging emerging developments is an increased willingness on the part of judges to use advisory juries. The rules of procedure permit judges to empanel a jury in cases where the Seventh Amendment does not require one. A judge who has empanelled an advisory jury must still make independent findings of fact and provide legal reasons for the decision, but a jury can be helpful in these tasks. The jury's presence may force a judge to grapple with differences in point of view, as the Justices of the Supreme Court should have done in *Scott v. Harris*. One judge advocated using advisory juries in criminal sentencing to "bridge the lifestyle and empathy gap between judge and criminal" and to "provid[e] insights and the opportunity for a more humane and effective administration of justice."[47] The same can be said of civil cases as well, especially in cases where participants in the litigation are likely to be the victims of a judge jaundiced by bitter experience.

One example of the usefulness of an advisory jury comes from *Floyd v. City of New York*. In that case, the parties were not entitled to a jury trial because the plaintiffs were seeking an injunction, which can only be issued by judges, not juries. But as the trial neared, the presiding judge, Shira Scheindlin, considered using an advisory jury. She expressed concern that a decision by a judge alone was "not the prefer-able route, because whatever the outcome, the criticism will be, 'This is one person.'" Her ruling, she explained, might be attacked as "not a verdict of the community." She added that it was "important to hear from the community," which, unlike the judge, could provide "many points of view." She recognized that the legal questions at the core of that lawsuit—whether the stop-and-frisk policy was reasonable under the Fourth Amendment and whether the policy violated equal pro-tection of the laws—are not answerable by expert knowledge alone.[48] Ultimately, Judge Scheindlin did not empanel an advisory jury. It would have been useful for her to know how a randomly selected group of ordi-nary New Yorkers reacted to the evidence about the stop-and-frisk prac-tices that affected their daily lives. Nevertheless, the dialogue inside and outside the courtroom spurred by the lawsuit was robust, and the lawsuit provided a catalyst for citizens who were illegally stopped and frisked to participate in the debate of how their neighborhoods should be policed.[49]

One of the important differences between the result of a judicial decision as opposed to one reached by a jury is that judicial deci-sions often explain in detail the basis for the decision whereas juries decide in a "black box"—that is, they are not asked to produce *public* reasons for their decision or to explain their deliberations. In a sense, juries reflect an image of a society in which the process of delibera-tion legitimates the decision rather than the soundness of the reasons for that decision being the measure of its validity. There is no way of judging the soundness of a jury's reasoning because jurors are not required to provide the reasons for their decision or to expose their deliberation to public view. The public part of the jury trial lies not in the decision-making process, but at trial when lawyers are required to present their competing proofs and arguments to the jury in lan-guage that ordinary people can understand. The arguments for the winning side can then be imputed as the basis for the jury's decision, but outside observers cannot know what the jurors really thought. The production of arguments by lawyers, as well as the process of deliberation itself, is a significant part of the jury's contribution to democracy. Perhaps juries ought to be empowered to give reasons as well, even if they are not required to do so.[50]

Because the jury is an important part of self-government, jury service should be more common, more effective, and more accessible. Instead of complaining about juror ignorance, we should do something about it. Instead of limiting juror access to information, judges need careful study of what information could make jurors better decision-makers. Rather than limiting the opportunities to serve on juries, judges ought to expand them. As the possibility of using an advisory jury demonstrates, it is possible for juries and judges to work together even in cases where a jury is not required.

LITIGATION, REASON GIVING, AND DEMOCRACY

It is no surprise that political theorists have focused on the courts as an example of deliberation and public reason. Litigation is a form of democratic deliberation because it requires parties to produce reasoned arguments, as the two sides present their evidence and justifications to the court. Unlike voters or parties negotiating a contract, participants in a lawsuit are required to present reasons for their positions, and those reasons are tested against arguments from the other side. We saw the effects of this testing of arguments in the marriage equality case discussed in chapter 2. In that case and in the stop-and-frisk litigation, this exchange of arguments happened at trial, but it can also occur at settlement hearings as the various cases arising out of the terrorist attacks of 9/11 demonstrate.[51]

Because litigation is an adversarial process, it depends on each side to present its arguments and proofs to best effect. In a society where income and educational inequality mean that people do not have equal capacities to hire lawyers and invest in litigation, the adversarial system cannot live up to its promise. Both lawyers and pro se litigants may be unable to provide good reasons or argue their points well because they are not sufficiently skilled or knowledgeable or do not invest the time in writing well-reasoned briefs. The next chapter considers the importance of equality in litigation, both as a way of enabling the values discussed so far—participation, transparency, and enforcement of the law—and as an independent value.

EQUALITY BEFORE THE LAW

In the previous chapters, we saw three core functions of litigation in democracy: it assists in enforcement of the law, encourages the revelation of important information, and promotes participation in self-government. Underlying all these things is a prerequisite we have only briefly discussed but which is at the heart of the legal system: equality before the law. In order for people to participate in the legal system, to obtain the information needed to prove their claims, and ultimately to enforce the law, they must be able to stand on equal footing with one another—or something close to it. The reason for this is that the US legal system is adversarial and the process of litigation is lawyer-driven. A litigant who is overwhelmed by the resources and skill of his adversary will find it more difficult to present good arguments, to uncover crucial information, and to win the case. It is also fundamental to a system of laws worthy of the name that the courts treat individuals equally, even those who are not worthy of esteem.

Equal treatment before the law, regardless of status, is what is generally meant by the phrase "a government of laws and not of men." Living under a government of laws requires that everyone's conduct be subject to legal rights and obligations that each of us can enforce. For these reasons, judges are expected to treat each person before the court with equal concern and respect. As a plaintiff side lawyer explained about his client's suit against the oil giant BP: "There is only one place where a waitress or a shrimper can be on equal footing with a company the size of BP, and that's a courtroom." Although this is not true as a matter of fact—indeed much of this chapter will be devoted to this problem—that lawyer's statement expresses a deeply held belief about what the process of litigation ought to be like.[1]

As we shall see, the commitment to equality before the law—what the philosopher Ronald Dworkin termed "equal concern and respect"—is found more in the rhetoric about the court system than in its practical operation. The words "Equal Justice Under Law" are engraved on the Supreme Court building, and the federal judicial oath of office requires judges to swear that they "will administer justice without respect to persons, and do equal right to the poor and the rich." These idealistic statements affirm the dignity and moral worth of every person by promising to all an avenue for the recognition and enforcement of their rights and obligations. For this reason, a person excluded from the court system is politically degraded. Such a person has no rights—not even the right to have rights. By the right to have rights, I mean the most basic of all rights: the ability to appear before a government official and argue that one is entitled to recognition as a potential holder of rights. A precondition to this kind of participation is that judges treat litigants with equal concern and respect. Equality, then, is both promoted by and vital to our court system. The endorsement and protection of principles of equality is the foundation for the other justifications for litigation. Without it, participation will be less meaningful, crucial information will remain hidden, and enforcement of the law will be diminished.[2]

The courts can provide a refuge of equal treatment for those otherwise denied political rights, such as, for example, the right to vote. The right to sue itself is a political right, somewhat like voting or jury service, and so must be protected. This is both because lawsuits are the primary way that individuals can enforce their rights and because the process of litigation is an independent form of participation in self-government. Consider that in many states convicted felons are not allowed to vote, yet they still have the right to sue. Children may not vote, but they can assert their rights in court. Rules that prohibited the poor, women, African Americans, and other classes of people from serving on juries have been overturned. These rulings recognized that every citizen, regardless of their station in life, is entitled to an equal right to sue and the opportunity to participate in jury service. The fact that people who are excluded or marginalized can sue when they cannot exercise other political rights makes litigation an irreplaceable avenue for the realization of equal treatment under law for everyone. Equal justice before the law is, in this way, a predicate to asserting rights and liberties. There can be a tension between liberty and equality, but in litigation equality before the court is what makes the assertion of liberties possible.[3]

Yet as we shall see, the right to equality before the law stands on unstable footing. The reason for this is that formal equality—that is, the idea that the rules of the game apply the same to all—is not sufficient to achieve equal justice before the law. Even if everyone is entitled to equal treatment before the court as a formal matter, their individual circumstances may make it impossible for them to take advantage of this promise. The formal procedures of litigation seem to apply the same to everyone, but exercising them requires also some modicum of material equality, that is, the resources to use the rules to one's advantage to the same extent as one's adversary.[4]

There are two types of equality that are important to think about. The first is equality of litigants. This idea encompasses both the issue of *access* to the courts—that every person should be entitled to his day in court—and the issue of relative *power* between litigants—that the judge should treat each litigant with equal concern and respect no matter what his station in life. Judges have struggled with the question of how much they should help litigants without resources stand on equal footing with the well-heeled. A second consideration is equality of outcomes, that is, the idea of consistent decisions across cases. When litigation is accused of producing unpredictable results, these accusations are serious and disturbing because both the rule of law and basic ideas of fairness require that like cases be treated alike. Just as inequality between adversaries in particular cases poses a challenge for the legal system, so too does inconsistency across cases, which highlights the need to balance individual case decisions with fairness across the board. This chapter will explore how the legal system can better provide equality before the law—both as between opponents and across the board—and to what extent it falls short.

WHY FORMAL EQUALITY IS NOT ENOUGH

Each person's case ought to be adjudicated based on the facts of that case and the applicable law, no matter who the litigant. This is the foundation of the rule of law. As Justice Frank Murphy wrote, "Only by zealously guarding the rights of the most humble, the most unorthodox and the most despised among us can freedom flourish and endure in our land."[5] It is easy to treat the powerful and respected in society well; society is tested by how we treat the least esteemed among us. Just as the substantive law should be applied equally to each case, so each litigant should benefit from the same procedural rules. Our system recognizes this for the most part and with a few exceptions does not create special, status-based rules for certain classes of litigants. Both sides of a lawsuit, for example, may seek to discover from their opponent private information relevant to the suit: a plaintiff alleging that a certain product caused her injury may be required to submit to a medical examination by a medical expert, while that plaintiff may be able to question the engineer of the offending product under oath.

Today most people understand that formal equality is a fundamental requirement of a just legal system. It is difficult to find contemporary examples of formal *inequality* in the US courts, although there are some. There were times, however, when formal inequality of procedure as well as substance was written into law. Consider, for example, the state of the law in 1850, when the Fugitive Slave Act provided that a commissioner deciding the status of a person would receive a ten-dollar fee if he returned the fugitive to slavery, but only a five-dollar fee if he freed that person. The act also forbade African Americans from testifying on their own behalf and allowed the commissioner to determine the fate of alleged slaves in their absence. The unequal treatment of African Americans was formalized in the legal system in the form of both substantive and procedural inequality. It is easy to see the link between equality before the court and the recognition of a person as a moral agent in such an extreme case. While some slaves had limited access to the courts—most conspicuously in those few southern states that permitted slaves to sue for their freedom—their right to sue diminished significantly in the decades before the Civil War. Moreover, slaves could not sue for any reason unless represented by a white lawyer; nor could they testify against white persons, or serve on juries.[6]

For the most part, these days all litigants are governed by the same rules. Of course, a person too poor to hire a good lawyer will not be able to take advantage of those rules to the same degree as a wealthy litigant. Poorer litigants may have difficulty explaining their legal claims to the court and will not know how to use available procedural rules to their advantage. For this reason, *formal equality*, that is, facial equality under which the same rules apply to everyone, may not necessarily confer *material equality*, that is, substantive equality in the process of litigation notwithstanding great differences between litigants outside the court.

To understand the difference between formal and material equality, recall *Casale v. Kelly*, the case discussed in chapter 3 in which a group of homeless people in New York, arrested for loitering and panhandling, sued the city for allegedly violating their First Amendment rights. An entire office of lawyers represents New York City (called "Corporation Counsel"), and these are an extremely experienced group, not least because the city is sued so frequently. On top of this legal fleet, the city can hire top-notch outside counsel for especially complicated or difficult cases, all paid for with tax revenue. In sum, New York City is a sophisticated legal actor. The homeless, by contrast, are a disempowered group with no easy access to legal representation nor the means to pay for lawyers. Even if a homeless person has sufficient legal knowledge to know when his or her rights have been violated, learning how to defend those rights in court takes experience, access to legal knowledge, and time—all things a homeless person is unlikely to have. As a result of these differences, New York City is in a much better position than the homeless to use procedures to its advantage, even though the same set of procedural rules apply to both. This is why formal equality is not sufficient to achieve material equality before the law.[7]

Achieving substantive justice, whether in the realm of contract, antidiscrimination, housing, or any other area of the law, requires more than a judge, a courtroom, and facially equal rules for all. The legal system needs something more to ensure that the powerless can also realize their right to be heard. Material equality requires giving some participants in the legal system, especially low-income and marginalized people, additional resources so that they can litigate on equal footing. But because material equality requires financial resources, it is in tension with many of the cost-cutting measures so enthusiastically embraced by critics of litigation, and it seems impossible in light of shrinking budgets. Judges, legislatures, and policymakers rarely consider the erosion of equality and the rule of law caused by budget cuts and limits on funding for legal services for the poor (as well as reduced access to legal counsel for the middle class). What these reformers fail to realize is that the courts need to be a special sphere where equal justice can be realized so that democracy can flourish.[8]

HOW INEQUALITY IN LITIGATION DISTORTS THE LAW

Those with few resources are at a severe disadvantage in the courts. In an adversarial system, cases are overseen by a neutral arbiter with no stake in the outcome of the lawsuit and little power to investigate independently. Consequently, each litigant is responsible for researching the law, developing evidence, and presenting arguments. The judge depends on both sides to do this work in order to decide the case correctly. If one side lacks the means to properly present the strongest arguments, the judge will not hear them and the integrity of the case outcome will be compromised.[9]

Individuals suffer when they cannot adequately protect their own rights, but the systemic effects of inequality are also destructive of the rule of law. For example, more powerful litigants may skew the development of the law in their favor. Some powerful litigants are repeat players and they find themselves defending suits brought by plaintiffs making similar claims. These institutions may decide to litigate weak cases and settle strong cases to prevent judicial decisions that will disfavor them in the future. Because of the precedential value of any given lawsuit, this kind of influence has serious consequences for the development of law in the long term. Further, since settlement value is often secret while the outcomes of litigated cases are public, a cherry-picking settlement strategy can also reduce the perceived value of similar lawsuits in the future in the sense that potential plaintiffs see only the value placed on the "weak" cases publicly litigated and not the strong cases that settled privately.[10]

Even when cases are litigated, if one side has ineffective lawyers, the law will develop in a distorted or unjust way. For example, in some employment discrimination cases, employers have argued that if the same person who hired the employee is also the one who fired them, that person probably did not discriminate against the employee in the firing. The idea behind this "same actor" inference is that if the manager was free from bias in the hiring of an employee, it is fair to conclude that the manager was also free from bias in firing that person. The evolution of the same actor inference is a fascinating study in the consequences of poor lawyering. Unsophisticated plaintiffs' lawyers in courts that had not accepted this inference nevertheless assumed its applicability without dispute, to the detriment of their clients. When those clients lost, judges wrote opinions solidifying the same actor defense in their jurisdiction—simply because the plaintiff's lawyer made no attempts, as a more competent lawyer would have, to challenge it. This is how bad lawyering distorts the law; had better lawyers been litigating, the law very well might have developed differently.[11]

HOW THE LAW PROTECTS EQUALITY

As we saw in chapter 3, economic inequality can keep litigants from participating meaningfully in their lawsuits. The Supreme Court case of *Boddie v. Connecticut* provides an apt example. That case involved two Connecticut residents, Mr. and Mrs. Boddie, seeking a divorce but unable to pay the fees the state required to officially end their marriage. Because only a court can grant a divorce, without a fee waiver they had to remain married. The Supreme Court held that the state's mandatory fee violated the Boddies' due process rights. In so doing, it recognized that formal equality is not enough to secure justice. Although the same law applied equally to everyone—that is, everyone was required to pay the same filing fee—that rule constituted a far greater burden for some individuals than for others, with the consequence of severely limiting life choices for people like the Boddies. The law on the books promised formal equality, but yielded material inequality. The *Boddie* decision was a victory for equality since the Court struck down the state's rule as to court fees for obtaining a divorce.[12]

The Supreme Court has rendered similar decisions in cases where monetary requirements, although facially equal, manifested in fundamental inequalities to litigants. In one example, the Court held unconstitutional the requirement of some states that would-be appellants in criminal cases pay for a trial transcript, which could run into the thousands of dollars, on the grounds that the practical consequence of such a requirement was that only wealthy defendants could appeal. The Supreme Court held the same—that the doors of the courthouse be open to indigent appellants—in civil proceedings involving loss of parental rights. A monetary requirement, the Court held in *M.L.B. v. S.L.J.*, cannot bar the appeal of an indigent parent seeking to dispute the termination of her parental rights just because she cannot afford a transcript.[13]

These cases mark a victory for equality, but that victory is a narrow one. The Justices have limited the protection of material equality under the United States Constitution to court fees in cases implicating a narrow set of rights labeled "fundamental": imprisonment, marriage, divorce, and parental rights. The Supreme Court has refused to impose a requirement that fees be waived for bankruptcy proceedings, for example, and for review of agency determinations.[14] And in any event, court fees are the smallest expense in litigation. Federal constitutional law has not been interpreted to ensure material equality in most lawsuits.

Some state constitutions extend material equality protection further than the minimal safeguards set forth by the Supreme Court. The Supreme Court of Washington State, for example, examined this issue in *Schroeder v. Weighall*. The case was brought after state tort reform legislation had shortened the statute of limitations for medical malpractice claims to one year. Usually statutes of limitations are tolled until the victim reaches the age of eighteen, because children cannot be expected to know their rights, much less exercise them, before that age. The particular legislation in Washington, however, did not provide such a carve-out for children, meaning that the time to bring a suit was not only shortened, but did not accommodate the special circumstances of minors. In reviewing the application of the statute of limitations to children, the Washington Supreme Court found that the law was unconstitutional because, although it treated everyone the same, the law caused special detriment to a particularly vulnerable population—children, and especially children in state care or those whose guardians did not have the knowledge or incentive to sue on their behalf. Treating this group of children the same as adults, the court said, resulted in unequal treatment before the law because of their particular vulnerability. The court concluded that the state could show no compelling interest for imposing such a draconian rule and it struck down the law. The Oklahoma Supreme Court reached a similar conclusion when it reviewed a legislative requirement that patients wishing to sue for medical malpractice produce an expert affidavit of the merit of their case. "A statute that so conditions one's right to litigate impermissibly denies equal protection," the Oklahoma court explained, "and closes the court house doors to those financially incapable of obtaining a pre-petition medical opinion." A number of state courts have held on similar grounds that damages caps violate equal protection because they arbitrarily limit damages for those who can least afford it, treating severely injured victims worse than those with lesser injuries.[15] But many other states' high courts have upheld provisions that limit statutes of limitations or cap damages, despite their disparate effects on litigants with higher value claims or without resources.

Federal and state statutes also ensure that even the very poor can still vindicate their rights in court. Federal statutes provide that inability to pay a court fee cannot keep a person from being able to vindicate her rights; courts are required to waive fees for indigent plaintiffs. Lawyers' fees, of course, are another matter. Paying a lawyer is one of the greatest costs of litigation, and, as we have seen, a good lawyer can be crucial to winning a case. The homeless people who sued the City of New York in *Casale v. Kelly*, for example, were able to sue because of a federal law which requires that the defendant in civil rights cases (in that case, a municipality) pay the plaintiffs' attorneys' fees if the plaintiff prevails. As a result, plaintiffs with strong cases can find good lawyers who are willing to take a case even if the plaintiff is unable to pay their fee.[16]

Pooling claims is another way to ensure that litigants who cannot pay a lawyer can finance their lawsuits. Class actions, for example, aggregate low-value suits under one larger umbrella. Often these are lawsuits that individual plaintiffs would not otherwise bring because the value of the suit is less than the cost of suing. The class action is vital to the rule of law because it forces defendants who commit small wrongs and are unjustly enriched—such as a bank that charges a minimal but illegal fee millions of times—to answer for their conduct. Since the filing fee for most small claims courts is twenty-five dollars, only a zealous (and somewhat impractical) customer would sue to recoup the fee they were charged. As Judge Richard Posner explained, "The realistic alternative to a class action is not 17 million individual suits, but zero individual suits, as only a lunatic or a fanatic sues for $30."[17]

Class actions do not only guarantee enforcement of the law in low-value cases, they also guarantee the equality of individuals against large enterprises. In the bank example above, the class action mechanism allows a single person, perhaps not very wealthy or sophisticated, to marshal resources that no individual consumer would ever rationally devote to a lawsuit because the collective suit is worth millions while each individual's claim is worth almost nothing. The result is the recognition and protection of individual rights through the class action.[18]

However, class actions may also compromise equality in a different way. In a class action, the lawyer gets paid a percentage of the overall fund won by the plaintiffs. This can often mean a payment of millions of dollars for the attorney. The idea that those harmed will get an award of only a few dollars while the lawyers will get millions is offensive to many people. The justification for this disparity is that fees encourage lawyers to enforce the laws through lawsuits that no individual could bring on their own. Nobody would go to the time and expense of bringing an individual lawsuit for $30, even if they knew they were entitled to compensation (and most people are not sure, at the outset of a suit, whether they will recover anything). In a class action lawsuit, the plaintiffs' lawyers take a significant risk that they will lose the suit and not receive any fee. They structure their business like a stock portfolio, taking on some risky cases and some that are more likely to win, and using the proceeds from one suit to support another. The riskier the case, the more the lawyers need to invest to see the case to its conclusion, and the more they need to be paid if they win to justify taking on that risk and up-front cost. Since many individuals are unaware of the kind of misconduct that lends itself to class actions, in some cases class actions can be the only way to enforce the law. Although some class action fee awards seem exorbitant—and some really are—in other cases high fees are justified because they create the incentives needed for the system to promote material equality between litigants and support the rule of law. Ultimately, whether any particular class action suit promotes material equality depends on whether the fee award genuinely reflects the risk that the attorney took in pursuing the case and whether the fee is used by the lawyer to finance collective suits that would otherwise be too expensive to bring.[19]

In sum, some modicum of material equality is necessary for courts to live up to the promise of equal treatment. Although courts and legislatures have taken steps in the direction of securing material equality, especially when it comes to court access fees, material equality remains the exception, rather than the rule. Even the particular protections provided in cases where material equality is most important because they involve challenges to abuses of governmental power and to subordination of minority groups—such as civil rights cases—are now under threat.[20]

CHALLENGES TO EQUALITY IN THE COURTS

At a general level, it is hard to be *against* equality in the sense of a general principle that courts should treat those who appear before them with equal concern and respect. Nevertheless, the idea of providing material equality before the courts is controversial, in part because it involves the distribution of resources and in part because it is hard to draw a line where the assistance should stop. The trend has been to roll back accommodations that promote material equality in areas where they already exist, rather than extending accommodations in the name of material equality to new areas. The justification, of course, is cost.[21]

Critics of laws that promote material equality between litigants argue that these laws increase the total number of lawsuits. This is true because these rules empower those who were otherwise unable to sue to do so. In the absence of waivers of court fees for the indigent, fee shifting, and class actions, one would predict fewer lawsuits. This argument is only damning if the type of litigation promoted by fee shifting, class actions, and other laws is worthless. Most people agree that increasing the legitimate enforcement of rights is good for society, and most people agree that litigation can be bad for society when it is not brought to enforce rights and obligations, but rather to harass or intimidate the other side. The critical question is whether the type of litigation that material equality promotes is the good kind or the bad kind, and the answer is context dependent and will likely be founded on one's views of the law at issue. There is no definitive answer to this question because there is no reliable empirical study that demonstrates whether litigation promoted by, for example, fee shifting regimes is largely filed to vindicate rights or for other, inappropriate reasons (such as to harass or merely to extract an attorney's fee). There are stories of particular lawsuits that sound silly or baseless, but these do not provide a sufficient basis for risking the erosion of the rule of law. There is no reason to think that the poor or powerless are more likely than the powerful to use litigation for bad ends rather than legitimately seeking to enforce their rights. In the absence of real proof of systemic abuse, the principle of equality before the court should trump unsupported assumptions about the quality of litigation brought by certain groups.[22]

Because of assumptions that a lot of litigation brought by the least fortunate in our society is worthless, courts and legislatures have altered or tightened laws meant to enhance material equality between litigants so that today the powerless are at a significant disadvantage in litigation. The worst of these reforms enact formal inequality into law by limiting access to the courts for unpopular groups. For example, in 1996 Congress passed a law called the Prison Litigation Reform Act (PLRA) that requires prisoners, who often file suit against the government, to pay filing fees regardless of their financial condition. If they cannot pay at once, prisoners must have the fee taken out of their bank accounts in installments. Further, the law has a "three strikes you're out" provision that forbids prisoners who have filed three cases that were dismissed from filing any more cases without paying filing fees—which can be as much as $400—up front. There is no safe harbor unless a prisoner can show a risk of imminent physical harm, a very rare situation. Congress hoped that the new rules would deter what many, including the federal judiciary, perceived as frivolous lawsuits clogging the courts by raising the bar to filing. The law is explicitly unequal in that it treats prisoners differently from everyone else, because anyone who is *not* a prisoner, even a person who was released from prison yesterday, can obtain a fee waiver if they are too poor to pay. This law reinforces the powerlessness of prisoners by depriving them of the procedural mechanisms that are available to all other litigants.[23]

The PLRA also changed the fee shifting laws in civil rights cases only for prisoners. In ordinary civil rights cases, if the plaintiffs' lawyer wins, the defendant must pay plaintiff's attorney's fees at a market rate. The reason for this is to encourage effective lawyers, who can market their services in the private sector, to represent clients in civil rights cases. In cases involving prison inmates, however, fees are limited by statute to very low rates, which discourages many attorneys from taking on prisoners' suits. Instead, as one jail supervisor explained, "The bigger impact is that the PLRA has shifted cases that would have had attorneys to the pro se docket, which has helped us with the potential damages and made them easier to defend." When prisoners bring suits on their own, the government has a better chance of winning, even when the case is meritorious, and when prisoners sue without lawyers they end up with lower damages awards, which benefits prison authorities at the expense of prisoners with winning claims. The PLRA has been in place since 1996, yet no court has ruled on the constitutionality of its provisions, although some have hinted that parts of the law may be unconstitutional.[24]

The PLRA succeeded in lowering the number of cases filed by prisoners. It did this by imposing onerous requirements (not only those described above), making it harder for prisoners to sue. The result was that even cases with merit, where prisoners allege serious violations of civil rights, have been kept out of court without being heard. This raises serious concerns for rule of law values because prisoners are among the least powerful segments of society and the most reviled; they have no political power, cannot vote, and cannot leave. Congress enacted a law that explicitly denies prisoners equal concern and respect, singling them out for unequal treatment before the courts, with higher barriers than those faced by other litigants. This law saved money because it reduced lawsuits, but its cost to a democratic society which values the rule of law is high.[25]

What of the allegation that most of these suits were frivolous? Even if they were, legislating formal inequality is the wrong approach. There is a tension between permitting prisoners to sue, unfettered, and the cost to the system of reviewing these suits. It is reasonable to be concerned about diverting judicial resources to frivolous cases because when a prisoner suit takes up judicial time, suits by others who have a fair claim to justice may be delayed. But the response to pressures on the legal system should not be to abandon fundamental values in favor of reducing costs. Legislation that mandates unequal treatment in the courts based on status, like the PLRA, is antithetical to the rule of law. In fact, litigation is more important to prisoners than other people because prisoners have so few avenues for redress. Indeed, prisoners' right to sue is a core example of the right to have rights.[26]

Other laws roll back equality in less obvious ways than the PLRA. For example, courts have been curtailing procedures that allow people with limited resources to band together and sue powerful institutions, eroding the possibility of material equality. By limiting class actions, courts have made it hard, sometimes impossible, to enforce consumer protection laws. Changes to the law of class actions have happened slowly and involve technical rules of procedure, but although they may be technical these changes are no less destructive of the rule of law. The justification for these changes is similar to that advocated in connection with prisoner suits: that there is too much frivolous litigation. Businesses, it is said, are attacked by greedy plaintiffs' lawyers and settle for large sums out of fear. This may be true some of the time, but there is no proof that most class action litigation is meritless and some class action litigation is certainly meritorious. Most importantly, in many cases where the amount at stake is very small, ordinary people with a legitimate suit will have no other avenue to defend their rights than collective litigation. The trade-off that society must make when deciding whether to restrict class actions is between the potential cost to business of overenforcement and equal justice before the court for individuals. Before that trade-off can be reasonably made, there needs to be reliable information about the extent of meritless litigation as distinct from the enforcement of existing laws. So far, no such evidence has been forthcoming.[27]

We have discussed how the Supreme Court, in a string of cases, held that arbitration contracts barring class action lawsuits are binding on consumers, even in standard form contracts that do not permit the consumer to negotiate terms. In one case, a California couple sued a mobile phone company because it advertised free phones but charged consumers a tax of, on average, around thirty dollars (as a result, the phone was not free). The company included in their nonnegotiable cell phone contract—the kind nobody ever reads—an arbitration clause forbidding customers from bringing their suits as class actions and requiring them to arbitrate individually. This meant paying an arbitrator, which is more expensive to the individual plaintiffs than filing a class action in court. Applying California contract law, the lower court held that contracts that both required arbitration and barred class actions were unconscionable. The Supreme Court reversed. Today, nearly every company has a similar provision in their consumer contracts, and as a result many consumers cannot depend on state contract laws to protect their right to public vindication.[28]

Arbitration can cost thousands of dollars since the parties pay for the arbitrators. By contrast, the courts are paid for by the state or federal governments. Even contracts forcing arbitration but promising to reimburse a winning plaintiff's costs deter suits; no one is going to risk losing thousands for the chance to win thirty dollars. As a result, ordinary consumers who wish to protect their rights are effectively barred from the courts and diverted instead to a secret and expensive private tribunal. When people cannot sue to enforce their rights, the rule of law is eroded: in a pure arbitration regime, laws will not be enforced except by those who already have power and resources.[29] That is how limitations on class actions produce inequality before the law.

Arbitration provisions and the bar on class actions have affected not only individual consumers, but also small businesses. In one case, a small restaurant in California wanted to sue American Express for violating the antitrust laws. The Supreme Court held in *American Express v. Italian Colors Restaurant* that an arbitration provision between the small restaurant and American Express barred class actions. The damages in question were around $25,000, but bringing a suit required an economic expert report, which cost $300,000. If the restaurant had been allowed to bring a class action suit, it would have been able to recoup this cost because it would have sued on behalf of the thousands of restaurants that accept American Express. For the individual small business, however, the numbers did not justify the effort required to vindicate its rights. The Supreme Court thus closed the doors of justice on this restaurant, and thousands of other small businesses, by ruling that an arbitration clause is always binding. Justice Scalia explained that "the fact that it is not worth the expense involved in *proving* a statutory remedy does not constitute the elimination of the *right to pursue* that remedy." A right to pursue a remedy, without the ability to pursue it in fact, is an empty right. The opinion upheld formal equality (each party to the contract can pursue its rights in arbitration) but ignored material equality because each party cannot assert its rights equally. The poorer party is at a distinct disadvantage because it simply cannot afford to enforce its rights. The result of this ruling is that the antitrust violation, if there was one, will continue, and that many other cases where an antitrust violation might have been found will never be brought because they are simply too costly for individual businesses to pursue. The only possible avenue left for businesses such as this restaurant is if the government decides to bring suit.[30]

Antitrust suits provide yet another example of procedural decisions where the courts ignored the effect of inequality on the rule of law. In a case called *Bell Atlantic v. Twombly,* the Supreme Court held that a plaintiff claiming an antitrust conspiracy must allege specific facts demonstrating that the conspiracy existed. The Court explained that the plaintiffs in that case had not pled sufficient facts for their case to go forward and that there was an alternative, reasonable explanation for conduct that appeared anticompetitive. But the problem for plaintiffs alleging conspiracy is that conspiracies are just that—secret agreements. Only access to communications between the relevant players would have revealed whether they in fact conspired to raise prices. And here is another example of inequality: because of an information asymmetry, individual consumers in court cannot stand on equal turf with corporations.[31]

By requiring plaintiffs to produce information they cannot reasonably obtain, the Supreme Court shut the door to justice on them. The

Court's concern was that the process of civil discovery would cost the corporation too much, especially if the case was without merit, a fact which was impossible to ascertain without more information. The Court reasoned that the cost of discovery will have an "in terrorem" effect on defendants so that they will settle even "anemic cases."[32] In *Ashcroft v. Iqbal*, a case applying heightened pleading in the civil rights context, the Court was even more explicit about elevating concerns about costs in articulating its view that government officials' need to be free of lawsuits is more important than the enforcement of constitutional rights. As we learned in previous chapters, a group of Muslim immigrants brought a suit alleging that in the aftermath of the terror attacks of 9/11 they had been arrested and held in harsh conditions on account of their religion and national origin. The key allegation was that then Attorney General John Ashcroft and FBI Director Robert Mueller had conspired to violate their civil rights. The Supreme Court struck down the suit before it even began. In so doing, the Court created a false trade-off between equality on the one hand and governmental efficiency on the other. Writing for the majority, Justice Kennedy explained that "Litigation, though necessary to ensure that officials comply with the law, exacts heavy costs in terms of efficiency and expenditure of valuable time and resources that might otherwise be directed to the proper execution of the work of the Government." Yet the proper execution of the work of the government also requires obeying the Constitution, which states that the president "shall take Care that the Laws be faithfully executed." Enforcing that requirement was the point of the lawsuit.[33]

A trade-off between equality and efficiency was unnecessary in these cases because the Court could have protected the officials in question with less draconian means that did not jeopardize equal justice under law, such as by careful judicial control of the discovery process. For example, in *Iqbal* plaintiffs might have been allowed to seek written documentary evidence or to question lower-level officials, and the district court might have limited their ability to depose high-ranking officials until they discovered through other means some basis to think there was in fact a conspiracy. Instead, in both these cases the Supreme

Court assumed that lower courts could not control discovery, although the procedural rules give judges substantial control over this process. It is hard to understand why the Supreme Court put the self-interested claims of government officers ahead of its faith in the abilities of district court judges without empirical proof of the judges' shortcomings. In cases where values as important as equal justice under law are at stake, the evidentiary burden for imposing barriers on the weaker side should be a high one.

When faced with the opportunity to improve the law by equalizing power between litigants before the court, the Supreme Court has instead favored the more powerful, systematically making it harder for the weak or underresourced to sue. At first blush, the examples are vastly different: the small businesses trying to assert the antitrust laws against larger, more powerful businesses; the individual consumers trying to enforce the promises of large corporations; the most powerless in society, immigrants and prisoners, trying to vindicate their constitutional rights. Yet they all share the same pattern. In each of these cases, one party faced an uphill battle and lacked the resources or ability to use the rules to enforce its rights, and in each case the judiciary could help them by enforcing the right to equal treatment in the courts through material equality, that is, by giving them the opportunity to use procedural rules on equal footing with their opponent.

When ordinary people lack the ability to protect their rights, the foundation of the rule of law—that all people are equal before the court—is eroded. At a minimum, the legislature and the courts should not single out classes of people (such as prisoners) for formally different treatment based on their status. Because formal equality is insufficient to guarantee equal treatment in the courts when the larger society is characterized by economic inequality, protecting the rule of law also requires some level of material equality in litigation. But how far should this ideal go? True equality before the court, a system in which judges in fact do "equal right to the poor and the rich" as the federal oath of judicial office promises, imposes costs. Those costs can be political, such as allowing unpopular groups like prisoners equal access to the courts or permitting high-level officials to be sued. The costs are also monetary. For example, fee shifting regimes not only require defendants to pay the plaintiffs' fees if plaintiffs prevail, but also increase time spent on litigation by enabling ordinary people to sue when they think they have been wronged. These are the costs that a society must pay in service of the rule of law.

It almost goes without saying that because economic inequality is part of the social fabric in the United States, it would be impossible to provide true universal material equality (even limited to the judicial sphere) without significant social change. This ideal is not realizable given the structure of modern life. The hard question, then, is how to fashion a satisfactory approach to material equality in the courts in a world characterized by fundamental material inequality among individuals outside the courthouse. Are there certain kinds of cases for which material equality is more important, and if so, what are they and how can we demarcate them? For example, money could be allocated to prioritize legal services for the worst off, such as the very poor facing eviction proceedings. Or it could be allocated to prioritize cases that fundamentally affect the rule of law, such as lawsuits against the government for violations of rights or against institutions engaging in large-scale illegal behavior. Our current regime, to the extent it still functions, is focused on the latter approach. Fee shifting is available in civil rights cases and in some consumer cases where consumers face a much larger and more sophisticated institution as an adversary. Class actions also target large-scale illegality, although in many cases the individual harm is small. But middle- or low-income people with individual suits have a difficult time affording legal assistance.[34]

One of the most difficult barriers to equality before the law, especially in the many cases where fee shifting or class actions are not available, is access to lawyers. Even if the fee for court filing is waived, navigating the confusing and complicated process of litigation is a barrier for most people. As we saw in the introduction, many cases where individuals are defendants end in default and there is little activity that might be fairly described as litigation in those cases. Hiring a lawyer is expensive, and access to legal services is limited by bar admission requirements, which create costly barriers to becoming a lawyer and maintaining a law license. Perhaps these requirements should be altered. Currently experiments are being conducted to determine what the effect of unbundling legal services will have on clients, including allowing nonlawyers to provide limited legal services so that more people can obtain legal advice to assist them with their problems and to help them assert their rights. Already courts are providing nonlawyers to assist some self-represented litigants in navigating the court system by providing information. Some states have launched pilot projects to evaluate whether providing free legal services to individuals in financial distress yields better outcomes than simply giving them information or providing no help at all. There are many great policy proposals out there, but what is needed to realize them is commitment on the part of courts and the legislatures who fund them to equal justice before the law.[35]

EQUALITY OF CASE OUTCOMES

So far this chapter has focused on equality among litigants and attempts to mitigate, where most important, the effects of considerable inequalities in resources on individuals' access to justice. Another important aspect of equality, however, is the concept that similar cases ought to yield similar outcomes. This form of equality is summed up in the common law maxim that like cases ought to be treated alike. Many complaints about litigation are not about the question of how poorer and weaker litigants can obtain their day in court, but instead focus on inconsistency in the results of adjudication. For example, on multiple occasions the Supreme Court has expressed concern about unpredictable liability. It is important to address these criticisms because when it comes to case outcomes, there are serious trade-offs to be made between equality and individualism.[36]

A court system that reaches consistent outcomes realizes one aspect of fairness. But our courts are not geared toward achieving consistency; instead, they are structured to provide individualized adjudication. For the most part, cases are brought one at a time, and that is how judges decide them. Judges rarely consider how a series of similar cases resolve longitudinally across different courts or jurisdictions, or even within their own courthouse. Juries, meanwhile, are not told how previous, similar cases were decided. On top of the inherent variation in results reached by different courts in different places, state laws may vary greatly, leading to different outcomes in different states for the same type of case. This raises the specter of inequality, but it also provides a very different kind of fairness. Giving personalized attention to individual cases ensures that even small variations in the facts of the case will be duly considered before judgment is made. As a consequence, courts must balance two values in tension: equal treatment on the one hand and individual treatment on the other.

Critics of litigation cite inconsistency across cases as an example of the "litigation lottery." Complaints that juries reach inconsistent decisions and that litigation is a lottery speak to the fact that consistent outcomes are an important part of justice and that this conception of justice is relational. It also reminds one of the importance of reason to a system of laws because a lottery invokes the specter of arbitrary or random decision-making. On a systemic level, part of the calculus of fairness is whether a litigant has received the same result as another, similarly situated litigant. The Vioxx litigation provides a good example. As we learned in chapter 1, in response to reliable medical studies finding that Vioxx increased the rates of heart attacks and strokes in patients, its manufacturer, Merck & Co., pulled the drug off the market, but not before many thousands of people had used it. Patients filed tens of thousands of lawsuits against Merck across the country. Sixteen cases were brought to trial. In five of those trials, Merck was found liable and juries awarded the plaintiffs multimillion-dollar damages. In the rest, plaintiffs lost. Why should there be such different outcomes for these patients, if all of them took Vioxx and suffered a heart attack?

The reason for different outcomes is that the issues jurors face in a trial are those where reasonable minds could differ in their interpretation of the facts. (After all, if the outcome was clear, the parties would likely settle their dispute before trial.) For this reason, disparate outcomes are not a basis for rejecting litigation as unreasonable, fundamentally unfair, or a lottery; reasonable decision-makers could reach different outcomes in a close case, yet still be applying the law to the facts of that case faithfully. As we saw in chapter 3, the Supreme Court recognizes that "decisionmaking in fact-intensive disputes necessarily requires judgment calls." Sometimes this means different decision-makers—whether judges or juries—will decide the application of law to the facts of a nearly identical case differently.[37]

A fair system cannot require that like cases always come out alike. It can only require that judges and juries apply the law accurately to the facts of the case. Even adjudicators who are sincerely applying the facts to the law in the case before them may reach different outcomes some of the time, because individual decision-makers will differ in their interpretation of the facts some of the time. In addition, judges may reach different conclusions about the law at different points in time, so that people whose cases were adjudicated earlier will have an outcome different from those adjudicated later. Such inconsistencies are inevitable.

Different outcomes in similar cases reflect a court system that values individual nuances of a case and decentralized decision-makers over consistency. This trade-off is a product of the fact that in the United States individualism is as important a value as equality. After all, it would be possible to obtain equal outcomes if, for example, a court tried all similar cases together and applied uniform standards with no recognition of special circumstances or awarded damages according to a predetermined schedule. Such innovations would be a significant departure from our current system. The best way for the courts to address the apparent unfairness of different outcomes for apparently similarly situated litigants under the current system is by requiring a reasoned decision to justify the outcome.[38]

Sometimes factual differences between cases that are not readily apparent to outsiders justify different outcomes. In the Vioxx litigation, for example, each plaintiff was required to prove that Vioxx caused *their* heart attack. A diabetic plaintiff—who because of his diabetes already faced an increased risk of heart attack—faced a more difficult burden in showing that Vioxx, not his diabetes, caused his heart attack. For this reason, a different outcome for a diabetic plaintiff and for an otherwise healthy plaintiff is in fact quite reasonable.[39] Of course, not every factual difference justifies a divergent outcome in an otherwise similar case. The best argument in favor of individual adjudication is that, by necessity, the determination of which differences matter is a case-specific enterprise. The law specifies to some extent which factors are relevant (such as a preexisting condition of diabetes) and which are not.

Individual determinations of injuries and damages are also important to the substantive underpinnings of particular laws. Damages are supposed to compensate the plaintiff for the harm done to him by the defendant. Even people subject to the same harm will suffer injuries of different types and extent. This is a product of natural variation between individuals. For example, an injury that puts a plaintiff out of work for six months can lead to widely different compensation if that plaintiff is an investment banker rather than a minimum wage employee at a fast food restaurant.

Many may find it unjust that our system awards an already wealthy family more money than a family that is struggling economically and has just lost its primary breadwinner. Indeed, renowned special master Kenneth Feinberg struggled with just this issue in administering the 9/11 Victim Compensation Fund to families and victims who opted out of the tort system and agreed to take a settlement instead. Some were very rich and others very poor, but all experienced terrible losses. In his book about the experience, Feinberg concluded that he would have preferred to give identical amounts to all claimants rather than to quantify the value of human life in the aftermath of such a disaster, especially when those valuations reflect existing economic inequality.[40]

Feinberg came up against the limits of the legal system in a society that tolerates significant income inequality. There is little the courts can do about this wealth gap (in the context of tort litigation, anyway) because the principle of compensation, which is the core of tort law, requires that the plaintiff who has proven fault be put back in the position he was in before he was injured. In this way substantive tort law reinforces inequality outside the courthouse, or at least preserves the status quo ante. One way that the tort law has inserted some modicum of equality is pain and suffering damages, which compensate the low (or no) wage earner for an injury that is more difficult to monetize than a loss of income. I pointed out earlier in this chapter that some state courts have struck down statutes that cap pain and suffering damages on equal protection grounds. A reason for doing so is that such caps disproportionately harm those who do not earn wages: children, the old, and the very poor.[41]

Another reason outcomes may differ is diversity of decision-makers. The United States is a country made up of many legal systems: one for each of the fifty states, plus the federal court system, as well as separate court systems in territories such as Puerto Rico, and tribal courts. Each state has different laws that affect outcomes of individual cases. A plaintiff in Wisconsin and a plaintiff in Georgia suing for the same wrong may achieve different outcomes because their states have different laws.[42]

Even within the same court system, judges differ in their interpretations of a law or their application of the law to the facts of a particular case. Sometimes these differences are corrected on appeal when the appellate court resolves differences by establishing a uniform view of the law. But not all lawsuits reach the appellate court, and even if they do, different appellate judges will themselves disagree. Judges and juries can also differ in their evaluation of a case. As we saw in chapter 3, juries are not told how cases similar to the one before them were decided, so they cannot reasonably be expected to produce consistent outcomes. Judges, who do have some insight into how similar cases came out, are also inconsistent in their damages awards.[43]

The problem of inconsistency among decision-makers is everywhere in the United States legal system. Critics of the legal system often argue that juries are particularly inconsistent in their verdicts, but in fact all decision-makers in our legal system reach inconsistent results. When researchers asked participants in the legal system to provide their assessment of how much compensation should be awarded in a medical malpractice case where the doctor had admitted liability, the answer varied across judges, lawyers, and jurors. The mean compensation was the same across every decision-maker: around $50,000. What was surprising was that the variance of awards was greater among legal professionals (judges and lawyers) than among mock juries made up of twelve people. The range of awards for legal professionals was from $22,000 to $82,000; for mock jury awards, the range was $29,500 to $69,000. It is likely that the variance among juries was less than that among legal professionals because they deliberate. This conclusion is based on the fact that when individual prospective jurors were asked to evaluate the case on their own, their awards showed more variance than those of legal professionals. What we learn from this is that people, even professional adjudicators, evaluate the same case differently. The decentralization of decision-making among judges and juries in different jurisdictions is a significant reason for differences in outcomes of otherwise similar cases. But these features of the legal landscape have their benefits, as I will explain shortly.[44]

Outcomes can also evolve over time as a result of changes in social thinking or available information, adding another dimension to variance in outcomes and another valuable justification for that variance. Consider, for example, lawsuits brought by smokers against tobacco companies claiming the companies did not adequately notify consumers of the dangers of their products. In early lawsuits, the tobacco companies largely prevailed. Over time, as more information about the dangers of tobacco and the misrepresentations of the tobacco companies to consumers became known, and as the tide of public opinion turned against smoking, smokers started to win their lawsuits. Later plaintiffs received different outcomes than the early plaintiffs, but we hardly want to lower the damage awards of those later cases to match up with those of the early ones in the name of equality. (Nor is it practicable to retroactively impose findings in later cases or to re-try cases from the past.) The variation here is not caused by injustice or inequality—it is the consequence of changing social mores. This variation is unavoidable, too, as social change is always on the horizon.[45]

This leads into another salient point in defense of variation in litigation. By valuing individualism and decentralization over consistency, our legal system limits error and bias. When an initial case is decided wrongly—as many think happened in the tobacco cases—that error need not be repeated in a second case because it is decided independently of the first. Decentralization can also counteract bias. If one type of decision-maker is biased against a certain group of litigants or kind of case, a variety of decision-makers limits the effects of this bias.[46] For example, our system allows juries, judges, and appellate courts to decide case outcomes and recovery amounts. Even in cases tried to a jury, the trial judge and the appellate court may review the verdict to determine whether it was reasonable and may reduce a verdict in some cases. Judicial review of jury verdicts is a useful backstop in extraordinary cases where variation among jury verdicts can cause severe inequalities between litigants. Because reducing or overturning a jury's verdict diminishes juror participation, however, that power should be exercised with great care.[47]

Often differences in outcomes are not the result of chance or an unjust system, but of the individual attention given to each case. This is the reason that critics who point to inconsistent outcomes as evidence of a so-called litigation lottery are misguided. But such differences are an important reason for judges to justify their decisions thoroughly, so that participants understand that differences in outcomes are not arbitrary but vary because of distinctions that lawfully permit divergent results.[48]

There will always be some trade-offs between reaching consistent outcomes across cases and providing individualized adjudication in each case. The question is how to strike the balance. With some innovation, courts could provide more consistent outcomes without sacrificing too much the participation benefits of individualism. For example, judges could base damages awards on sample trials, but this can only be done in large-scale lawsuits, such as those involving similar conduct by a defendant against a group of plaintiffs who suffered similar injuries. In those types of cases, judges can conduct coordinated sample trials across the country and then use the results of these trials to develop a matrix of damages that could be a benchmark for settlements. While not everyone will get their individual day in court under this scenario, each plaintiff obtains a result informed by a jury trial and which attempt to take into account salient factors about his individual case. This type of resolution is possible when cases are consolidated and judges in different jurisdictions coordinate their work. For example, the many thousands of Vioxx cases filed in federal court were consolidated in Louisiana, and lawsuits that had been filed in state courts were similarly consolidated before a single judge in each state. These judges collaborated on a process in which they tried a number of cases to juries in several jurisdictions. That process was somewhat decentralized because even though a single judge was managing it, many juries from different parts of the country decided the outcomes. Because the cases were settled using a matrix, similarly situated plaintiffs received the same amount. Ultimately, the outcomes were consistent across cases while still respecting the plaintiffs' individuality.[49]

Giving juries similar cases to compare to the case before them or creating a compensation matrix based on sample cases may seem radical, but in fact these practices have a long history. Insurance companies have been using similar techniques to price settlement for over one hundred years. Beginning in the 1880s, companies paid for work injuries using standardized payment schedules. Today, ordinary cases involving car accidents are settled according to a type of going rate that is negotiated between lawyers and insurance companies. Although each case may be negotiated individually, the participants understand that the settlement in one case will inform and be informed by a portfolio of similar cases.[50]

When settlements are based on the facts of the individual case as compared to similar cases, they are able to balance the values of individualism and equality. Fairness requires not only that the decision is legally correct as to this individual, but also that it be comparable to what others received. But it is a real problem that there is no information about the substance of matrix-based settlements in individual cases. Although jury verdicts and judicial decisions are published, and settlement matrixes in mass tort cases are sometimes publicized, ordinary settlements are not. Returning to the theme of imbalance of power and resources from the beginning of this chapter, large insurers are able to retain vast amounts of information about previously settled cases to use in determining what they are willing to pay in each individual case brought. But individuals lack access to this type of information and so may settle for less than the going rate. Equal treatment in litigation, then, requires not only that individuals have an opportunity to participate on equal footing with their opponent, but also that they have access to information.

THE MEANING OF EQUALITY BEFORE THE LAW

The idea that people should receive equal treatment in the court system is well established and long recognized. It is based in a deeper ideal that characterizes modern democracy: the ideal of status equality. As the philosopher Elizabeth Anderson explains, democracy presupposes equality between the governed in discussions of collective self-determination: "To stand as an equal before others in discussion means that one is entitled to participate, that others recognize an obligation to listen respectfully and respond to one's arguments, that no one need bow and scrape before others or represent themselves as inferior to others as a condition of having their claim heard."[51] The courts are a crucial sphere where it ought to be possible for the otherwise excluded and stigmatized to be recognized as having the type of equal standing Anderson describes.

The ideal of status equality in the courts seems as though it ought to be taken for granted, except that even today certain classes of indivi duals such as prisoners are singled out for worse treatment. For everyone else, wealth inequality outside the courthouse and decentralized adjudication, both features of our social structure that are unlikely to change, contribute to the problem of inequality before the law. The challenge is to develop procedural innovations that can achieve a better balance between equality and other values, such as individualism, than our current system has done.

EPILOGUE

Litigation is more than a process of dispute resolution, although of course resolving a dispute is part of its purpose. It is a process through which individuals, groups, organizations, and corporations promote and protect democratic values. Litigation allows people to enforce the law, force crucial information into the open, and participate in self-government by presenting and disputing proofs and reasoned arguments. To do all this requires that people be able to present their case on equal footing, no matter what their social standing outside the courtroom, and that they be treated by the court with equal concern and respect.

It is sometimes hard to see litigation as a social good because lawsuits are usually brought when something bad has happened. The introduction explained that litigation occurs when there is a tear in the fabric of society. Accidents happen; people and institutions make poor choices, and others suffer for those choices. This book has explored many such cases. It is important not to confuse the fact that we live in an imperfect world with the result that these imperfections sometimes require people to assert and defend their rights by filing lawsuits. The way we react to these tears in the social fabric—including whether we choose to give people access to the courts to voice their concerns and articulate their arguments to a governmental official—is a test of the kind of society we live in.

The process of litigation will not always yield just results, but it can produce an informative dialogue grounded in facts and reason. Some lawsuits seek to achieve ends that many find disagreeable, and some arguments made in court seem wrongheaded. Lawsuits may be aimed at expanding individual rights or limiting them, broadening access to the ballot or curtailing it, increasing regulation to promote health and safety or curbing it. Which arguments succeed and which rights are vindicated is the ultimate measure of justice. The debates over the most profound questions of equality and liberty, as well as more mundane questions raised by commonplace tort and contract cases, will continue. However these disputes are resolved for the moment, no side should be able to pull up the ladder behind it—yet that is just what is happening today.

Litigation as a democratic institution is under attack in a variety of ways, largely through procedural changes limiting people's ability to sue without adequate justification. Supreme Court decisions have tightened the requirements for bringing a case to court by limiting standing doctrine so that it is harder and harder for litigants to show that they are entitled to be heard in federal court and by requiring that the plaintiff present information in pleadings that is not accessible without court-ordered discovery. The Court has also tightened the requirements for personal jurisdiction, making it harder to sue out-of-staters or foreigners in both state and federal court. Rule-makers continually add restrictions to the civil discovery rules. Indeed, the length of these rules has metastasized to enormous proportions in an effort to curb perceived excesses—yet there is no reliable empirical evidence that discovery is out of control, unmoored to the underlying value of cases, or that the addition of new restrictions has made civil discovery more fair, resulted in more important information being unearthed, or even made life easier for federal district court judges. Quite the opposite: we saw in chapter 2 that if anything there is too little discovery rather than too much in most cases.

Increasingly, summary judgment has done the work of trial, with judges taking on more and more decision-making. Public trials, including jury trials, are now a rare event in the American justice system. This phenomenon, while producing reasoned arguments and decisions in some cases, can in other cases obscure important factual disputes, divert decisions from juries to judges, hide the workings of the justice system that are revealed at trial, and prevent the elaboration of narratives that are important for public debate. Limitations on the class action device have made it harder for consumers and public interest groups to bring suits to remedy wrongs they have suffered. Statutory limits on damages and attorneys' fees have made it harder for people to obtain lawyers, even when they have a good case and have suffered grave harm. The encouragement of secrecy in civil discovery and in settlement has limited access to information as well as law enforcement. Other procedural changes have moved litigation entirely out of the public sphere, such as the Supreme Court's decisions upholding arbitration in take-it-or-leave-it consumer contracts. As Justice Ginsburg noted in a dissent in a recent case upholding an arbitration agreement, such provisions leave consumers "without effective access to justice."[1] Taken together, these developments constitute a procedural assault on litigation despite the lack of empirical evidence supporting many of the criticisms of litigation that have spurred these changes.[2]

The troubling thing about these developments is that they restrict or even eliminate legal rights *indirectly*. While the erosion of rights has at other historical moments been more direct and evident even to the casual observer of the courts, today the battle requires explanation because it is happening around procedure more than substance. Rights remain on the books, but people cannot realize these rights because of procedural impediments. If people cannot sue, in many cases they will not be able to enforce the law, obtain and reveal information that will discipline wrongdoers and spur legislative action, or participate in self-government; they will even be on their own in resolving disputes. The background norms that smooth day-to-day interactions, the belief that rights and obligations are enforceable and that liberties will be protected, are endangered by the growing restrictions on litigation.

Complaints about the wheels of justice have been consistent in American history, but there is something novel about the current assault on litigation in that it focuses not on rights but on procedures. As early as 1713, colonists complained when lay pleading was transforming into pleading dominated by lawyers. In the 1850s, concerns about complexity and ossification led to revisions of the procedural law. In an influential lecture to the bar in 1906 entitled "The Causes of Popular Dissatisfaction with the Administration of Justice," Roscoe Pound decried the rigid and complex procedural system, a system he believed was too adversarial and prevented cases from being heard on the merits. In the 1930s the procedural regime was overhauled to make it easier for litigants to obtain that merits determination. These previous calls for procedural change were not to keep cases *out* of the courts; rather, reformers wanted to make the courts a better place for cases to be litigated.

The movement to keep cases out of court has been a response to the rights revolution of the 1960s. From 1930 to 1960, case filing rates in the federal courts were at a low ebb, but they rose with the creation of new statutory causes of action in the 1960s and 1970s; these statutes protected civil rights, consumer rights, and the environment and, as we have seen, gave individuals private rights of action to pursue violations of the law. In comparison to a historic low of the mid-twentieth century, per capita filing rates seemed high in the 1970s and 1980s, but they were not high in comparison to historic rates, and they soon stabilized. Indeed, per capita filing rates were higher earlier in our history than they are today. For example, per capita litigation rates in the early nineteenth century were about double those of the 1970s. What changed in the 1960s and 1970s were two things. First, more people had rights than ever before; access to the courts became broader than at any other time in United States history. Second, by comparison to the immediately preceding period, filing rates seemed out of control, although they were consistent with or below historic per capita rates.[3]

The arguments in favor of limiting litigation today, unlike in prior generations, seek to curb litigation as a way to limit the law's reach.[4] The overlap between debates about rights and obligations and debates about the litigation process obscure what constraints on litigation do to democracy. If it is to be honest, the conversation should shift to what is really at stake: what rights and obligations ought individuals and institutions have in the type of society we want to be?

The purpose of this book has been to illuminate the democratic value of litigation so that we can begin a conversation about procedural reforms that would truly improve this institution. One example of how this conversation might move forward concerns judicial attitudes toward litigation and toward parties. We saw in the cases of Abby Gail Lassiter and Michael Turner how poorly justice is administered when judges express contempt for litigants. The problem of judicial attitudes is expressed in how the work of judges is evaluated. For example, today federal judges are measured by how many motions they decide and how many cases they close quickly. By statute, every six months the Administrative Office of the Courts publishes a list of judges who have motions pending more than six months or cases pending more than three years. The message of this method of measuring judicial productivity is that the judge is to resolve cases in the fastest way possible.[5]

Even though the speed of decisions is one measure of productivity, it does not tell us how well cases are decided, what information was produced in the course of litigation, whether the judge afforded the parties an opportunity to participate, or whether litigants were treated with dignity and respect. This measure does not even ask how complex the case that was resolved was or what was produced for society as a part of adjudicating it. A case which reached a multiday trial (and was much more work for the judge) is treated just the same as a case that the judge dismissed right after it was filed from the perspective of judicial productivity. A case that resulted in the discovery and publication of important information that improved consumer safety is treated the same as a case that was settled with a secrecy agreement that prevented critical information from getting out. Yet these cases differ in their contribution to our democracy, and they should be measured differently. This is not to say that speed of resolution is not an important issue—delay can have considerable costs—but speed should not be the sole measure of productivity.

Judge William Young has suggested a new measure for judicial productivity, which he called "bench presence." The idea is to measure judicial productivity based on the amount of time the judge spends publicly adjudicating disputes, because open, public court proceedings promote transparency, are more likely to induce both litigants and judges to give reasons, and provide a forum for litigants to be treated with equal concern and respect. When there is a public hearing in the courtroom, rather than exchange of paper motions, there can also be a dynamic conversation between judge and litigants that encourages the type of reasoned dialogue that ought to be the distinctive contribution of litigation to democracy. Judge Young's coauthored study measuring bench presence showed that judicial hours in the courtroom are on the decline. The main cost to increasing bench presence, one would think, would be delay in resolving cases. But Judge Young found that judges spending more time on the bench did not resolve cases more slowly on the whole.[6]

Measuring the amount of time a judge spends on the bench does not capture the full interaction of judges with litigants because that interaction can happen outside the courtroom. Motions can be heard and argued more informally in the judges' chambers. Even if there were an oral argument in the courtroom, there is no guarantee that there will be anyone to see that public spectacle. A measure of bench presence that would encourage judges to hear more motions in the courtroom rather than privately, however, opens up the possibility of bringing the public into the courtroom in a way that back-room exchanges do not. There is also some evidence that formality in litigation contexts improves litigant satisfaction and increases the perception of legitimacy. Given the benefits of public justice, judges ought to be encouraged to hear motions in the courtroom rather than in their chambers.[7]

This brings us to the key point: if you make what you measure, court systems should be measured by their success at promoting and protecting democratic values, not merely by their ability to close cases. Judicial productivity should be measured by the extent to which judges reach decisions on the merits, enable the revelation of information needed for individual and democratic decision-making, facilitate participation in the public airing (and testing) of proofs and arguments, and treat all litigants with equal concern and respect. Bench presence is a good beginning, even if it does not fully capture these qualitative measures.

This book has suggested a number of other policy changes, including limiting certain types of secret settlements as well as confidentiality orders in cases where the information at issue would impact public safety, creating a database of settlements so that litigants could know if their settlement was fair, finding ways to create more opportunities for individuals to participate in adjudication as jurors, and providing more opportunities for representation for those who cannot afford a lawyer. There are many other potential changes to the court system that would promote democratic values. This book has laid out those values in order to provide the starting point for such a conversation.[8]

Any policy reform will require trading off some of these democratic values because they sometimes conflict. For example, although many times enforcement of the law is best achieved through settlement, settlements can also limit both transparency and people's participation in the litigation process. The challenge is how to balance these democratic values fairly. Perhaps a way can be devised to increase participation and transparency while still settling cases to achieve the enforcement goal. In chapter 3, I suggested bellwether trials as one such compromise. In order to start a discussion about the best balance between these values, the first step is to recognize their import.

Litigation is a social good and promotes democracy; just as democracy is a messy business, so is litigation. Nevertheless, the democracy-promoting value of litigation is why it continues to be a great honor to be a trial judge and why litigants continue to turn to the courts to decide their disputes instead of resorting to self-help. It is a process that maintains civil society. It is not naïve to expect that the process of litigation be democracy-promoting, indeed, there are concrete ways that our system can and often does advance democratic values. Still, there is plenty of room for improvement, especially in light of recent trends that have endangered democratic values instead of promoting them.

What shape our court system should take and how accessible it should be to ordinary people are political questions in the most basic sense of the term—that is, they are questions about the appropriate framework for governance in our society. This is why it is important to think carefully about the contribution of litigation to the social fabric and the values that litigation ought to promote, which is what this book has tried to do. Litigation is a civilized response to the difficult disagreements that often crop up in a pluralist society. The process of litigation does more than resolve disputes; it contributes to democratic deliberation. This is the key to understanding what this process is supposed to be about and what should be done to improve it. By appreciating the democratic values people protect and promote when they sue—enforcement of the law, transparency, participation, and social equality—reformers can work toward a court system that is truly democracy promoting.

NOTES

PREFACE

1. The phrase "exacts heavy costs" is from *Ashcroft v. Iqbal*, 556 U.S. 662, 685–86 (2009); "in terrorem" settlements is from *AT&T Mobility v. Concepcion*, 563 U.S. 333, 350 (2011). The Lawsuit Abuse Reduction Act of 2013, H.R. 2655 (113th Congress 2013–14) was intended to "prevent frivolous lawsuits and help dispel the legal culture of fear that has come to permeate American society," H. Rept. 113–255, by requiring mandatory monetary sanctions of persons found to have made a frivolous claim. The law does not define the term "frivolous." The Fairness in Class Action Litigation Act, H.R. 1927, sought to limit the availability of consumer class actions because these suits "undermine the proper administration of justice and hurt the U.S. economy by lumping uninjured people and injured into the same classes, greatly inflating class size, and unduly pressuring companies to settle, at the expense of consumers who are forced to pay higher prices in order to offset the cost of litigation to U.S. companies." H. Rept. 114–328. Laws attempting to make bringing suits more difficult, but not altering the substantive law, include the Prison Litigation Reform Act, 42 U.S.C. § 1997(e) and Private Securities Litigation Reform Act of 1995, 15 U.S.C. § 78u–4. For bestselling books against litigation see PHILIP K. HOWARD, THE DEATH OF COMMON SENSE: HOW LAW IS SUFFOCATING AMERICA (2011). Other books against litigation, although not on the bestseller list, have had a profound influence on the debate. Of these the one that stands out is WALTER K. OLSON, THE LITIGATION EXPLOSION: WHAT HAPPENED WHEN AMERICA UNLEASHED THE LAWSUIT (1992).

2. Learned Hand, *The Deficiencies of Trials to Reach the Heart of the Matter* in 3 LECTURES ON LEGAL TOPICS, ASSOCIATION OF THE BAR OF THE CITY OF NEW YORK 105 (1926). The first sentence is quoted in *Zauderer v. Office of Disciplinary Counsel of Supreme Court of Ohio*, 471 U.S. 626, 642–43 (1985) (followed by the statement "But we cannot endorse the proposition that a lawsuit, as such, is an evil"); *Nixon v. Fitzgerald*, 457 U.S. 731 (1982) (holding former president was entitled to immunity from damages liability based on his official acts); *Johnson v. Louisiana*, 406 U.S. 380, 393 (1972) (Douglas, J., dissenting); *Ullman v. U.S.*,

350 U.S. 422, 444 (1956) (Douglas, J., dissenting). I have found no evidence of Judge Hand's second sentence being quoted in any judicial opinion.

3. The quote in the text is from JOHN RAWLS, POLITICAL LIBERALISM xx (2d ed. 1996). On the legal process school see generally Neil Duxbury, *Faith in Reason: The Process Tradition in American Jurisprudence*, 15 CARDOZO L. REV. 601 (1993). On the complex relationship between law and violence see Robert M. Cover, *Violence and the Word*, 95 YALE L. J. 1601 (1986). For a critique of legalism see JUDITH N. SHKLAR, LEGALISM: LAW, MORALS, AND POLITICAL TRIALS (1986).

4. For a general statement on deliberative democracy, see AMY GUTMANN & DENNIS THOMPSON, DEMOCRACY AND DISAGREEMENT (1998).

INTRODUCTION

1. The case of the child who died as a result of eating contaminated meat is described in JEFF BENEDICT, POISONED: THE TRUE STORY OF THE DEADLY E. COLI OUTBREAK THAT CHANGED THE WAY AMERICANS EAT (2013). The case of the woman who was paid less than her male counterpart refers to Lilly Ledbetter. Ledbetter v. Goodyear Tire & Rubber Co., 550 U.S. 618, 643 (2007) (Ginsburg, J., dissenting), *overturned by legislative action*, Lilly Ledbetter Fair Pay Act of 2009, Public Law No. 111–2, 123 Stat. 5 (2009). ("By the end of 1997, Ledbetter was the only woman working as an area manager and the pay discrepancy between Ledbetter and her 15 male counterparts was stark: Ledbetter was paid $3,727 per month; the lowest paid male area manager received $4,286 per month, the highest paid, $5,236.") The oil spill refers to the Deepwater Horizon disaster in the Gulf of Mexico in 2010, but could just as easily refer to the Exxon Valdez oil spill in 1989. For a description of both of these disasters, accompanying litigation, and regulatory responses see Ronen Perry, *The Deepwater Horizon Oil Spill and the Limits of Civil Liability*, 86 WASH. L. REV. 1 (2011).

2. It is not always clear what counts as "costs" when critics say lawsuits are too costly. Mostly the costs that reformers seek to reduce are transactions costs—such as the cost of paying lawyers, filing fees, and money spent on judicial administration—but sometimes the costs complained of also include the costs imposed by law enforcement, that is, the cost of having to pay for alleged wrongdoing or of complying with the law. For example, the US Chamber of Commerce explains on its website that businesses suffer "not only from the costs of fighting sometimes frivolous lawsuits," but also because the system of law enforcement has "turned into a shakedown operation." Jan. 16, 2016: http://web.archive.org/web/20161029194233/https://www.uschamber.com/legal-reform?tab=position.

3. As the US Chamber of Commerce argued in an amicus brief to the Supreme Court, certifying the employment class action at issue "would bury American businesses in abusive class-action lawsuits to the detriment of consumers, the U.S. economy and the judicial system itself." Brief of the Chamber of Commerce of the United States of America as Amicus Curiae in Support of Petitioner at 4–5, Wal-Mart Stores, Inc. v. Dukes, 131 S. Ct. 2541 (2011) (No. 10–277). *See*

also HOWARD, THE DEATH OF COMMON SENSE, Preface note 1 (a *New York Times* bestseller articulating many of these criticisms); Barack Obama, State of the Union Address (2011) ("I'm willing to look at other ideas to bring down costs, including . . . medical malpractice reform to rein in frivolous suits"). For a description of hostility to litigation in Supreme Court jurisprudence see Andrew M. Siegel, *The Court Against the Courts: Hostility to Litigation as an Organizing Theme in the Rehnquist Court's Jurisprudence*, 84 TEX. L. REV. 1097 (2006). One study found that between 1973 and 2010, 59 percent of members of Congress supported at least one litigation reform provision. Stephen B. Burbank & Sean Farhang, *Litigation Reform: An Institutional Approach*, 162 U. PA. L. REV. 1543, 1558 (2014). That study also found that the attempt to curb litigation through legislation was not very effective as compared to later attempts to curb litigation through court decisions. *Id.* at 1652, 1670. For examples of portrayals of the legal system as pathological and detrimental to business interests because businesses are forced to pay unnecessary or unfair judgments or take needless precautions to avoid the costs of litigation, see Theodore Eisenberg, Sital Kalantry, & Nick Robinson, *Litigation as a Measure of Well-Being*, 62 DEPAUL L. REV. 247, 247 (2013); WILLIAM HALTOM & MICHAEL MCCANN, DISTORTING THE LAW: POLITICS, MEDIA, AND THE LITIGATION CRISIS (2004). For critiques of the dominant narrative (none of which have become bestsellers) see Carl T. BOGUS, WHY LAWSUITS ARE GOOD FOR AMERICA: DISCIPLINED DEMOCRACY, BIG BUSINESS, AND THE COMMON LAW (2003); JAY FEINMAN, UN-MAKING LAW: THE CONSERVATIVE CAMPAIGN TO ROLL BACK THE COMMON LAW (2004); HAZEL GENN, JUDGING CIVIL JUSTICE (2010); JUDITH RESNIK & DENNIS CURTIS, REPRESENTING JUSTICE: INVENTION, CONTROVERSY, AND RIGHTS IN CITY-STATES AND DEMOCRATIC COURTROOMS (2011). *See also* Marc Galanter, *The Turn Against Law: The Recoil Against Expanding Accountability*, 81 TEX. L. REV. 285 (2002). The observation that litigation rates are related to wrongs in the world brings us to a key insight: the right way to make a normative judgment about the litigation rate is by reference to actionable injuries. *See* Theodore Eisenberg, *The Need for a National Civil Justice Survey of Incidence and Claiming Behavior*, 37 FORDHAM URB. L. J. 17, 23 (2010); Sachin S. Pandya & Peter Siegelman, *Underclaiming and Overclaiming*, 38 LAW & SOC. INQUIRY 836 (2013) (explaining the difficulty in measuring claim rates). However, there is also evidence that litigation rates are responsive to broader macroeconomic trends. *See* John J. Donohue III & Peter Siegelman, *Law and Macroeconomics: Employment Discrimination Litigation over the Business Cycle*, 66 S. CAL. L. REV. 709 (1993). The complaint that many lawsuits are frivolous is addressed later in the chapter, but suffice it to say for now that anecdotes of specific frivolous suits cannot take the place of sustained empirical analysis, and there is no reliable empirical study documenting that there is large-scale filing of frivolous litigation. There is some evidence, however, that in mass tort cases, plaintiffs' attorneys will file weak suits in greater numbers when the cases are consolidated. As one judge recently noted, plaintiffs were filing suits where the statute of limitations had run because "the evolution of the MDL process toward providing an alternative dispute resolution forum for global settlements has produced incentives for the filing of cases that otherwise would not be filed if they had to stand on their own merit as a stand-alone action." In re Mentor Corp. Obtape Transobturator Sling Prod. Liab. Litig., No. 2004408MD2004CDL, 2016 WL 4705807, at *1 (M.D. Ga. Sept. 7, 2016).

4. It is notable that there were almost as many opinions as Supreme Court justices. Although a majority agreed that the paper could not be restrained, they did not agree about the limits of this principle. New York Times Co. v. United States, 403 U.S. 713 (1971). For a full-length study of the case see DAVID RUDENSTINE, THE DAY THE PRESSES STOPPED: A HISTORY OF THE PENTAGON PAPERS CASE (1996).

5. Although the government has asked newspapers not to publish information that would be detrimental to national security, that is different than bringing a lawsuit because it leaves the decision up to the editors (whether they make the right decision is a different question). For example, in 2004 the *New York Times* decided to delay publishing information it obtained regarding National Security Administration surveillance for thirteen months (spanning a presidential election) at the request of the presidential administration. The Washington bureau chief said he later regretted the decision. *See* Margaret Sullivan, *Lessons in a Surveillance Drama Redux*, N.Y. TIMES, Nov. 10, 2013, at SR 12. For discussions of leaks in the modern age, with special reference to the troves of documents released by Edward Snowden and Chelsea Manning, see David E. Pozen, *The Leaky Leviathan: Why the Government Condemns and Condones Unlawful Disclosures of Information*, 127 HARV. L. REV. 512, 528–42 (2013) (describing the scope, nature, and legal response to leaks); Mary-Rose Papandrea, *Leaker Traitor Whistleblower Spy: National Security Leaks and the First Amendment*, 94 B.U. L. REV. 449 (2014) (describing the different ways the press and others have characterized Snowden). On the creed that the United States is a government of laws and not of men, see *Marbury v. Madison*, 5. U.S. (1 Cranch) 137, 163 (1803); JOHN ADAMS, *Novanglus Letter No. 7, in,* NOVANGLUS, AND MASSACHUSETTENSIS; OR, POLITICAL ESSAYS (1819).

6. *See* Boddie v. Connecticut, 401 U.S. 371, 374–74 (1971) ("Perhaps no characteristic of an organized and cohesive society is more fundamental than its erection and enforcement of a system of rules defining the various rights and duties of its members, enabling them to govern their affairs and definitively settle their differences in an orderly, predictable manner. Without such a 'legal system,' social organization and cohesion are virtually impossible; with the ability to seek regularized resolution of conflicts individuals are capable of interdependent action that enables them to strive for achievements without the anxieties that would beset them in a disorganized society. Put more succinctly, it is this injection of the rule of law that allows society to reap the benefits of rejecting what political theorists call 'the state of nature' "). *See also* Frank I. Michelman, *The Supreme Court and Litigation Access Fees: The Right to Protect One's Rights–Part II*, 1974 DUKE L. J. 527, 536 (1974).

7. As noted in the Preface, this book is in the traditional of the legal process school, which emphasized that the processes of lawmaking and enforcement, if correctly followed, would lead to just outcomes. *See generally* Neil Duxbury, *Faith*

in Reason: The Process Tradition in American Jurisprudence, 15 CARDOZO L. REV. 601 (1993). As Lon Fuller wrote: "We demand of an adjudicative decision a kind of rationality we do not expect of the results of contract or of voting. This higher responsibility toward rationality is at once the strength and the weakness of adjudication as a form of social ordering." Lon L. Fuller, *The Forms and Limits of Adjudication*, 92 HARV. L. REV. 353, 367 (1978) (emphasis omitted). *See also* Lawrence Lessig, *The Regulation of Social Meaning*, 62 U. CHI. L. REV. 943 (1995). My views here also share affinity with philosophers writing about deliberative democracy, who focus on the process of deliberation as serving a legitimating function for government and argue for the possibility of changing values subject to that deliberative process. GUTMANN & THOMPSON, DEMOCRACY AND DISAGREEMENT, Preface, note 4. The values articulated here are contested values; they are not neutral, but I do claim that they are widely held and that they are beneficial. Two things bear note: the fact that values are widely held does not always make them just, and the fact that these values are just does not make them a sufficient condition for a just society.

8. Selected academic writings making the point that procedure has become more restrictive include Stephen B. Burbank & Sean Farhang, *Litigation Reform: An Institutional Approach*, 162 U. PA. L. REV. 1543 (2014); Arthur R. Miller, *Simplified Pleading, Meaningful Days in Court, and Trials on the Merits: Reflections on the Deformation of Federal Procedure*, 88 N.Y.U. L. REV. 286 (2013); Judith Resnik, *The Privatization of Process: Requiem for and Celebration of the Federal Rules of Civil Procedure at 75*, 162 U. PA. L. REV. 1793 (2014); A. Benjamin Spencer, *The Restrictive Ethos in Civil Procedure*, 78 GEO. WASH. L. REV. 353 (2010). SARAH STASZAK, NO DAY IN COURT: ACCESS TO JUSTICE AND THE POLITICS OF JUDICIAL RETRENCHMENT (2015). On the claim that the uses of procedure to limit rights goes unnoticed, see Stephen B. Burbank & Sean Farhang, *The Subterranean Counterrevolution: The Supreme Court, the Media, and Litigation Retrenchment*, 65 DEPAUL L. REV. 293 (2016).

9. Matt Apuzzo, *Students Joining Battle to Upend Laws on Voter ID*, N.Y. TIMES, July 6, 2014, at A1. The fact that the proceedings are public and that the debate is brought into the public realm is a way to perform democracy and the rule of law. In other words, the idea of the rule of law is performed through the process of participating in and watching court proceedings. For a discussion of performativity in a different context see JUDITH BUTLER, GENDER TROUBLE: FEMINISM AND THE SUBVERSION OF IDENTITY (1990).

10. Marc Galanter, *Contract in Court; Or Almost Everything You May or May Not Want to Know about Contract Litigation*, 2001 WISC. L. REV. 577, 593 (2001) (describing cases of individuals against corporations as "uphill" cases and cases of corporations against individuals as "downhill" cases and demonstrating which is more likely to take longer and result in a plaintiff victory).

11. The story is described in Douglas NeJaime, *Winning through Losing*, 96 IOWA L. REV. 941, 979–81 (2011). *See also* Ben Depoorter, *The Upside of Losing*, 113 COLUM. L. REV. 817 (2013) (arguing that losing can increase mobilization and bring attention to the plight of the losing party, resulting in political backlash). For a discussion on how activists use the courts to develop narratives of

resistance and oppression see Jules Lobel, *Courts as Forums for Protest*, 52 UCLA L. Rev. 477, 487–88, 490 (2004); Jules Lobel, *Losers, Fools & Prophets: Justice as Struggle*, 80 Cornell L. Rev. 1331, 1343 (1995); and Jules Lobel, Success without Victory: Lost Legal Battles and the Long Road to Justice in America (2003). Another example of conservative impact litigation includes the lawsuits aimed at expanding the scope of the Second Amendment. *See, e.g.,* D.C. v. Heller, 554 U.S. 570, 635 (2008); Adam Liptak, *Carefully Plotted Course Propels Gun Case to Top*, N.Y. Times, Dec. 3, 2007, at A16 (explaining how libertarian lawyers behind the Heller case "carefully select[ed]" the plaintiffs and "were inspired by" the work of Thurgood Marshall). Of course, litigation also allows corporations and organizations to enforce their rights against individuals.

12. A settlement required the New York City Police Department to periodically produce information regarding stops and frisks from its database. The settlement and background are described in *Daniels v. City of New York*, No. 99 Civ. 1695, 2007 WL 2077150, at *1 (S.D.N.Y. July 16, 2007). *See also* The New York City Police Department's "Stop & Frisk" Practices: A Report to the People of the State of New York from the Office of the Attorney General (1999). The fact that information produced in litigation can result in more lawsuits may spur institutions to hide information or not create it in order to avoid liability. I have found no good empirical studies on how often or under what conditions this occurs. In some cases, companies are required to keep particular types of records by statute. *See, e.g.,* 29 U.S.C. § 211(c) (requiring employers to keep certain records of employee time).

13. For an overview of judicial review and the conditions that make it legitimate, see Barry Friedman, *The Birth of an Academic Obsession: The History of the Countermajoritarian Difficulty, Part Five*, 112 Yale L. J. 153 (2002). For some prominent theories see Cass R. Sunstein, The Partial Constitution (1993) (proposing deliberative democratic theory of judicial review); John Hart Ely, Democracy and Distrust: A Theory of Judicial Review (1981) (proposing a representation-reinforcing theory of judicial review). For influential critiques of Ely's theory see Lawrence H. Tribe, *The Puzzling Persistence of Process-Based Constitutional Theories*, 89 Yale L. J. 1063 (1980); Michael C. Dorf, *The Coherentism of Democracy and Distrust*, 114 Yale L.J. 1237, 1253 (2005); James E. Fleming, *Constructing the Substantive Constitution*, 72 Tex. L. Rev. 211, 304 (1993). This book adds little to the argument over the scope of judicial review but instead shifts the focus to the process of an individual bringing a constitutional violation to the courts, which is a form of political participation usually ignored by theorists. I should also note that although the text discusses appointed judges, in many states judges are elected, leading to a different set of concerns. For a history of judicial elections, see Jed Handelsman Shugerman, The People's Courts: Pursuing Judicial Independence in America (2012).

14. The data on whether and how much people lump their losses is limited. Medical malpractice claim rates are very low, according to a number of studies that I will investigate in chapter 1. The enforcement of the law through litigation depends

on people suing when they are wronged. Although scholarship on claiming in other areas is rather limited, low claiming rates are consistent with my lived experience. *See* R.E. Miller & Austin Sarat, *Grievances, Claims, and Disputes: Assessing the Adversary Culture*, 15 Law & Soc'y. Rev. 525 (1980–81); Herbert M. Kritzer et al., *To Confront or Not to Confront: Measuring Claiming Rates in Discrimination Grievances*, 25 Law & Soc'y. Rev. 875 (1991); Herbert M. Kritzer, *The Antecedents of Disputes: Complaining and Claiming*, 1 Oñati Socio-Leg. Series 1 (2011).

15. While filings rose in the period leading up to the 1990s, since filings have stabilized or even decreased. A 2014 report on the state courts found that 2012 filings for civil cases were down approximately 7.7 percent since 2008. It is notable that most cases are heard in state courts (about 98 percent), and this is where the small claims that make up half the cases in the United States are filed. In 2012, for example, there were about 17 million civil cases filed in the state courts, compared to only 285,000 in federal courts. Of these more than half (about 9.4 million) were filed in courts of limited jurisdiction, such as small claims courts, which may only hear claims under a certain dollar amount and offer simplified procedures. R. LaFountain et al., National Center for State Courts, National Court Statistics Project, Examining the Work of the State Courts: An Overview of 2012 State Trial Court Caseloads 8 (2014) (available at www.courtstatistics.org/~/media/Microsites/Files/CSP/ NCSC_EWSC_WEB_NOV_25_14.ashx). The federal courts, which hear less than 2 percent of the cases filed, have a different makeup, but still about half of the cases filed are transactional. Commercial cases broadly construed (that is, intellectual property, contracts, antitrust, commercial law, and consumer law) make up about 22 percent of the federal docket. Tort cases make up about 20 to 25 percent of the federal docket, prisoner cases make up another 20 percent (about half of these involve civil rights allegations), and other civil rights are approximately 12 percent. Gillian K. Hadfield, *Exploring Economic and Democratic Theories of Civil Litigation: Differences between Individual and Organizational Litigants in the Disposition of Federal Civil Cases*, 57 Stan. L. Rev. 1275, 1289–90 (2005). Data on civil filings in the federal courts for 2012 is available at www.uscourts.gov/statistics/table/jci/federal-judicial-caseload-statistics/2012/03/31.

16. R. LaFountain et al., National Center for State Courts, Examining the Work of the State Courts: An Overview of 2010 State Court Caseloads 11 (2012) (available at www.courtstatistics.org/~/media/ Microsites/Files/CSP/DATA%20PDF/CSP_DEC.ashx). Hawai'i seems to be an outlier here—the greater share of civil cases in that state involve contract, probate, and real property, as well as the catch-all category of "other civil cases." By contrast, in Connecticut small claims and contract cases make up 87 percent of the civil docket (43 percent for small claims, 44 percent for contract).

17. For empirical data, see Theodore Eisenberg, *Mandatory Arbitration for Customers but Not for Peers: A Study of Arbitration Clauses in Consumer and Non-Consumer Contracts*, 92 Judicature 118 (2008). This study evaluated firm contracts and

found that the same firms that preferred arbitration clauses in contracts with consumers did not prefer arbitration clauses in contracts with other businesses. However, the data set was relatively small (under 200 contracts).

18. For a history of the relationship between tort litigation and societal changes, see JOHN FABIAN WITT, THE ACCIDENTAL REPUBLIC: CRIPPLED WORKINGMEN, DESTITUTE WIDOWS, AND THE REMAKING OF AMERICAN LAW (2006). For description of the ebb and flow of mass torts more recently, see Alexandra D. Lahav, *The Law and Large Numbers: Preserving Adjudication in Complex Litigation*, 59 FLA. L. REV. 383 (2007). For a description of the development in civil rights litigation, see SEAN FARHANG, THE LITIGATION STATE: PUBLIC REGULATION AND PRIVATE LAWSUITS IN THE U.S. 10 (2010).

19. The data discussed in this and the following paragraph is taken from Hadfield, *Exploring Economic and Democratic Theories of Civil Litigation, supra* note 14 at 1298 (2005).

20. *Id.* at 1301. The empirical support for this claim is not robust. For example, studies have reached different conclusions on the effect of pleadings standards, although they are also testing different things. *Compare* Alexander A. Reinert, *Measuring the Impact of Plausibility Pleading*, 101 VA. L. REV. 2117 (2015) (testing refiling as well as dismissals and finding an effect) *with* William H. J. Hubbard, *Testing for Change in Procedural Standards, with Application to* Bell Atlantic v. Twombly, 42 J. LEGAL STUD. 35 (2013) (testing only dismissals and finding no effect). There is little reliable information on the effect of changes to the summary judgment standard on particular groups, but for an economic analysis showing an advantage to defendants, see Samuel Issacharoff & George Loewenstein, *Second Thoughts about Summary Judgment*, 107 YALE L. J. 73 (1990).

21. For discussions of the legal profession's tilt toward legal services for organizations and corporations, see Gillian K. Hadfield, *The Price of Law: How the Market for Lawyers Distorts the Justice System*, 98 MICH. L. REV. 953 (2000); John P. Heinz et al., *The Changing Character of Lawyers' Work: Chicago in 1975 and 1995*, 32 LAW & SOC'Y REV. 751 (1998). Heinz et al. found that legal effort on behalf of corporations in 1995 was about 64 percent where it was about 16 percent on behalf of individuals in cases involving family law, personal injury, criminal representation and the like. *Id.* at 765–67.

22. In the federal courts, one study found that settlement rates vary between 36 percent and 46 percent for all cases, and cases brought by organizations tend to settle more often than those brought by individual plaintiffs. Settlement rates are higher when we only look at contested cases, that is, cases where the defendant did not default and the plaintiff did not abandon the case. In those cases, individuals settle about 50 percent of the time, while organizational plaintiffs settle around 70 percent of the time. Adjudication rates are higher when individuals sue: judges decide those cases before trial about 23 percent of the time, whereas judges decide cases brought by organizations only about 13 percent of the time. Hadfield, *Exploring Economic and Democratic Theories of Civil Litigation, supra* note 15, 57 STAN. L. REV. at 1309–17. An earlier study found that 63 percent of randomly selected cases in state and federal court settle. Herbert M. Kritzer, *Adjudication to Settlement: Shading in the Gray*, 70 JUDICATURE 161,

163 (1986). On the effect of pretrial motions on plaintiffs and defendants, see Theodore Eisenberg & Kevin M. Clermont, *Plaintiphobia in the Supreme Court*, 100 CORNELL L. REV. 193 (2014); Reinert, *Measuring the Impact of Plausibility Pleading, supra* note 20.

23. Marc Galanter, *The Vanishing Trial: An Examination of Trials and Related Matters in Federal and State Courts*, 1 J. EMP. LEGAL STUD. 459, 459–60, 466–68, 510 (2004).

24. Punitive damages are only awarded in 5 percent of tort (and 6 percent of contract) trials in which plaintiffs *prevail* (which itself represents a small subset of the total number of cases filed or of cases tried), and punitive damages have average values of $47,000 in tort cases and $80,000 in contracts cases. There are outlier cases with large punitive damages awards, of course, and although they are very few they cast an inordinately long shadow over the conversation about litigation. For an overview of these statistics see Robert C. LaFountain & Neal B. Kauder, *Caseload Highlights: Examining the Work of the State Courts* 11 NATIONAL CENTER FOR STATE COURTS (2005) (available at www.courtstatistics.org/FlashMicrosites/CSP/images/ch-11-1.pdf); Galanter, *The Vanishing Trial, supra* note 23 at 468–80.

25. Galanter, *The Vanishing Trial, supra* note 23, at 517–18, 520 (and sources cited therein).

26. However, this book does not provide a comparative account of different enforcement institutions. The point of the book is to say what values we should promote, and further study can be done on whether other institutions promote these values better than litigation.

27. Ariel Sabar & Suevon Lee, *Judge Tries Suing the Pants off Dry Cleaners*, N.Y. TIMES, June 13, 2007 (describing lawsuit by administrative law judge against drycleaner); Bryan Chambers, *School System Removing Swings*, WEST VIRGINIA HERALD-DISPATCH, August 30, 2010; Kyla Ashbury, *Cabell Schools Now Keeping Swing Sets*, WEST VIRGINIA RECORD, September 3, 2010. Sometimes rising insurance premiums are a function of litigation: the more costs the insurer must pay due to litigation, the higher the premiums will rise. (Sometimes insurance costs are also a function of the insurance market.) But the debate here is about a trade-off between the cost of safer surfaces and the cost of injury, with insurance costs standing in for the cost of injury. Replacing old asphalt with new materials is a cost, creating a trade-off between safety and expense. We should be explicit about what is at stake rather than blaming "litigation" as an institution. What is really at stake is whether we think municipalities should pay for safer playground surfaces. If municipalities pay, ultimately this means taxpayers pay to protect our children. Suppose a softer surface under a swing set costs $5,000 and settling a lawsuit for a broken arm costs $20,000. It would be more efficient to choose the softer surface. I have read accusations that some parents now want playgrounds to be *too* safe and that some danger on the playground is a good thing for children's development. That position is less powerful when the choice is between asphalt or more expensive rubber surfaces under swings. The democratic contribution of the courts is that they give individuals the possibility of being heard (about an unsafe playground, for example) when those in power

will not listen. There is something at once profoundly democratic about letting individuals have their full say before a government official, and profoundly anti-democratic in the clash between elected officials and individuals happening in the courts. Legislatures, of course, can respond to court decisions by changing the legal rules governing playground liability, for example. For a discussion of how lawsuits, in combination with parental activism, changed the face of the nation's playgrounds see CHARLES R. EPP, MAKING RIGHTS REAL: ACTIVISTS, BUREAUCRATS AND THE CREATION OF THE LEGALISTIC STATE 197–214 (2009).

28. Adam Liptak, *From a Book Review to a Criminal Trial in France*, N.Y. TIMES, February 22, 2011, at A14. The libel action was brought as a criminal action in France, although the penalties available are all monetary. The judgment in the case is available at www.ejiltalk.org/wp-content/uploads/2011/03/judgement-3-mars-2011.pdf.

29. JACK M. BALKIN, CONSTITUTIONAL REDEMPTION: POLITICAL FAITH IN AN UNJUST WORLD 12, 177–83 (2011). For example, many law professors were certain that the constitutional case against the Affordable Care Act was without merit on its face, but the arguments nevertheless gained traction in the Supreme Court. For a description from the perspective of an architect of the theory, see Randy E. Barnett, *No Small Feat: Who Won the Health Care Case (and Why Did So Many Law Professors Miss the Boat?)*, 65 FLA. L. REV. 1331, 1344 (2013). *See also* Suzanne B. Goldberg, *Constitutional Tipping Points: Civil Rights, Social Change, and Fact-Based Adjudication*, 106 COLUM. L. REV. 1955 (2006); Suzanne B. Goldberg, *Risky Arguments in Social-Justice Litigation: The Case of Sex Discrimination and Marriage Equality*, 114 COLUM. L. REV. 2087, 2153 (2014).

30. FED. R. CIV. P. 11 establishes the standards for sanctions for frivolous litigation in civil cases in federal court. For a thoughtful discussion of the economic and fairness implications, see Robert G. Bone, *Modeling Frivolous Suits*, 145 U. PA. L. REV. 519 (1997). It has been often noted that there is no evidence that there is widespread frivolous litigation or even any evidence of the extent of cases that are frivolous. *Id.* at 596.

31. Chaplin v. Du Pont Advance Fiber Sys., 303 F. Supp. 2d 766, 770–72 (E.D. Va. 2004) *aff'd*, 124 F. App'x 771 (4th Cir. 2005). The court did sanction the lawyer for bringing some claims that had no basis in fact, particularly his claim that the Confederate Southern American employees were discriminated against on the basis of race when they were of multiple races, and where they alleged no adverse employment action, which is required to bring a discrimination claim.

32. As Charles Yablon wisely explained: "[T]he Holy Grail of policymakers in this area, a rule that will deter frivolous litigation without inhibiting meritorious cases, is simply not attainable. Deterring low-probability claims, by definition, means the loss of some meritorious claims." Charles M. Yablon, *The Good, the Bad, and the Frivolous Case: An Essay on Probability and Rule 11*, 44 UCLA L. REV. 65, 68 (1996).

33. *See generally* HALTOM & MCCANN, DISTORTING THE LAW, *supra* note 3.

34. *Capitol Records v. Thomas-Rassett*, 692 F.3d 899 (8th Cir. 2012). The case describes the recording industry's arguments in favor of high penalties, which is that they deter copying and copying cumulatively damages their ability to maintain profitable businesses. In any individual case, however, the penalties are indubitably high. For a procedural solution to the problem that penalties can far exceed the actual damage in copyright cases, see Peter S. Menell & Ben Depoorter, *Using Fee Shifting to Promote Fair Use and Fair Licensing*, 102 CAL. L. REV. 53 (2014). An example of a national news story on the subject is a 2003 Fox News story titled "12-Year-Old Sued for Music Downloading," available at www.foxnews .com/story/2003/09/09/12-year-old-sued-for-music-downloading.html.

35. I AN EDITOR'S TREASURY: A CONTINUING ANTHOLOGY OF PROSE, VERSE, AND LITERARY CURIOSA 1032 (H. Mayes ed. 1968).

36. For a discussion of the question of discrimination plaintiffs' experiences with the legal system as silencing and reinforcing helplessness, see Martha Minow, *Speaking of Silence*, 43 U. MIAMI L. REV. 493 (1988). *See also* Ellen Berrey, Steve G. Hoffman, & Laura Beth Nielsen, *Situated Justice: A Contextual Analysis of Fairness and Inequality in Employment Discrimination Litigation*, 46 LAW & SOC'Y REV. 1 (2012) (describing structural asymmetries that benefit employer defendants in employment discrimination suits as well as perceptions of fairness among both sides in these lawsuits). For a nuanced discussion of people's experience with, and resistance to, the law and the complex ways individuals react to the process of litigation, see PATRICIA EWICK & SUSAN SILBEY, THE COMMON PLACE OF LAW: STORIES FROM EVERYDAY LIFE (1998).

37. *See* Alexandra D. Lahav, *Are Class Actions Unconstitutional?*, 109 MICH. L. REV. 993, 1009 (2011) (discussing the problem of salience and accountability in laws that limit access to the courts). For a discussion of the idea of a norm of nonenforcement, see Minow, *Speaking of Silence*, *supra* note 36 at 496; Galanter, *The Turn Against Law*, *supra* note 3.

38. "Relatively low barriers to entry have . . . generated an undesirable result—a deluge of frivolous or vexatious claims filed by the uninformed, the misinformed, and the unscrupulous." Lepucki v. Van Wormer, 765 F.2d 86, 87 (7th Cir. 1985) (per curiam), quoted in A. Benjamin Spencer, *The Restrictive Ethos in Civil Procedure*, 78 GEO. WASH. L. REV. 353, 359 (2010). *See also* Judith Resnik, *Trial as Error, Jurisdiction as Injury: Transforming the Meaning of Article III*, 113 HARV. L. REV. 924, 929 (2000) (describing how judges "redefine their jobs by adding the management and settlement of civil cases to their judicial role"); Marc Galanter, *The Hundred-Year Decline of Trials and the Thirty Years War*, 57 STAN. L. REV. 1255, 1266 (2005) (describing the change in adjudication from trial to pretrial as a function, in part, of ideology: "The primary role of courts, in this emerging view, is less enunciating and enforcing public norms and more facilitating resolution of disputes").

39. City of Los Angeles v. Lyons, 461 U.S. 95 (1983).

40. For an articulation of the three-part test, see *Lujan v. Defenders of Wildlife*, 504 U.S. 555, 560–61 (1992). The Court in *Lyons* explained, "In order to establish an actual controversy in this case, Lyons would have had not only to allege that he would have another encounter with the police but also to make the incredible

assertion either, (1) that *all* police officers in Los Angeles *always* choke any citizen with whom they happen to have an encounter, whether for the purpose of arrest, issuing a citation or for questioning or, (2) that the City ordered or authorized police officers to act in such manner." City of Los Angeles v. Lyons, 461 U.S. at 105–6. Because chokeholds might sometimes be legal, the Court articulated a standard that would be impossible for a victim of civil rights abuses to meet. This is a restrictive move because it limits people's ability to obtain redress in the courts. This restrictive interpretation, moreover, is part of a larger development. As now Judge William Fletcher has explained, "The creation of a separately artic-ulated and self-conscious law of standing can be traced to two overlapping devel-opments in the last half-century: the growth of the administrative state and an increase in litigation to articulate and enforce public, primarily constitutional, values." William A. Fletcher, *The Structure of Standing*, 98 YALE L.J. 221, 225 (1988). In some countries, standing is a far looser requirement. Aharon Barak, *Foreword: A Judge on Judging: The Role of a Supreme Court in a Democracy*, 116 HARV. L. REV. 16, 106 (2002) (discussing the more open approach to standing doctrine in Israel).

41. J. McIntyre Mach., Ltd. v. Nicastro, 131 S. Ct. 2780 (2011). For a discussion of the significance of the case and personal jurisdiction more generally see Stephen E. Sachs, *How Congress Should Fix Personal Jurisdiction*, 108 Nw. U. L. REV. 1301 (2014); Paul D. Carrington, *Business Interests and the Long Arm in 2011*, 63 S.C. L. Rev. 637, 638–39 (2012) (describing the *Nicastro* decision as unfair both to tort victims and domestic businesses). We will discuss in greater detail in the chapter on enforcement the extent to which tort is effective as a deter-rent of misconduct. For a theoretical debate on the question of the effectiveness of products liability law, *compare* A. Mitchell Polinsky & Steven Shavell, *The Uneasy Case for Product Liability*, 123 HARV. L. REV. 1437 (2010) *with* Benjamin C. Zipursky & John C.P. Goldberg, *The Easy Case for Products Liability Law: A Response to Professors Polinsky and Shavell*, 123 HARV. L. REV. 1919 (2010). Note that this debate takes a view of the law that is focused on whether markets are better at regulating product safety than law, and does not consider some of the more intangible factors addressed in this book such as promoting participation, answerability, transparency, and equality.

42. The pleading rule states that the plaintiff needs to provide a "a short and plain statement of the claim showing that the pleader is entitled to relief" and the remedy sought. Fed. R. Civ. P. 8(a). The interpretation of this pleading rule was changed by two cases, *Ashcroft v. Iqbal*, 556 U.S. 662 (2009), and *Bell Atlantic v. Twombly*, 550 U.S. 544 (2007). There is no scholarly consensus as to the effect of this change in pleading rules on court access. For an analysis of some of the difficulties of studying the question empirically, see David Freeman Engstrom, *The* Twiqbal *Puzzle and the Empirical Study of Civil Procedure*, 65 STAN. L. REV. 1203 (2013). For some contrasting studies of the effect of this doctrinal change see Jonah B. Gelbach, *Material Facts in the Debate over* Twombly *and* Iqbal, 68 STAN. L. REV. 369 (2016) (documenting difficulty in determining the effect of these cases using data analysis); Reinert, *Measuring the Impact of Plausibility Pleading, supra* note 20 (describing results of a qualitative study that plausibility

pleading has a disproportionately negative effect on civil rights cases). No doubt the empirical debate will continue, but in the meantime the normative vision espoused by these cases is clear: it is better to screen cases early than to impose on defendants the costs of revealing information.

43. For empirical support for the proposition that small claims diverted to arbitration are not brought see Judith Resnik, *Diffusing Disputes: The Public in the Private of Arbitration, The Private in the Courts, and the Erasure of Rights*, 124 YALE L. J. 2804, 2893–914 (2015) (finding approximately 134 arbitration filings against AT&T in the period between 2009 and 2014 whereas a class action would have included millions of customers charged illegal fees, but noting the limited access to data); *Arbitration Study: Report to Congress, Pursuant to Dodd-Frank Wall Street and Consumer Protection Act* § 1028(a), CONSUMER FIN. PROTECTION BUREAU (2015) (finding low arbitration filing rates as well as low rates for filing individual lawsuits). As we shall see in chapter 3, class actions allow for collective vindication of rights but, at the same time, limit each individual's ability to participate in their lawsuit because they become one of many. For a discussion of the doctrinal developments limiting class actions see Robert H. Klonoff, *The Decline of Class Actions*, 90 WASH. U. L. REV. 729 (2013). The effort to limit class action litigation has been driven by two arguments. First, that tightening the standards for class certification protects individuals' right to a day in court by making sure that the class is homogenous. Second, that class actions unfairly threaten defendants with catastrophic liability, effectively "blackmailing" them to capitulate to settlement. As a result, the courts made it more difficult for individuals to enforce their rights, because if they cannot bring a case collectively there is little point in bringing it at all. For evaluation of these arguments see Bruce Hay & David Rosenberg, *"Sweetheart" and "Blackmail" Settlements in Class Actions: Reality and Remedy*, 75 NOTRE DAME L. REV. 1377, 1379 (2000) ("[T]he risks of . . . blackmail settlements have been overstated"); Charles Silver, *"We're Scared to Death": Class Certification and Blackmail*, 78 N.Y.U. L. REV. 1357, 1357 (2003) (observing that "the charge that class actions subject defendants to excessive settlement pressure" relies on "factual assertions that are questionable or unproven").

44. Brown v. Board of Educ. of Topeka, Kan., 347 U.S. 483 (1954); David Marcus, *The Public Interest Class Action*, 104 GEO. L. J. 777 (2016). The most recent decision denying appeal is M.D. *ex rel. Stukenberg v. Perry*, 547 Fed. Appx. 543 (5th Cir. 2013) (per curiam). For the decision granting class certification see M.D. *ex rel. Stuekenberg v. Perry*, 294 F.R.D. 7 (S.D. Tex. 2013).

45. The best general discussion of the public and private costs of litigation is Steven Shavell, *The Fundamental Divergence between the Private and the Social Motive to Use the Legal System*, 26 J. LEGAL STUD. 575 (1997). This article does not consider (and in some cases rejects) the public benefits of the kind that are presented in this book, but is a very useful starting point. *Id.* at 596. For a discussion of arbitration as privatization, see J. Maria Glover, *Disappearing Claims and the Erosion of Substantive Law*, 124 YALE L. J. 3052 (2015); Judith Resnik, *Fairness in Numbers: A Comment on* AT&T v. Concepcion, Wal-Mart v. Dukes, *and* Turner v.

Rogers, 125 HARV. L. REV. 78 (2011). For a discussion of this historical context of arbitration's growth, see Amalia D. Kessler, *Arbitration and Americanization: The Paternalism of Progressive Procedural Reform*, 124 YALE L. J. 2940 (2015). For a sociological look at how entities use arbitration to their advantage, see Shauhin A. Talesh, *The Privatization of Public Legal Rights: How Manufacturers Construct the Meaning of Consumer Law*, 43 LAW & SOC'Y REV. 527 (2009) (describing manufacturer reaction to California "lemon" laws); Shauhin Talesh, *Rule-Intermediaries in Action: How State and Business Stakeholders Influence the Meaning of Consumer Rights in Regulatory Governance Arrangements*, 37 LAW & POL'Y 1 (2015) (describing case studies showing that private dispute resolution has affected the law and limited rights in allowing those regulated to enforce, and change, the rules). For an incisive analysis of consumer contracts with analysis of particular markets, see OREN BAR-GILL, SEDUCTION BY CONTRACT: LAW, ECONOMICS, AND PSYCHOLOGY IN CONSUMER MARKETS (2012).

46. Edward Brunet, *Replacing Folklore Arbitration with a Contract Model of Arbitration*, 74 TUL. L. REV. 39, 42–47 (1999) (describing "the demise of folklore arbitration" and noting that "[t]oday, many arbitrations resemble litigation"); Thomas J. Stipanowich, *Arbitration: The "New Litigation,"* 2010 U. ILL. L. REV. 1. On the preference for arbitration in the consumer context as a way to eliminate liability, see Samuel Issacharoff & Erin F. Delaney, *Credit Card Accountability*, 73 U. CHI. L. REV. 157, 158 (2006); Jean R. Sternlight & Elizabeth J. Jensen, *Using Arbitration to Eliminate Consumer Class Actions: Efficient Business Practice or Unconscionable Abuse?*, 67 LAW & CONTEMP. PROBS. 75, 103 (2004).

47. For a discussion of these doctrinal changes and their relationship to the history of the Federal Arbitration Act see Hiro N. Aragaki, *The Federal Arbitration Act as Procedural Reform*, 89 N.Y.U. L. REV. 1939, 2024–26 (2014) (discussing the idea of arbitration as a form of procedural reform rather than an attempt to erase litigation through contract). Much has been written recently on consumer contracts that we do not read. For some alternatives see Ian Ayres & Alan Schwartz, *The No-Reading Problem in Consumer Contract Law*, 66 STAN. L. REV. 545 (2014) (suggesting field-based comprehension tests); Lauren E. Willis, *Performance-Based Consumer Law*, 82 U. CHI. L. REV. 1309 (2015) (suggesting a performance standard for consumer contracts that ensures consumer comprehension). For more on these issues see OREN BAR-GILL, SEDUCTION BY CONTRACT: LAW, ECONOMICS, AND PSYCHOLOGY IN CONSUMER MARKETS (2012).

48. For an overall discussion of these developments, see Resnik, *Fairness in Numbers, supra* note 45. In *AT&T Mobility LLC v. Concepcion*, 563 U.S. 333, 131 S. Ct. 1740 (2011), the Supreme Court upheld an arbitration contract that forbade class actions. Part of the reasoning in the case was that the terms of the arbitration agreement were not so expensive and onerous that individual consumers would be without a remedy. *Id.* at 1753. For an examination and critique of such consumer-friendly agreements, see Myriam Gilles, *Killing Them with Kindness: Examining "Consumer-Friendly" Arbitration Clauses after AT&T Mobility v. Concepcion*, 88 NOTRE DAME L. REV. 825 (2013). In *American Express Co. v. Italian Colors Restaurant*, 133 S.Ct. 2304 (2013), the Supreme Court upheld an

arbitration clause that barred class actions and resulted in the plaintiff being unable to vindicate their rights under the antitrust laws.

49. *See* FED. R. CIV. P. 16 (settlement conferences); FED. R. CIV. P. 56 (summary judgment). For a general look at these developments see Stephen N. Subrin & Thomas O. Main, *The Fourth Era of American Civil Procedure*, 162 U. PA. L. REV. 1839 (2014). The most famous critique of settlement is Owen Fiss, *Against Settlement*, 93 YALE L. J. 1073 (1984). For an analysis of how summary judgment is more beneficial to defendants than plaintiffs, see Issacharoff & Loewenstein, *Second Thoughts about Summary Judgment, supra* note 20; John Bronsteen, *Against Summary Judgment*, 75 GEO. WASH. L. REV. 522 (2007).

50. For a discussion of these limitations see Pamela S. Karlan, *Disarming the Private Attorney General*, 2003 U. ILL. L. REV. 183. For cases limiting fees, see, e.g., *Buckhannon Board & Care Home, Inc. v. West Virginia Department of Health & Human Services*, 532 U.S. 598 (2001) (rejecting the "catalyst theory" for obtaining attorneys' fees and holding that a judgment altering the parties' preexisting relationship is required for fee shifting). The Supreme Court has recognized that lawyers bringing private civil rights suits can help enforce broader social policy. *See* Newman v. Piggie Park Enterprises, 390 U.S. 400, 401–2 (1968) (per curiam). For a discussion of the concept, see William B. Rubenstein, *On What a "Private Attorney General" Is—And Why It Matters*, 57 VAND. L. REV. 2129 (2004).

51. On the challenges of defining what a "tort" is, see Thomas C. Grey, *Accidental Torts*, 54 VAND. L. REV. 1225, 1227 (2001). Statistics of the breakdown of cases in the state courts, where most cases are filed, can be found at R. LaFOUNTAIN ET AL., NATIONAL CENTER FOR STATE COURTS, NATIONAL COURT STATISTICS PROJECT, EXAMINING THE WORK OF THE STATE COURTS: AN OVERVIEW OF 2012 STATE TRIAL COURT CASELOADS 8 (2014) (available at www.courtstatistics.org/~/media/Microsites/Files/CSP/NCSC_EWSC_WEB_NOV_25_14.ashx). On limitations on tort damages and other economic barriers to filing, see Joanna M. Shepherd, *Uncovering the Silent Victims of the American Medical Liability System*, 67 VAND. L. REV. 151 (2014). For a contrary, physician perspective on medical malpractice and the need for tort reform see Daniel P. Kessler, *Evaluating the Medical Malpractice System and Options for Reform*, 25 J. ECON. PERSP. 93 (Spring 2011). In some states, statutes of limitations in medical malpractice are as short as six months from the discovery of the injury or within two years of the event. *See, e.g.,* Ala. Code §6.5.482; Mich. Comp. Laws §600.5805, §600.5838a, and §600.5851. In others, patients have three years or longer. *See, e.g.,* Md. Courts & Judicial Proceedings Code Ann. §5–109 (three years from discovery or five years from the act causing injury).

52. The most common reasons given for adopting damages caps include concerns about unpredictable (or overly generous) juries and rising insurance premiums. As we shall see when we discuss juries in chapter 3, there is no reliable evidence that juries are out of control or that they are more unpredictable decision-makers than judges are across the board. An arbitrary damages cap will reduce the amount that a wrongdoer has to pay, especially in the worst cases where people

have suffered the most, and one would assume this would also reduce insurance premiums (although the evidence on this is conflicted). For a short survey of some of the arguments and literature on the role of insurance in tort law see Tom Baker, *Liability Insurance as Tort Regulation: Six Ways That Liability Insurance Shapes Tort Law in Action*, 12 CONN. INS. L.J. 1, 2 (2006). *See also* KENNETH S. ABRAHAM, THE LIABILITY CENTURY: INSURANCE AND TORT LAW FROM THE PROGRESSIVE ERA TO 9/11 (2008).

53. ROSCOE POUND, THE SPIRIT OF THE COMMON LAW 13 (1921).

CHAPTER 1

1. *Moeller v. Taco Bell Corp.*, U.S. Dist. Ct. – N.D. Ca, No. C 02-5849 (MJJ); Beth Winegarner, *Taco Bell Ends Customer ADA Suit as $5.4M Settlement OK'd*, LAW 360, June 4, 2014.

2. The categories of answerability, accountability, and deterrence overlap somewhat, and the justifications for wanting each can overlap as well. A consequentialist would say that being forced to answer for alleged wrongs leads to accountability, and being held accountable in turn can deter future conduct. On answerability see Scott Hershovitz, *Harry Potter and the Trouble with Tort Theory*, 63 STAN. L. REV. 67, 101 (2010). I learned of it through a discussion with Scott Shapiro of the Yale Law School and am indebted to him for bringing this concept into my analysis. The ideas of accountability and deterrence correspond roughly to two prevalent rationales for tort law: corrective justice and deterrence, but as noted they have significant overlap and it is not clear to me that one must choose between them. For a description of corrective justice as a reason for tort law, John C.P. Goldberg & Benjamin Zipursky, *Torts as Wrongs*, 88 TEXAS L. REV. 917 (2010). The classic statement of the deterrence rational for torts can be found in GUIDO CALABRESI, THE COST OF ACCIDENTS (1970), and there have been many others since. Much of the empirical literature on tort law, which we will consider later in this chapter, concerns the question of whether tort law actually deters misconduct and looks at whether defendants were forced to pay as corollary to this (the idea being that if defendants are forced to internalize the full cost of their conduct, they will only engage in socially beneficial conduct). There are few satisfactory studies of what people want from litigation, as many studies of procedural justice do not use actual litigants as subjects. *See, e.g.,* TOM R. TYLER, WHY PEOPLE OBEY THE LAW: PROCEDURAL JUSTICE, LEGITIMACY AND COMPLIANCE (1990). In addition, as Gillian Hadfield points out, these studies look at people as subjects of the law rather than as active participants. For a qualitative empirical study showing that one of the things people want out of litigation is answers based on interviews of actual litigants, see Gillian K. Hadfield, *Framing the Choice between Cash and the Courthouse: Experiences with the 9/11 Victim Compensation Fund*, 42 LAW & SOC'Y REV. 645 (2008).

3. For a discussion of some critiques from the left see Laura Beth Nielsen & Robert L. Nelson, *Rights Realized? An Empirical Analysis of Employment Discrimination Litigation as a Claiming System*, 2005 WISC. L. REV. 663–711; THOMAS F. BURKE, LAWYERS, LAWSUITS, AND LEGAL RIGHTS: THE BATTLE OVER LITIGATION IN

AMERICAN SOCIETY 23–24 (2002); Anthony J. Sebok, *Dispatches from the Tort Wars*, 85 TEX. L. REV. 1465, 1468 (2007). For a critique of tort litigation and an argument for markets as a replacement, see Polinsky & Shavell, *The Uneasy Case for Product Liability*, introduction, note 41. I assume here that regulation is worthwhile and that markets have not done a good job of regulating public goods such as product safety. The question I ask is *how* to regulate the market, but of course there are those who take the position that there need not be any regulation.

4. Churchill's aphorism was "Indeed it has been said that democracy is the worst form of Government except all those other forms that have been tried from time to time." 7 WINSTON S. CHURCHILL: HIS COMPLETE SPEECHES, 1897–1963 (Robert Rhodes James, ed. 1974) at 7566.

5. For a general summary of the comparison between litigation versus regulation from an economic point of view, see Richard Posner, *Regulation (Agencies) versus Litigation (Courts)* in REGULATION VERSUS LITIGATION: PERSPECTIVES FROM ECONOMICS AND LAW (Daniel P. Kessler, ed., 2011). Posner does not address government lawsuits as a separate form of regulation, turning his attention only to the two ideal types: agency regulation and common law suits. On the regulation of juice (as an example of food regulation) see 21 CFR § 120.1–120.25 (2014). In *Alexander v. Sandoval*, the Supreme Court held that only the government can bring disparate impact claims under Title VI of the Civil Rights Act with respect to government benefit programs. 532 U.S. 275, 279 (2001). *See also* 42 U.S.C.A. § 2000d (prohibiting the denial of assistance based on race, color, or national origin). For a critical discussion of American exceptionalism in permitting private rights of action, see ROBERT A. KAGAN, ADVERSARIAL LEGALISM: THE AMERICAN WAY OF LAW (2001).

6. There is a rich scholarly literature in administrative law and the role of expertise and executive control that I cannot do justice to here. For an overview of the debates on expertise in administration and its relationship to politics, see Elena Kagan, *Presidential Administration*, 114 HARV. L. REV. 2245, 2253 (2001); Jodie Freeman & Adrien Vermeule, Massachusetts v. EPA: *From Politics to Expertise*, 2007 SUP. CT. REV. 51. On the evolution of the question of expertise, see generally, EDWARD A. PURCELL JR., THE CRISIS OF DEMOCRATIC THEORY: SCIENTIFIC NATURALISM AND THE PROBLEM OF VALUE (1973). On the Consumer Protection Finance Bureau's regulation of debt practices see CFPB Press Release, *47 States and D.C. Take Action Against JPMorgan Chase for Selling Bad Credit Card Debt and Robo-Signing Court Documents*, July 8, 2015.

7. *See* Marcia Angell, *Your Dangerous Drugstore*, NEW YORK REVIEW OF BOOKS, June 8, 2006. It is beyond the scope of this book but important to note that there has been an ongoing battle over whether the legislation enabling the FDA also preempts state tort laws. I do not address the issue of preemption of state tort and other law by federal regulation here, but it is an important and related issue. For a discussion see Catherine M. Sharkey, *Products Liability Preemption: An Institutional Approach*, 76 GEO. WASH. L. REV. 449 (2008).

8. Of course what is "best for society as a whole" is contested. *See, e.g.*, Cass R. Sunstein, *Naked Preferences and the Constitution*, 84 COLUM. L. REV. 1689,

1694 (1984). For a more nuanced view of regulatory capture see David Freeman Engstrom, *Corralling Capture*, 36 HARV. J.L. & PUB. POL'Y 31 (2013). For arguments in favor of the revolving door on empirical and normative grounds, see David Zaring, *Against Being Against the Revolving Door*, 2013 U. ILL. L. REV. 507 (2013).

9. The story is told in Angell, *Your Dangerous Drugstore*, *supra* note 7. For a longer discussion of these issues, see MARCIA ANGELL, THE TRUTH ABOUT THE DRUG COMPANIES (2005).

10. For a discussion of some of these arguments in context, see David Freeman Engstrom, *Public Regulation of Private Enforcement: Empirical Analysis of DOJ Oversight of Qui Tam Litigation under the False Claims Act*, 107 Nw. U. L. REV. 1689 (2013); David Freeman Engstrom, *Private Enforcement's Pathways: Lessons from Qui Tam Litigation*, 114 COLUM. L. REV. 1913 (2014). Politicians and the high-level government officials they appoint are also self-interested, however, so it is rarely the case in public life that we can find an actor completely free of self-interest. Sometimes government lawyers can also hire private lawyers to pursue cases on their behalf. *See* State v. Lead Indus. Assoc. Inc., 951 A.2d 428 (R.I. 2008). That practice has been criticized by academics and the press. *See, e.g.,* Margaret H. Lemos & Max Minzner, *For-Profit Public Enforcement*, 127 HARV. L. REV. 853 (2014). Some argue that the burden of bringing antitrust actions should rest entirely with the government, not private attorneys. This raises questions of both resource allocation and trust in governmental power. The government supported the private parties' right to sue in the *Italian Colors* case, discussed in the introduction. *See* Brief of the United States as Amicus Curiae Supporting Respondents, *American Express et al. v. Italian Colors Restaurant*, No. 12–133 (January 2013). The Supreme Court held that the plaintiffs were bound by an arbitration clause, which meant they would have to proceed individually, making it impossible for them to maintain that lawsuit. The government did bring an action against American Express and the company was found to have violated the antitrust laws after a bench trial, but for a different practice than that alleged in the *Italian Colors* case. United States v. Am. Exp. Co., 88 F.Supp.3d 143 (E.D.N.Y. 2015).

11. Benjamin Weiser, *New York City Settles Suit over Abuses at Rikers Island*, NY TIMES, June 22, 2015; First Amended Complaint, *Nunez v. City of New York et al.*, 11-CV-5845 (dated May 24, 2012); UNITED STATES DEPARTMENT OF JUSTICE, CIVIL RIGHTS DIVISION, INVESTIGATION OF FERGUSON POLICE DEPARTMENT (March 4, 2015); Jed S. Rakoff, *The Financial Crisis: Why Have No High-Level Executives Been Prosecuted?* NEW YORK REVIEW OF BOOKS, Jan. 9, 2014; Jed S. Rakoff, *Justice Deferred Is Justice Denied* (reviewing BRENDAN L. GARRETT, TOO BIG TO JAIL: HOW PROSECUTORS COMPROMISE WITH CORPORATIONS (2015)), NEW YORK REVIEW OF BOOKS, Feb. 19, 2015.

12. *See* SEAN FARHANG, THE LITIGATION STATE, introduction, note 18 at 10.

13. For a summary of the argument, see FARHANG, THE LITIGATION STATE, *id.* at 16–18, 227–32.

14. For an analysis of the development of litigation and the risks associated with private enforcement regimes, see Engstrom, *Private Enforcement's Pathways, supra*

note 10 at 1924–31. For an example of a lawsuit that held an agency to account for failing to regulate adequately and to rely on expertise, see *Massachusetts v. E.P.A.*, 549 U.S. 497 (2007), in which the state of Massachusetts sued the EPA for failing to engage in a rulemaking process with respect to greenhouse gas emissions from automobiles. For a discussion of the significance of the case, see Freeman & Vermeule, Massachusetts v. EPA, *supra* note 6. For an analysis of the relationship between litigation and agency rulemaking based on empirical evidence of how interest groups, especially regulated parties, use litigation to amend regulations, see Wendy Wagner et al., *Rulemaking in the Shade: An Empirical Study of EPA's Air Toxic Emissions Standards*, 63 Admin. L. Rev. 99, 133–35 (2011).

15. For support of this view see Wendy Wagner, *When All Else Fails: Regulating Risky Products through Tort Litigation*, 95 Geo. L. J. 693 (2007) (arguing that limitations on agency information and describing the symbiotic relationship between agency regulation and tort suits). A classic scholarly critique of litigation along the lines that it deforms bureaucratic response is Kagan, Adversarial Legalism, *supra* note 5. *See also* Burke, Lawyers, Lawsuits and Legal Rights, *supra* note 3. For the argument that litigation is ineffectual, see Gerald N. Rosenberg, The Hollow Hope: Can Courts Bring About Social Change (2nd ed., 2007), and for the argument that court decisions cause a backlash see Michael J. Klarman, From Jim Crow to Civil Rights: The Supreme Court and the Struggle for Racial Equality (2004).

16. Joanna Schwartz, *What Police Learn from Lawsuits*, 33 Cardozo L. Rev. 841, 855–56 (2012) (describing police departments use of information from lawsuits to improve performance); Charles R. Epp, Making Rights Real, introduction, note 27 at 115–37 (demonstrating that the greater a police department's experience with litigation, the more the department is likely to take corrective action). But other scholars show how in the employment context, institutional incorporation of legal norms can result in excessive judicial deference to internal governance, so that in the end victims of discrimination where the employer has a policy against discrimination lose their cases, weakening the impact of law. In other words, a policy that seems to respond to liability can be just so much window dressing, allowing real wrongs to continue. *See* Lauren B. Edelman et al., *When Organizations Rule: Judicial Deference to Institutionalized Employment Structures*, 117 J. of Soc. 888–954 (2011). One admittedly small study found that organizations respond differently to real or threatened litigation, running the gamut from mere symbolic policies, to grudging acceptance of change, to internalization and adoption of accommodation norms. Jeb Barnes & Thomas F. Burke, *Making Way: Legal Mobilization, Organizational Response, and Wheelchair Access*, 46 Law & Soc'y Rev. 167–98 (2012).

17. Brown v. Bd. of Educ. of Topeka, Kan., 349 U.S. 294 (1955). The argument that *Brown* did little or nothing at the time is presented most famously in Rosenberg, The Hollow Hope, *supra* note 15. His answer to the question posed in the title is "no." The argument that it was really the backlash against Brown that resulted in widespread social change is made in Klarman, From Jim Crow to Civil Rights, *supra* note 15. Klarman's other work shows that

litigation can have different roles for different social questions at different historical moments. *See* MICHAEL J. KLARMAN, FROM THE CLOSET TO THE ALTAR:
COURTS, BACKLASH, AND THE STRUGGLE FOR SAME-SEX MARRIAGE (2014).

18. Brown v. Bd. of Educ. of Topeka, Kan., 349 U.S. 294, 301 (1955) (instructing
courts to "enter such orders and decrees consistent with this opinion as are necessary and proper to admit to public schools on a racially nondiscriminatory
basis *with all deliberate speed* the parties to these cases") (emphasis added). The
Civil Rights Act of 1964 is codified at 42 U.S.C. §§ 2000a–2000h–6 (2015).
For a short discussion of this history see MARTHA MINOW, IN *BROWN'S* WAKE:
LEGACIES OF AMERICA'S EDUCATIONAL LANDMARK 19–31 (2010). For a lon-
ger treatment, the classic work is RICHARD KLUGER, SIMPLE JUSTICE: THE
HISTORY OF *BROWN V. BOARD OF EDUCATION* AND AMERICA'S STRUGGLE FOR
EQUALITY (1976). *See also* KLARMAN, FROM JIM CROW TO CIVIL RIGHTS,
supra note 15. For a history of the passage of the Civil Rights Act of 1964, see
TODD S. PURDUM, AN IDEA WHOSE TIME HAS COME: TWO PRESIDENTS, TWO
PARTIES, AND THE BATTLE FOR THE CIVIL RIGHTS ACT OF 1964 (2014).

19. Parents Involved in Community Schools v. Seattle School District No. 1, 551
U.S. 701 (2007). In *Parents Involved*, Justice Roberts writing for the plurality
evoked *Brown*, stating, "The way to stop discrimination on the basis of race is to
stop discriminating on the basis of race." *Id.* at 748. Martha Minow writes, correctly: "The ring of an aphorism cannot hide the distortion of the past implied by
this analysis." MINOW, IN *BROWN'S* WAKE, *supra* note 18 at 29–30. For criticisms
of *Brown's* legacy from the left see CHARLES J. OGLETREE JR., ALL DELIBERATE
SPEED: REFLECTIONS ON THE FIRST HALF CENTURY OF *BROWN V. BOARD OF
EDUCATION*, at xi (2004); DEREK BELL, SILENT COVENANTS: *BROWN V. BOARD
OF EDUCATION* AND THE UNFULFILLED HOPES FOR RACIAL REFORM 196
(2004).

20. This narrative is explained with great nuance and detail in KLARMAN, FROM
JIM CROW TO CIVIL RIGHTS, *supra* note 15. For a counterhistory, see Paul
Finkelman, *Book Review: Civil Rights in Historical Context: In Defense of* Brown,
118 HARV. L. REV. 973 (2005).

21. On the lesson of *Brown* being to stay away from litigation: Martin Luther King Jr.
was quoted saying of litigation as a strategy, activists should "not get involved in
legalism [and] needless fights in lower courts," for that is "exactly what the white
man wants the Negro to do. Then he can draw out the fight. . . . We must move on
to mass action." Quoted in D. GARROW, BEARING THE CROSS: MARTIN LUTHER
KING JR. AND THE SOUTHERN CHRISTIAN LEADERSHIP CONFERENCE 91
(1986). Not addressed here is the potential for disagreement between litigants
and one another and between litigants and their counsel. For discussions of that
important issue see Derek Bell, *Serving Two Masters: Integration Ideals and Client
Interests in School Desegregation Litigation*, 85 YALE L. J. 470 (1976); Deborah L.
Rhode, *Class Conflicts in Class Actions*, 34 STAN. L. REV. 1183 (1982); William B.
Rubenstein, *Divided We Litigate: Addressing Disputes among Group Members and
Lawyers in Civil Rights Campaigns*, 106 YALE L. J. 1623 (1997).

22. Randall Kennedy, *Martin Luther King's Constitution: A Legal History of the
Montgomery Bus Boycott*, 98 YALE L.J. 999, 1000 (1989).

23. The story here is taken from Kennedy, *Martin Luther King's Constitution, id.,* where it is recounted in greater detail.

24. Some do not agree that *Brown* was the impetus for these protests. For a discussion of the thesis that *Brown* did not inspire protests, but macroeconomic and social factors did, see KLARMAN, FROM JIM CROW TO CIVIL RIGHTS, *supra* note 15 at 374.

25. *Gayle v. Browder,* 352 U.S. 903 (1957) (the decision was a per curiam affirmation of the decision below, part of the Supreme Court's strategy to make few waves as it struck down provision after provision of Jim Crow). *See also* Kennedy, *Martin Luther King's Constitution, supra* note 22 at 1051–53; KLARMAN, FROM JIM CROW TO CIVIL RIGHTS, *supra* note 15 at 372–73 (explaining that regardless of the Supreme Court's decision in Gayle, the boycott "demonstrated black agency, resolve, courage, resourcefulness and leadership"). A different decision, Klarman writes, "hardly would have negated, or even greatly tarnished" these accomplishments. *Id.* Even so, getting Supreme Court support couldn't have hurt.

26. Kennedy, *Martin Luther King's Constitution, supra* note 22 at 1055–56.

27. For a historical study on how these two strategies can work together, see TOMIKO BROWN-NAGIN, COURAGE TO DISSENT: ATLANTA AND THE LONG HISTORY OF THE CIVIL RIGHTS MOVEMENT (2011). *See also* Kenneth W. Mack, *Law and Local Knowledge in the History of the Civil Rights Movement,* 125 HARV. L. REV. 1018 (2012).

28. Kennedy, *Martin Luther King's Constitution, supra* note 22 at 1047 (discussing *City of Montgomery v. Montgomery Improvement Ass'n,* reprinted in 2 RACE REL. L. REP. 123 (1957)).

29. For example, one study attempted to show that where courts were forced to rule on the scope of constitutional rights, courts tend to rule more narrowly than when they are permitted to avoid such rulings. Nancy Leong, *The Saucier Qualified Immunity Experiment: An Empirical Analysis,* 36 PEPP. L. REV. 667, 670–71 (2009). For a contrary finding see Paul W. Hughes, *Not a Failed Experiment: Wilson-Saucier Sequencing and the Articulation of Constitutional Rights,* 80 U. COLO. L. REV 401 (2009). For a discussion of these studies, see John C. Jeffries Jr., *Reversing the Order of Battle in Constitutional Torts,* 2009 SUP. CT. REV. 115, 137 (2009). For a list of the various procedural ways the Supreme Court has limited substantive rights using procedural means, see Burbank & Farhang, *Litigation Reform: An Institutional Approach,* introduction, note 8 at 1543 (demonstrating that the movement toward limiting litigation has come largely from the courts through procedural rules since 1960). As noted in the text, some argue that an unfriendly federal court is a reason to promote abstention doctrines. *Compare* Thomas Healy, *The Rise of Unnecessary Constitutional Rulings,* 83 N.C. L. REV. 847, 857 (2005) *with* Jeffries, *Reversing the Order of Battle,* at 123, n. 29 ("The partisan of expansive readings of constitutional rights, who prefers the avoidance doctrine, today may find himself in an embarrassing position when a new President names a raft of new judges"). Although the doctrine of preclusion limits individuals from refiling a case once a final judgment has been reached, it does not prevent a new plaintiff from filing a new suit about

the same subject matter to change the law. *See* Taylor v. Sturgell, 553 U.S. 880 (2008).

30. The most recent state court trial statistics show that the median award is $32,000. Robert C. LaFountain & Neal B. Kauder, Caseload Highlights: Examining the Work of the State Courts, National Center for State Courts, February 2005. For an analysis of the extent of underclaiming, and why there is not enough information to say with certainty, see Pandya & Siegelman, *Underclaiming and Overclaiming*, introduction, note 3. On too few claims, see, e.g., Richard L. Abel, *The Real Tort Crisis—Too Few Claims*, 48 Ohio State L. J. 443–67 (1987); Tracey E. George & Chris Guthrie, *Induced Litigation*, 98 Nw. U. L. Rev. 545, 575–76 (2004). Media reporting plays a significant role in this perception. One study found that products liability verdicts in plaintiffs' favor are reported in newspapers much more often than those in defendants' favor, although there were many more verdicts in favor of defendants than plaintiffs. Steven Garber & Anthony G. Bower, *Newspaper Coverage of Automotive Product Liability Verdicts*, 33 Law & Soc'y Rev. 93 (1999). For a study looking beyond newspapers and at reports other than verdicts and finding a more varied landscape, see Herbert M. Kritzer & Robert E. Dreschsel, *Local News of Civil Litigation*, 96 Judicature 16 (2012). These researchers found that often media reports do not include verdicts or dollar figures, but when they do they tend to be much bigger than the median award—two-thirds of the media clips involved verdicts over $1 million, whereas the median award was $28,000. *Id.* at 21.

31. Barry Meier & Hilary Stout, *Falling through the Legal Cracks*, NY Times, Dec. 30, 2014, at B1.

32. Anton R. Valukas, Report to Board of Directors of General Motors Company Regarding Ignition Switch Recalls (May 29, 2014) at 168, 182–83.

33. The full story is told in Benedict, Poisoned, introduction, note 1. *See id.* at 80–81, 84–88.

34. Benedict, Poisoned, *id.* at 113–16.

35. Benedict, Poisoned, *id.* at 240–42, 119–21, 160–61.

36. Wil S. Hylton, *A Bug in the System: Why Last Night's Chicken Made You Sick*, The New Yorker, February 2, 2015. One interesting thing about Bill Marler, the lawyer who brought the suit, is that he both litigates and speaks to businesses about safe practices and how to prevent outbreaks before they happen so that they can avoid lawsuits.

37. Joanna C. Schwartz, *A Dose of Reality for Medical Malpractice Reform*, 88 N.Y.U. L. Rev. 1224, 1262, 1268, 1273 (2013) (describing uses of departments of risk management and patient safety within hospitals that use litigation data—both closed claims and ongoing litigation—to assess risk and propose changes); Tom Baker & Timothy D. Lytton, *Allowing Patients to Waive the Right to Sue for Medical Malpractice: A Response to Thaler and Sunstein*, 104 Nw. U. L. Rev. 233, 242 (2010). Risk management data collection is protected from discovery and by evidentiary laws in many states. *Id.* at 1265; David A. Hyman & Charles Silver, *The Poor State of Health Care Quality in the U.S.: Is Malpractice Liability*

Part of the Problem or Part of the Solution?, 90 CORNELL L. REV. 893, 909 (2005). Numerous studies have used closed claims to measure quality of patient care and suggest improvements. For some studies of closed claims see Frederick W. Cheney, *The American Society of Anesthesiologists Closed Claims Project: What Have We Learned, How Has It Affected Practice, and How Will It Affect Practice in the Future?*, 91 ANESTHESIOLOGY 552, 552 (1999); Atul A. Gawande et al., *Risk Factors for Retained Instruments and Sponges after Surgery*, 348 NEW ENG. J. MED. 229 (2003) (studying incidence of retained sponges after surgery); Allen Kachalia et al., *Missed and Delayed Diagnoses in the Emergency Department: A Study of Closed Malpractice Claims from 4 Liability Insurers*, 49 ANNALS EMERGENCY MED. 196, 196–97 (2007). Schwartz tells us a story of one case in which the doctors in the hospital agreed there was no negligence, but in the lawsuit the hospital was unable to find an outside expert to support their position, requiring an internal reevaluation of problems in quality of care. Schwartz, *A Dose of Reality, id.* at 1284–85. On the lack of fit between systemic problems and individual cases, see Michelle M. Mello & David Studdert, *Deconstructing Negligence: The Role of Individual and Systemic Factors in Causing Medical Injuries*, 96 GEO. L.J. 599 (2008).

38. Troyen Brennan et al., *Incidence of Adverse Events and Negligence in Hospitalized Patients*, 324 N. ENG. J. MED. 370–76 (1991); Troyen Brennan et al., *Relation Between Negligent Adverse Events and the Outcomes of Medical-Malpractice Litigation*, 335 N. ENG. J. MED. 1963–67 (1996); PATIENTS, DOCTORS, AND LAWYERS: MEDICAL INJURY, MALPRACTICE LITIGATION AND PATIENT COMPENSATION IN NEW YORK: THE REPORT OF THE HARVARD MEDICAL PRACTICE STUDY TO THE STATE OF NEW YORK (1990). For confirming studies see Eric J. Thomas et al., *Incidence and Types of Adverse Events and Negligent Care in Utah and Colorado*, 38 MED. CARE 261–71 (2000); Tom Baker, *Reconsidering the Harvard Medical Practice Study about the Validity of Medical Malpractice Claims*, 33 J. OF LAW, MEDICINE, AND ETHICS 501–14 (2005). For a discussion of the methodology used by Brennan et al., see Pandya & Siegelman, *Underclaiming and Overclaiming*, introduction, note 3 at 10–11.

39. The study finding a gradual effect of damages caps on patient safety is Zenon Zabinski & Bernard S. Black, *The Deterrent Effect of Tort Law: Evidence from Medical Malpractice Reform* (January 15, 2015), available at http://ssrn.com/abstract=2161362. Studies finding no effect include Michael Frakes & Anupam B. Jena, *Tort Liability and Health Care Quality: The Divergent Impacts of Remedy-Focused and Substantive Tort Reforms*, available at http://ssrn.com/abstract=2374599 (2014) (finding no effect of noneconomic damages caps on birth outcomes); Allen Kachalia & Michelle M. Mello, *New Directions in Medical Liability Reform*, 364 N. ENG. J. MED. 1564–72 (2011) (finding that the evidence is inconclusive).

40. David Studdert et al., *Claims, Errors, and Compensation Payments in Medical Malpractice Litigation*, 354 N. ENG. J. MED. 2024–33 (2006). This study has some significant flaws, like every study. For example, there is no reason to think that the claims reviewed are in fact representative of other malpractice claims all over the country. Furthermore, the researchers were doctors who did not apply

the governing legal standard to the claims they reviewed, but instead applied a medical standard. Nor did the researchers always agree with one another in how to rate each claim. Nevertheless, their findings still provide real food for thought.

41. Studdert et al., *Claims, Errors and Compensation, id.* at 2024–33. Perhaps the most telling thing that arose from the Harvard study is the way the study was treated by the medical community. Instead of taking the researchers' recommendations for better treatment of injured patients seriously, the American Medical Association produced the following press release: "The costs of these meritless lawsuits are borne by patients who have decreased access to care as physicians are forced to spend significant time and money defending against meritless lawsuits." Press Release, AMA, *Harvard Study Shows 40 Percent of Medical Liability Claims Filed without Merit* (May 10, 2006) (quoted in Tom Baker & Timothy D. Lytton, *Allowing Patients to Waive the Right to Sue for Medical Malpractice: A Response to Thaler and Sunstein*, 104 Nw. U. L. Rev. 233, 251 n. 33 (2010)).

42. "Thus, the door of the state court is open for the vacatur of the default judgments en masse, without class certification, subclasses, hungry lawyers, or issues of process and statutes of limitations. . . . The countervailing benefits of a class action accrue almost entirely to the lawyers in a fee-rich environment, and leave trivial benefits for consumption by the class." Sykes v. Mel S. Harris & Associates LLC, 780 F.3d 70, 103 (2d Cir. 2015) (Judge Jacobs, dissenting). It was not at all clear that the state court remedy the judge proposed was in fact available or that there was anyone who would help the plaintiffs secure this remedy. Nor would remedy of vacating the judgment require the defendants to pay for what they had done, and it would have left them free to try it again. For a more general discussion of these practices see Blake Halpern, Bad Paper: Inside the Secret World of Debt Collectors (2015); Dalié Jimenéz, *Dirty Debts Sold Dirt Cheap*, 52 Harv. J. on Legis. 41 (2015).

CHAPTER 2

1. Copies of the documents and explanation of the discovery process from the plaintiffs' attorney's point of view can be found at: Bill Marler, *Another Lesson Learned the Hard Way: Odwalla E. coli Outbreak 1996*, Marler Blog (Jan. 23, 2013), www.marlerblog.com/legal-cases/another-lesson-learned-the-hard-way-odwalla-e-coli-outbreak-1996/#_ftn1.

2. *But see* Robert M. Cover, *Nomos and Narrative*, 97 Harv. L. Rev. 4, 40–44 (1983) (arguing that law can be jurispathic as well as jurisgenerative).

3. Many state courts track the federal rules of procedure, including those relating to discovery. Fed. R. Civ. P. 26–37.

4. For example, in a recent opinion the 9th Circuit Court of Appeals held that documents relating to a motion for a preliminary injunction in an automobile defect case may not be kept confidential pursuant to a stipulated discovery order. In that case the Center for Auto Safety intervened, claiming that the documents revealed a dangerous condition in the cars. *See* Center for Auto Safety v. Chrysler Group, 809 F.3d 1092 (9th Cir. 2016). The dissenting

opinion in that case argued that litigants have a right under the procedural rules to keep certain documents private, and that the common law presumption that the public has a right to access public documents should be more narrowly construed. For articles arguing against a broad right of publicity, see Arthur R. Miller, *Confidentiality, Protective Orders, and Public Access to the Courts*, 105 HARV. L. REV. 427 (1991) (arguing that litigation is a means of resolving private disputes, and that publicity would undermine this goal); Richard L. Marcus, *The Discovery Confidentiality Controversy*, 991 U. ILL. L. REV. 457, 470 (1991) (arguing that revelation of important information through civil litigation is a side effect of litigation, but not its purpose, and "the collateral effects of litigation should not be allowed to supplant its primary purpose" and pointing out that plenty of information gathered by governmental agencies is not publicly available). The basis of these arguments, which this book aims to dispel, is that litigation is fundamentally a private dispute resolution process.

5. The most often cited article critiquing discovery because of the cost asymmetry is Frank H. Easterbrook, *Discovery as Abuse*, 69 B.U. L. REV. 635, 635 (1989). This article, by a very well respected jurist, was cited by the Supreme Court in support of greater scrutiny of cases at the motion to dismiss stage to avoid discovery. Bell Atl. Corp. v. Twombly, 550 U.S. 544, 559 (2007). There is little empirical support for the claims it makes, although they are logical. For an analysis of information asymmetry and suggestions for reform, see Scott A. Moss, *Litigation Discovery Cannot Be Optimal But Could Be Better: The Economics of Improving Discovery Timing in a Digital Age*, 58 DUKE L.J. 889, 910 (2009).

6. David Luban, *Lawfare and Legal Ethics in Guantánamo*, 60 STAN. L. REV. 1981, 1989 (2008); Alexandra D. Lahav, *Rites without Rights: A Tale of Two Military Commissions*, 24 YALE J. OF L. & HUM. 439, 461–62 (2012) (quoting interview with anonymous lawyer).

7. Allen Kachalia et al., *Liability Claims and Costs before and after Implementation of a Medical Error Disclosure Program*, 153 ANNALS INTERNAL MED. 213 (2010); Richard C. Boothman et al., *A Better Approach to Medical Malpractice Claims? The University of Michigan Experience*, 2 J. HEALTH & LIFE SCI. L. 125–59 (2009); Tamara Relis, *"It's Not About the Money!": A Theory on Misconceptions of Plaintiffs' Litigation Aims*, 68 U. PITT. L. REV. 701, 722–28 (2007) (documenting plaintiffs' reasons for suing); Kathleen M. Mazor et al., *Communicating with Patients about Medical Errors: A Review of the Literature*, 164 ARCHIVES INTERNAL MED. 1690–97 (2004). A study of victims of 9/11 similarly found that they wanted answers (and answerability, discussed in chapter 1) from the legal process. Hadfield, *Framing the Choice between Cash and the Courthouse*, chapter 1, note 2 at 645–82. On hospitals' use of information for risk management, see generally Schwartz, *A Dose of Reality for Medical Malpractice Reform*, chapter 1, note 37.

8. TOM BAKER, THE MEDICAL MALPRACTICE MYTH 108–9 (2005); Robert A. Caplan et al., *Adverse Respiratory Events in Anesthesia: A Closed Claim Analysis*, 72 ANESTHESIOLOGY 828–33 (1990); Frederick W. Cheney, *ASA Closed Claim Project: Where Have We Been and Where Are We Going?* 57 ASA NEWSLETTER

8–22 (1993); Stephen Schoenbaum & Randall R. Bovbjerg, *Malpractice Reform Must Include Steps to Prevent Medical Injury*, 140 ANNALS INTERNAL MED. 51–53 (2004).

9. Bill Vlasic, *Inquiry by G.M. Is Said to Focus on Its Lawyers*, N.Y. TIMES, May 18, 2014, at A1; ANTON R. VALUKAS, REPORT TO BOARD OF DIRECTORS OF GENERAL MOTORS COMPANY REGARDING IGNITION SWITCH RECALLS (May 29, 2014).

10. Matt Richtel, *U.S. Withheld Data Showing Driving Risks*, N.Y. TIMES, July 21, 2009, at A1; *Center for Auto Safety v. National Highway Traffic Safety Administration*, No. 08CV02057 (D.D.C. filed Dec. 1, 2008).

11. *See* Floyd v. City of New York, 959 F.Supp.2d 540 (S.D.N.Y. 2013). *See also* Joseph Goldstein, *Trial to Start in Class-Action Suit on Constitutionality of Stop-and-Frisk Tactic*, N.Y. TIMES, March 18, 2013, at A15.

12. It was not only the plaintiffs who analyzed this data, the New York Office of the Attorney General did as well. The quote is from their report. OFFICE OF THE NEW YORK ATTORNEY GENERAL, CIVIL RIGHTS BUREAU, NEW YORK CITY POLICE DEPARTMENT'S "STOP & FRISK" PRACTICES: A REPORT TO THE PEOPLE OF THE STATE OF NEW YORK FROM THE OFFICE OF THE ATTORNEY GENERAL 136 (1999) (citation omitted), available at www.oag.state.ny.us/sites/default/files/pdfs/bureaus/civil_rights/stp_frsk.pdf. The decision ruling that the stop-and-frisk practices were unconstitutional is *Floyd v. City of New York*, 959 F. Supp. 2d 540 (S.D.N.Y. 2013), *appeal dismissed* (Sept. 25, 2013).

13. Robert Brauneis, *Copyright and the World's Most Popular Song*, 56 J. COPYRIGHT SOC'Y U.S.A. 335 (2009); Ben Sisario, *"Happy Birthday" Copyright Case Reaches a Settlement*, N.Y. TIMES, Dec. 10, 2015, at B8.

14. Lane v. Franks, 134 S. Ct. 2369 (2014) (holding that retaliation against a public employee for testifying at a criminal proceeding violates the First Amendment); *V.L. v. E.L.*, 136 S. Ct. 1017 (2016) (holding that state must recognize same-sex adoption under the Full Faith and Credit clause). For examples of litigation brought by conservative groups, see *Top Ten Victories in Becket Fund History*, THE BECKET FUND FOR RELIGIOUS LIBERTY, www.becketfund.org/top-ten-victories; *Our Cases*, PROJECT ON FAIR REPRESENTATION, www.projectonfair-representation.org/cases/.

15. Ledbetter v. Goodyear Tire & Rubber Co., Inc., 550 U.S. 618 (2007) *overturned by legislative action*, Lilly Ledbetter Fair Pay Act of 2009, Public Law No. 111–2, 123 Stat. 5 (2009).

16. Tehan v. U.S. ex rel. Shott, 382 U.S. 406, 416 (1966). On the ability of trials to produce competing narratives, see ROBERT P. BURNS, A THEORY OF THE TRIAL (1999); ROBERT A. FERGUSON, THE TRIAL IN AMERICAN LIFE (2008). See also Paul Schiff Berman, *An Observation and a Strange but True "Tale": What Might the Historical Trials of Animals Tell Us about the Transformative Potential of Law in American Culture?*, 52 HASTINGS L.J. 123, 144–45 (2000). For a summary of the competing narratives in the stop-and-frisk case, see *Floyd v. City of New York*, 959 F. Supp. 2d 540 (S.D.N.Y. 2013).

17. KENJI YOSHINO, SPEAK NOW: MARRIAGE EQUALITY ON TRIAL—THE STORY OF HOLLINGSWORTH V. PERRY 7–10 (2015). I don't have proof that the trial was

a specific catalyst that changed public perception. The trial was in 2010, and in either 2010 or 2011 support exceeded opposition to same-sex marriage for the first time. The overall trend is increasing support for marriage equality, so that shift may not be a result of the trial itself but more a general zeitgeist to which the trial contributed. For an analysis of the polls on this issue see Nate Silver, *How Opinion on Same-Sex Marriage Is Changing and What It Means*, N.Y. TIMES FIVETHIRTYEIGHT BLOG (March 26, 2013), http://fivethirtyeight.blogs. nytimes.com/2013/03/26/how-opinion-on-same-sex-marriage-is-changing-and-what-it-means/.

18. Michael J. Bazyler, *www.swissbankclaims.com: The Legacy and Morality of the Holocaust-Era Settlement with the Swiss Banks*, 25 FORDHAM INT'L L.J. 64 (2001) (summarizing the obstacles faced by lawyers and class members in the Holocaust Victim Assets Litigation); MICHAEL R. MARRUS, SOME MEASURE OF JUSTICE: THE HOLOCAUST ERA RESTITUTION CAMPAIGN OF THE 1990S (2009); Leora Bilsky & Talia Fisher, *Rethinking Settlement*, 15 THEORETICAL INQUIRIES IN L. 77 (2014); Leora Bilsky, *Transnational Holocaust Litigation*, 23 EUR. J. INT'L L. 349 (2012).

19. Leora Bilsky, *The Judge and the Historian: Transnational Holocaust Litigation as a New Model*, 24 HISTORY & MEMORY 117, 132 (2012); MICHAEL J. BAZYLER, HOLOCAUST JUSTICE: THE BATTLE FOR RESTITUTION IN AMERICA'S COURTS 15–16 (2003). Michael Marrus argues that litigation distorts historical narratives. MARRUS, SOME MEASURE OF JUSTICE, *id.* For a discussion of "law office history" as compared with the more nuanced narratives historians construct, see LAURA KALMAN, THE STRANGE CAREER OF LEGAL LIBERALISM 195–97 (1996). Kalman describes the consternation of a historian whose work was used in a sex discrimination case to show that women did not want commissioned jobs and therefore the employer was not liable for discrimination.

20. Bilsky, *The Judge and the Historian, supra* note 19 at 133–34.

21. Kiobel v. Royal Dutch Petroleum Co., 133 S. Ct. 1659 (2013) (holding that the Alien Tort Statute does not generally apply to violations of international law occurring outside the United States); Daimler AG v. Bauman, 134 S. Ct. 746 (2014) (rejecting jurisdiction over-multinational corporation in California concerning human rights violations occurring in Argentina); Wal-Mart Stores, Inc. v. Dukes, 131 S.Ct. 2541, 2551 (2011) (holding that class members must show that they share a common issue that will resolve all of their claims "in one stroke"). For an academic treatment see Pamela K. Bookman, *Litigation Isolationism*, 67 STAN. L. REV. 1081 (2015). For a somewhat contrary view justifying limiting jurisdiction see Daniel Klerman, *Rethinking Personal Jurisdiction*, 6 J. LEGAL ANALYSIS 245, 246 (2014).

22. Justice Kennedy explained: "Litigation, though necessary to ensure that officials comply with the law, exacts heavy costs in terms of efficiency and expenditure of valuable time and resources that might otherwise be directed to the proper execution of the work of the Government." Ashcroft v. Iqbal, 556 U.S. 662, 685 (2009). Along similar lines, Judge Posner wrote in a dissent: "Behind both *Twombly* and *Iqbal* lurks a concern with asymmetric discovery burdens and the

potential for extortionate litigation." Swanson v. Citibank, N.A., 614 F.3d 400, 411 (7th Cir. 2010). This, he explained, is due to the fact that modern technology creates vast troves of information kept by defendant corporations, but not by individual plaintiffs. *Id.*

23. These statistics and those that follow are taken from EMERY G. LEE III & THOMAS E. WILLGING, FEDERAL JUDICIAL CENTER NATIONAL, CASE-BASED CIVIL RULES SURVEY: PRELIMINARY REPORT TO THE JUDICIAL CONFERENCE ADVISORY COMMITTEE ON CIVIL RULES (2009). The great strength of this study is that it asked lawyers about their most recent resolved case, rather than about litigation in general, to distinguish between general impressions about discovery and the facts in the run of cases.

24. Wayne D. Brazil, *Civil Discovery: Lawyers' Views of Its Effectiveness, Its Principal Problems and Abuses*, 1980 AM. B. FOUND. RES. J. 787, 811 (1980).

25. Kurt Eichenwald, *The Great Smartphone War*, VANITY FAIR, June 2014; Dimitra Kessenides, *When Apple and Samsung Fight, The Lawyers Win*, BLOOMBERG BUSINESS, Dec. 9, 2013.

26. As Judge Jon O. Newman suggested in his opinion in *Iqbal* at the appellate level: "In a case such as this where some of the defendants are current or former senior officials of the Government, against whom broad-ranging allegations of knowledge and personal involvement are easily made, a district court might wish to structure such limited discovery by examining written responses to interrogatories and requests to admit before authorizing depositions, and by deferring discovery directed to high-level officials until discovery of front-line officials has been completed and has demonstrated the need for discovery higher up the ranks." Iqbal v. Hasty, 490 F.3d 143, 158 (2d Cir. 2007) *rev'd and remanded sub nom.* Ashcroft v. Iqbal, 556 U.S. 662 (2009). That suggestion was rejected by the Supreme Court. Perhaps as disturbing is the fact that when that part of the case settled, the government negotiated that the amount of the settlement be kept confidential. One more data point is worth adding: the Supreme Court decided in *Clinton v. Jones*, 520 U.S. 681 (1997), that a sitting president could be sued civilly for events that occurred before he took office.

27. AT&T Mobility LLC v. Concepcion, 563 U.S. 333 (2011); Am. Exp. Co. v. Italian Colors Rest., 133 S. Ct. 2304 (2013). Yochai Benkler, *Free as the Air to Common Use: First Amendment Constraints on Enclosure of the Public Domain*, 74 N.Y.U. L. REV. 354 (1999) (arguing that the increase in privatization of information reinforces the existing power structure and hinders society's information production and exchange process); Resnik, *Diffusing Disputes*, introduction, note 43 (describing how arbitration eviscerates rights and analyzing the constitutionality of forced arbitration).

28. United States v. Reynolds, 345 U.S. 1 (1953). For book-length treatments of the case see BARRY SIEGEL, CLAIM OF PRIVILEGE: A MYSTERIOUS PLANE CRASH, A SUPREME COURT CASE AND THE RISE OF STATE SECRETS (2009); LOUIS FISHER, IN THE NAME OF NATIONAL SECURITY: UNCHECKED PRESIDENTIAL POWER AND THE REYNOLDS CASE (2006).

29. Reynolds, 345 U.S. at 10. David Rudenstine, *The Irony of a Faustian Bargain: A Reconsideration of the Supreme Court's 1953* United States v. Reynolds *Decision,*

34 CARDOZO L. REV. 1283, 1390–91 (2013) (describing the increased use of the privilege and the irony that, contrary to the intent of the Justices at the time, it has embroiled the courts in national security controversies). The widows attempted to reopen the case on grounds of fraud after the documents were declassified, but the appellate court held that even information about the safety problems with the B-29 could have been construed as implicating national security concerns. Herring v. United States, 424 F.3d 384 (3d Cir. 2005).

30. The case is *Jewel v. NSA*, 965 F. Supp. 2d 1090 (N.D. Cal. 2013). Electronic Communications Privacy Act, 18 USC § 2510 et seq; Foreign Intelligence Surveillance Act, 50 USC § 1810 et seq. The provision for in camera review of documents in FISA is 50 U.S.C. § 1806(f). Charlie Savage, Edward Wyatt & Peter Baker, *U.S. Confirms Gathering of Web Data Overseas*, N.Y. TIMES, June 7, 2013, at A1. For a broader discussion see DAVID RUDENSTINE, THE AGE OF DEFERENCE: THE SUPREME COURT, NATIONAL SECURITY, AND THE CONSTITUTIONAL ORDER (2016).

31. TIMOTHY D. LYTTON, HOLDING BISHOPS ACCOUNTABLE: HOW LAWSUITS HELPED THE CATHOLIC CHURCH CONFRONT CLERGY SEXUAL ABUSE (2008). The story was revealed by the *Boston Globe*. Globe Spotlight Team, *Church Allowed Abuse by Priest for Years*, BOSTON GLOBE, January 6, 2002.

32. Jon Bauer, *Buying Witness Silence: Evidence-Suppressing Settlements and Lawyers' Ethics*, 87 OR. L. REV. 481 (2008) (arguing that secret settlements that prohibit future testimony violate the Model Rules of Professional Conduct).

33. Ashley Gauthier, *Secret Settlements*, in THE NEWS MEDIA AND THE LAW 3 (2000).

34. Laurie Goodstein, *Albany Diocese Settled Abuse Case for Almost $1 Million*, N.Y. TIMES, June 27, 2002 ("As the sexual abuse scandal has escalated, many victims and lawyers have broken their confidentiality agreements. Father Doyle said that in this climate 'it's probably a good gamble' that there will be no repercussions"). BAKER, MEDICAL MALPRACTICE MYTH, *supra* note 8 at 101; David M. Herszenhorn, *Hospital Drops Legal Action to Stem Tide of Bad Publicity*, N.Y. TIMES, July 27, 2002.

35. A number of states have enacted sunshine litigation acts. Fla. Stat. Ann. § 69.081 (West); La. Code Civ. Proc. Ann. art. 1426(c); S.C. R. CIV. P. 41.1; Wash. Rev. Code Ann. § 4.24.611(2) (West); TEX. R. CIV. P. 76a. Editorial, *Secrecy That Kills*, N.Y. TIMES, June 1, 2014, at SR10 (describing a proposed federal law limiting secret settlements in light of the GM case). We need more empirical data on how often judges grant protective orders keeping information confidential, and under what circumstances such orders are requested. Such data could help in considering what limits courts should place on publicity.

36. *Tom Baker, Transparency through Insurance: Mandates Dominate Discretion*, in CONFIDENTIALITY, TRANSPARENCY, AND THE U.S. CIVIL JUSTICE SYSTEM, 184–99 (Joseph W. Doherty et al., eds., 2012).

37. Stephen Yeazell, *Transparency for Civil Settlements: A NASDAQ for Lawsuits?* in CONFIDENTIALITY, TRANSPARENCY AND THE U.S. CIVIL JUSTICE SYSTEM, *id*. at 148–49, 155–56. This proposal is further discussed in the last chapter.

38. Kenneth Feinberg, *Transparency and Civil Justice: The Internal and External Value of Sunlight*, 58 DEPAUL L. REV. 473, 477 (2010).
39. Wood v. Moss, 134 S. Ct. 2056 (2014). For a critical discussion of qualified immunity see Karen M. Blum, *Section 1983 Litigation: The Maze, the Mud, and the Madness*, 23 WM. & MARY BILL RTS. J. 913, 924 (2015). I addressed the implications in chapter 1. See chapter 1, note 29 for sources.
40. Stephen R. Reinhardt, *The Demise of Habeas Corpus and the Rise of Qualified Immunity: The Court's Ever Increasing Limitations on the Development and Enforcement of Constitutional Rights and Some Particularly Unfortunate Consequences*, 113 MICH. L. REV. 1219 (2015). There is an argument that when courts fail to decide a constitutional question, they leave room for other branches of government to act, and this is democracy-promoting because the other branches are more representative than the courts. That argument raises the basic question of what justifies judicial review, which this book does not tackle. I will only say that it seems to me that a judicial decision is sometimes the beginning of a conversation, not the end.
41. Henry Paul Monaghan, *On Avoiding Avoidance, Agenda Control, and Related Matters*, 112 COLUM. L. REV. 665, 668 (2012) (Monaghan demonstrates how the Supreme Court sometimes adheres to a law declaration model in deciding whether to avoid decisions). Too much has been written about how broad or narrow court decisions should be, and the relationship between this question and inherited tradition, to be discussed at any length here. For an introduction, see Cass R. Sunstein, *The Supreme Court, 1995 Term—Foreword: Leaving Things Undecided*, 110 HARV. L. REV. 4 (1996).
42. For an analysis of the shared production of goods in the context of technological development, see YOCHAI BENKLER, THE WEALTH OF NETWORKS (2006).

CHAPTER 3

1. On the question of democratic deliberation in the courts, see HANNAH ARENDT, THE HUMAN CONDITION 192–212 (1958) (discussing the role of democracy in fostering communication regarding issues that shape social life); GUTMANN & THOMPSON, DEMOCRACY AND DISAGREEMENT, Preface, note 4 at 45 ("Many constitutional democrats focus on the importance of extensive moral deliberation within one of our democratic institutions—the Supreme Court. They argue that judges cannot interpret constitutional principles without engaging in deliberation, not least for the purpose of constructing a coherent view out of the many moral values that our constitutional tradition expresses"). For further readings on deliberation and political life see HUGH BAXTER, HABERMAS: THE DISCOURSE THEORY OF LAW AND DEMOCRACY (2011); Joshua Cohen, *An Epistemic Conception of Democracy*, 97 ETHICS 26 (1986); HENRY S. RICHARDSON, DEMOCRATIC AUTONOMY: PUBLIC REASONING ABOUT THE ENDS OF POLICY (2003). For a counterargument see Maya Sen, *Courting Deliberation: An Essay on Deliberative Democracy in the American Judicial System*, 27 NOTRE DAME J.L. ETHICS & PUB. POL'Y 303, 304 (2013) (arguing that "contributions both from social sciences and from doctrinal scholarship suggest that judges are strategic

(and oftentimes political) actors, and that their 'deliberations' might be more similar to quid pro quo bargaining than to reasoned intellectual exchanges"). All engagements with the legal system, even those ostensibly about private relationships, have a public dimension. For a discussion of this idea see David Luban, *Settlements and the Erosion of the Public Realm*, 83 GEO. L.J. 2619, 2634 (1995) (discussing a "public-life conception" of litigation in which "even ostensibly private disputes between apolitical citizens may have a public dimension engaging these values"). For a discussion of the public/private distinction see Morton J. Horwitz, *The History of the Public/Private Distinction*, 130 U. PA. L. REV. 1423 (1982); Duncan Kennedy, *Form and Substance in Private Law Adjudication*, 89 HARV. L. REV. 1685, 1769 (1976); Joseph William Singer, *Legal Realism Now*, 76 CAL. L. REV. 465, 477 (1988) (reviewing LAURA KALMAN, LEGAL REALISM AT YALE: 1927–1960 (1986)); Jack M. Balkin, *Populism and Progressivism as Constitutional Categories*, 104 YALE L.J. 1935, 1968–69 (1995) (reviewing CASS SUNSTEIN, DEMOCRACY AND THE PROBLEM OF FREE SPEECH (1993)) (explaining our inability to be free of the idea of public and private spheres).

2. Blakely v. Washington, 542 U.S. 296, 305–6 (2004). The context of that case was sentencing in the criminal context, and there are reasons to be concerned about that context, raising as it does the history of juror prejudice in the United States, especially of all-white juries against black defendants. The principle articulated, however, is the same and the risk the same as well in the civil context.

3. On the low rates of jury trials, see Galanter, *The Vanishing Trial*, introduction, note 23 at 506–10. On the historical question, including attitudes toward the jury right in the founding era and later, see Stephan Landsman, *The Civil Jury in America: Scenes from an Unappreciated History*, 44 HASTINGS L.J. 579, 598–600 (1993). On the question of who was permitted to serve on the jury and exclusions based on race and gender see NEIL VIDMAR & VALERIE P. HANS, AMERICAN JURIES: THE VERDICT 66–67 (2007).

4. *See, e.g.,* Campbell-Ewald v. Gomez, 136 S.Ct. 663 (2016) (Roberts, C.J., dissenting) (stating that "the federal courts exist to resolve real disputes, not to rule on a plaintiff's entitlement for relief there for the taking"). *See also* John H. Langbein, *The Disappearance of Civil Trial in the United States*, 122 YALE L.J. 522 (2012) (explaining the decline of the civil trial as a response to the fact that it is no longer needed to resolve disputes). For a discussion of the dominance of the dispute resolution model, see Monaghan, *On Avoiding Avoidance,* chapter 2, note 41 at 668. On the importance of adjudication as a process for reason giving, a function I see as also applicable to the litigation process, see Fuller, *The Forms and Limits of Adjudication*, introduction, note 7 at 367 ("We demand of an adjudicative decision a kind of rationality we do not expect of the results of contract or of voting. This higher responsibility toward rationality is at once the strength and the weakness of adjudication as a form of social ordering"). Deliberative democrats also use the courts as a primary example of public deliberation. GUTMANN & THOMPSON, DEMOCRACY AND DISAGREEMENT, Preface, note 4 at 45. For critiques of reason in adjudication, see Maya Sen, *Courting Deliberation: An Essay on Deliberative Democracy in the American Judicial System*, 27 NOTRE DAME J.L. ETHICS & PUB. POL'Y 303 (2013) (arguing that "contributions both from social

sciences and from doctrinal scholarship suggest that judges are strategic (and oftentimes political) actors, and that their 'deliberations' might be more similar to quid pro quo bargaining than to reasoned intellectual exchanges"); Mathilde Cohen, *When Judges Have Reasons Not to Give Reasons—A Comparative Law Approach*, 72 WASHINGTON & LEE L. REV. 483 (2015).

5. The long history of the litigation is told in *Casale v. Kelly*, 710 F. Supp. 2d 347 (S.D.N.Y. 2010).

6. For a detailed story of the *E. coli* outbreak, the lawsuits, and the restaurant's response, see BENEDICT, POISONED, introduction, note 1.

7. Elaine Porterfield & Adam Berliant, *Jack-in-the-Box Ignored Safety Rules*, THE NEWS TRIBUNE, June 16, 1995; Patrick O'Neill, *State Applauds Substantial Drop in E. Coli Cases*, THE OREGONIAN, Jan. 28, 1995 (quoting William Keene, a communicable disease epidemiologist with the Oregon Health Division).

8. Frank Michelman explained, to a "notable degree the panorama of our public life and human interaction occurs against a backdrop" of legal rights, "all potentially realizable through litigation." This knowledge makes "a significant contribution to whatever sense of security people feel in entering into relationships with others." Michelman, *The Supreme Court and Litigation Access Fees*, introduction, note 6 at 536. For a discussion of what we know about contract doctrine and the fact that most people do not bring their contract disputes to court, see Marc Galanter, *Contract in Court; Or Almost Everything You May or May Not Want to Know About Contract Litigation*, 2001 WISC. L. REV. 577. *See also* Stuart Macaulay, *Non-Contractual Relations in Business*, 28 AM. SOC. REV. 55 (1963) (demonstrating that resort to the courts was overshadowed by other, informal controls).

9. As Owen Fiss wrote: "[a]djudication is the social process by which judges give meaning to our public values." Owen M. Fiss, *Foreword: The Forms of Justice*, 93 HARV. L. REV. 1, 2 (1979). Similarly, Lon Fuller argued that adjudication is "a device which gives formal and institutional expression to the influence of reasoned argument in human affairs." Fuller, *The Forms and Limits of Adjudication*, introduction, note 7 at 366. They were writing of adjudication, but the statements also describe the performative aspect of the litigation process.

10. *See* Stephan Landsman, *The Growing Challenge of Pro Se Litigation*, 13 LEWIS & CLARK L. REV. 439 (2009). For a wide-ranging discussion and suggestions for reform see DEBORAH RHODE, ACCESS TO JUSTICE (2004). For examples of State Supreme Court Justices speaking out on the problem see the Hon. Wallace B. Jefferson, *Liberty and Justice for Some: How the Legal System Falls Short in Protecting Basic Rights*, 88 N.Y.U. L. REV. 1953 (2013); Chief Justice Chase T. Rogers, Connecticut Supreme Court, Connecticut Bar Association Keynote Address (June 11, 2012) (available at www.ncsc.org/~/media/Files/PDF/Information%20and%20Resources/Budget%20Resource%20Center/CBA%20Annual%20Meeting%20Dinner%202012.ashx). Whether a lawyer is necessary in a particular legal process is very context-dependent. *See, e.g.,* D. James Greiner et al., *The Limits of Unbundled Legal Assistance: A Randomized Study in Massachusetts District Court and Prospects for the Future*, 126 HARV. L. REV. 901 (2013). For a sustained discussion of the question of the right to

self-representation, reaching the contrary result to that advocated here, see RABEEA ASSY, INJUSTICE IN PERSON: THE RIGHT TO SELF-REPRESENTATION (2015). The case involving Jack Weinstein quoted in the text is *Floyd v. Cosi, Inc.,* 78 F. Supp. 3d 558, 561–62 (E.D.N.Y. 2015).

11. Lassiter v. Dep't of Soc. Serv. of Durham County, N.C., 452 U.S. 18 (1981).

12. In all but six states parents have an absolute right to counsel in termination proceedings. However, problems remain because of low attorney compensation, poor training, and other factors. VIVEK SANKARAN, A NATIONAL SURVEY ON A PARENT'S RIGHT TO COUNSEL IN TERMINATION OF PARENTAL RIGHTS AND DEPENDENCY CASES, available at http://youthrightsjustice.org/Documents/SurveyParentRighttoCounsel.pdf. European countries provide a much broader right to counsel. Airey v. Ireland, 32 Eur. Ct. H.R. (ser. A) at 12–13 (1979) (holding that the right to a fair hearing in civil cases may include a right to counsel). For a recent case see *In re T.M.,* 131 Haw. 419, 433, 319 P.3d 338, 352 (2014).

13. Some argue that legal representation alienates the client from their own case. This is certainly possible and requires sensitivity on the part of the lawyer. A classic article discussing this problem is Lucie E. White, *Subordination, Rhetorical Survival Skills, and Sunday Shoes: Notes on the Hearing of Mrs. G.,* 38 BUFF. L. REV. 1 (1990). *See also* William H. Simon, *Lawyer Advice and Client Autonomy: Mrs. Jones's Case,* 50 MD. L. REV. 213 (1991) (discussing the complex relationship between client autonomy and deference to expertise).

14. Alexandra D. Lahav, *Participation and Procedure,* 64 DEPAUL L. REV. 513 (2015) (quoting Judge Jack Weinstein on his experience in the Zyprexia litigation). For critiques of aggregation see Linda Mullenix, *Reflections of a Recovering Aggregationist,* 15 NEV. L. J. 1455 (2015); Elizabeth Chamblee Burch, *Disaggregation,* 90 WASH. U. L. REV. 667 (2013); Eduardo C. Roberno, *The Federal Asbestos Product Liability Multidistrict Litigation (MDL-875): Black Hole or New Paradigm?,* 23 WIDENER L. J. 97 (2013); Alan B. Morrison & Brian Wolfman, *Representing the Unrepresented in Class Actions Seeking Monetary Relief,* 71 N.Y.U. L. REV. 439 (1996). A critique based in constitutional law (albeit out of the mainstream) can be found in MARTIN H. REDISH, WHOLESALE JUSTICE: CONSTITUTIONAL DEMOCRACY AND THE PROBLEM OF THE CLASS ACTION LAWSUIT (2009).

15. The class action for economic damages arising out of the oil spill was settled. See *In re: Oil Spill by the Oil Rig "Deepwater Horizon" in the Gulf of Mexico, on April 20,* 910 F.Supp.2d 891 (E.D. La. 2012). The lawsuits against Merck relating to the drug Vioxx were consolidated in both state and federal courts. For a description see Alexandra D. Lahav, *The Case for "Trial by Formula,"* 90 TEX. L. REV. 571, 592 (2012); Howard M. Erichson & Benjamin C. Zipursky, *Consent Versus Closure,* 96 CORNELL L. REV. 265, 277–78 (2011). For a description of a small claims suit, see Brian T. Fitzpatrick & Robert C. Gilbert, *An Empirical Look at Compensation in Consumer Class Actions,* 11 N.Y.U. J. L. & BUS. 767 (2015).

16. It is important to understand that in aggregated cases in either state or federal court the practice is not to settle cases individually, but rather to structure an aggregate settlement that will include most, if not all, of the plaintiffs. There is an economic reason for this—what makes bringing these suits financially viable

is aggregation, and lawyers often have large numbers of cases (called inventory cases). A class action provides a procedural rule for doing this, but many cases are settled outside of the class action context. For a general overview of the issues that is dated but still relevant, see JACK B. WEINSTEIN, INDIVIDUAL JUSTICE IN MASS TORT LITIGATION: THE EFFECT OF CLASS ACTIONS, CONSOLIDATIONS AND OTHER MULTIPARTY DEVICES (1995). For an explanation of the ethical issues created by this structure see Nancy J. Moore, *Ethical Issues in Mass Tort Plaintiffs' Representation: Beyond the Aggregate Settlement Rule*, 81 FORDHAM L. REV. 3233 (2013). For a discussion of judicial responses to this structure, see Elizabeth Chamblee Burch, *Judging Multidistrict Litigation*, 90 N.Y.U. L. REV. 71 (2015).

17. For a journalistic account of both sides see Jesse Alejandro Cottrell, *"Stop and Frisk" May Be Working—But Is It Racist?*, THE ATLANTIC, January 23, 2013. For a description of the political battles around the issue, see Jennifer Fermino, *Mayor Bloomberg on Stop-and-Frisk: It Can Be Argued "We Disproportionately Stop Whites Too Much. And Minorities Too Little."* N.Y. DAILY NEWS, June 28, 2013.

18. Floyd v. City of New York, 959 F.Supp.2d 540 (S.D.N.Y. 2013); Floyd v. City of New York, 959 F.Supp.2d 691 (S.D.N.Y. 2013). The case was appealed to the Second Circuit but with the election of a new mayor, the city dropped the appeal. Floyd v. City of New York, 770 F.3d 1051 (2d Cir. 2014).

19. For a description of the Vioxx litigation and the role of bellwether trials, see Lahav, *The Case for "Trial by Formula,"* supra note 15; Alexandra D. Lahav, *Bellwether Trials*, 76 GEO. WASH. L. REV. 576 (2008); Hon. Eldon E. Fallon et al., *Bellwether Trials in Multidistrict Litigation*, 82 TUL. L. REV. 2323 (2008).

20. The hearings in the Agent Orange case and desegregation cases are described and analyzed in Martha Minow, *Judge for the Situation: Judge Jack Weinstein, Creator of Temporary Administrative Agencies*, 97 COLUM. L. REV. 2010 (1997). *See also* PETER H. SCHUCK, AGENT ORANGE ON TRIAL: MASS TOXIC DISASTERS IN THE COURTS (1988); Curtis J. Berger, *Away from the Court House and into the Field: The Odyssey of a Special Master*, 78 COLUM. L. REV. 707 (1978) (describing the experience of a special master holding hearings in the community in *Hart v. Cmty. Sch. Bd. of Brooklyn*, 383 F. Supp. 699 (E.D.N.Y. 1974), *supplemented*, 383 F. Supp. 769 (E.D.N.Y. 1974), *aff'd*, 512 F.2d 37 (2d Cir. 1975)).

21. This is not to say that legal ideas encompass every aspect of justice. There are often cases where we need to look beyond the constraints of trials to tell a story and beyond constraints of existing laws to determine what is morally just. The point here is that litigation is one important way to participate in the creation of narratives and the formation of justice. For a critique of civil rights laws, see, e.g., Richard Thompson Ford, *Rethinking Rights after the Second Reconstruction*, 123 YALE L.J. 2942, 2960 (2014).

22. For a description of this proposal see AM. LAW INST., PRINCIPLES OF THE LAW OF AGGREGATE LITIGATION § 3.17 (2010). But the lawyers are likely to want to convince everyone to agree to a settlement they have worked hard to negotiate, and discussions are more likely to happen in a law office than publicly. *See* Erichson & Zipursky, *Consent versus Closure, supra* note 15 at 301–4.

23. One study of tort litigation found that litigants prefer more formal proceedings such as trial, mediation, and arbitration over resolution by settlement. E. Allan Lind et al., *In the Eye of the Beholder: Tort Litigants' Evaluations of Their Experiences in the Civil Justice System*, 24 LAW & SOC'Y REV. 953, 976 (1990). *See generally* JOHN THIBAUT & LAURENS WALKER, PROCEDURAL JUSTICE: A PSYCHOLOGICAL ANALYSIS (1975). For an update summarizing the large procedural justice literature and empirical findings since 1975, see Nourit Zimerman & Tom R. Tyler, *Between Access to Counsel and Access to Justice: A Psychological Perspective*, 37 FORDHAM URB. L.J. 473 (2010). A valid critique of many of the psychological studies of procedural fairness is that the study subjects are not people engaged in an actual dispute. These studies also only consider what people report they perceive as fair and do not address the normative question of whether what is fair can be solely determined by these reports.

24. The lawyers did not need the court's approval of the settlement. Each individual client had the right to decide whether or not to accept it regardless of what the judge said. But since it was a collective settlement that needed most of the plaintiffs to agree if it was to go forward, the lawyers probably thought that having judicial approval would be helpful in convincing clients to join in. For a discussion of the process, see Alvin K. Hellerstein et al., *Managerial Judging: The 9/11 Responders' Tort Litigation*, 98 CORNELL L. REV. 127, 157 (2012). For a critique of the use of judicial power to oversee nonclass settlements, see Howard M. Erichson, *The Role of the Judges in Non-Class Settlements*, 90 WASH. U. L. REV. 1015 (2013).

25. Hadfield, *Framing the Choice Between Cash and the Courthouse*, chapter 1, note 2. The lawsuits of the small group of families that chose to sue ended up settling. Benjamin Weiser, *Family and United Airlines Settle Last 9/11 Wrongful Death Lawsuit*, N.Y. TIMES, Sept. 20, 2011, at A28.

26. Hon. William G. Young & Jordan M. Singer, *Bench Presence: Toward a More Complete Model of Federal District Court Productivity*, 118 PENN ST. L. REV. 55, 58, 73 (2013).

27. Hon. William G. Young, *Vanishing Trials, Vanishing Juries, Vanishing Constitution*, 40 SUFFOLK U. L. REV. 67, 71 (2006) ("within her proper fact-finding sphere, an American juror is a constitutional officer—the constitutional equal of the President, a Senator or Representative, or the Chief Justice of the United States"). The Supreme Court quote is from *Powers v. Ohio*, 499 U.S. 400, 407 (1991) (quoting 1 ALEXIS DE TOCQUEVILLE, DEMOCRACY IN AMERICA 334–37 (1835)). Not addressed here, although relevant, is the issue of juries determining the law as well as the facts of the case. For an analysis see Jenny E. Carroll, *The Jury's Second Coming*, 100 GEO. L.J. 657 (2012); Edith Guild Henderson, *The Background of the Seventh Amendment*, 80 HARV. L. REV. 289, 299 (1966) (discussing the claim that the jury can decide law as well as fact).

28. See the earlier quote from *Blakely v. Washington*, 542 U.S. at 305–6 ("Just as suffrage ensures the people's ultimate control in the legislative and executive branches, jury trial is meant to ensure their control in the judiciary"); Vikram David Amar, *Jury Service as Political Participation Akin to Voting*, 80 CORNELL

L. Rev. 203 (1995) (using the analogy with respect to juror exclusion). *See also* John Gastil et al., The Jury and Democracy: How Jury Deliberation Promotes Civil Engagement and Political Participation 46–47 (2010) (discussing results of study which showed higher voting rates among persons who had served on a criminal jury, but no such correlation among persons who had served in a civil jury).

29. Scott v. Harris, 550 U.S. 372, 378 (2007). For the first time ever in a Supreme Court opinion, the video was appended to the opinion and is available on the Supreme Court website.

30. "The landmark English search-and-seizure cases that inspired the framers were themselves civil-damage suits where juries helped determine whether government officials had acted reasonably." Akhil Reed Amar, *An Unreasonable View of the 4th Amendment*, L.A. Times, Apr. 29, 2001. The study debunking the Supreme Court's certainty that no reasonable person could see the case from the plaintiff's point of view is Dan Kahan et al., *Whose Eyes Are You Going to Believe? Scott v. Harris and the Perils of Cognitive Illiberalism*, 122 Harv. L. Rev. 837, 838 (2009).

31. Neil Vidmar & Valerie P. Hans, American Juries: The Verdict 226 (2007) (discussing juror review of law as a means to check governmental power); Shari Seidman Diamond et al., *The "Kettleful of Law" in Real Jury Deliberations: Successes, Failures and Next Steps*, 106 Nw. U. L. Rev. 1537 (2012) (describing juror deliberations). For a critique see Adrian Vermeule, *Many-Minds Arguments in Legal Theory*, 1 J. Legal Analysis 1 (2009); Jason M. Solomon, *Juries, Social Norms, and Civil Justice*, 65 Ala. L. Rev. 1125, 1185–87 (2014). In *Colgrove v. Battin*, 413 U.S. 149 (1973), the Supreme Court authorized six-member juries in civil cases. This decision has been much criticized. *See* Shari Seidman Diamond & Andrea Ryken, *The Modern American Jury: A One-Hundred-Year Journey*, 96 Judicature 315, 319 (2013) ("Overall, the research found that twelve-member juries tend to produce less variable awards, recall more testimony, and include a more representative mix of members than six-member juries"); *IV. Unshrinking the Federal Civil Jury*, 110 Harv. L. Rev. 1466, 1480 (1997) (summarizing studies and critiques).

32. There are three main objections to civil juries: jurors cannot understand complex cases, jurors are inconsistent in their determination of cases, and juries are biased against certain kinds of litigants. For a discussion of these objections see Alexandra D. Lahav, *The Jury and Participatory Democracy*, 55 Wm. & Mary L. Rev. 1029, 1046–51 (2014).

33. Galanter, *The Vanishing Trial*, introduction, note 23.

34. Concerns about consistency of jury verdicts express anxiety about pluralism. But why it is that judges, not juries, are considered the baseline correct decision-maker on liability? If the question is one of fact, we should be just as concerned about the judge disagreeing with the jury as the jury disagreeing with the judge. *See* Jennifer K. Robbennolt, *Evaluating Juries by Comparison to Judges: A Benchmark for Judging?* 32 Fla. St. U.L. Rev. 469, 502–6 (2005). For studies of jury inconsistency see Harry Kalven Jr. & Hans Zeisel, The American Jury 58, 63 (1966) (finding 78 percent agreement on verdict between judges

and juries in both civil and criminal cases); Shari Seidman Diamond et al., *Juror Judgments about Liability and Damages: Sources of Variability and Ways to Increase Consistency*, 48 DePaul L. Rev. 301, 303 (1998); Larry Heuer & Steven Penrod, *Trial Complexity: A Field Investigation of Its Meaning and Effects*, 18 Law & Hum. Behav. 29, 48 (1994); Michael J. Saks et al., *Reducing Variability in Civil Jury Awards*, 21 Law & Hum. Behav. 243, 246 (1997); Neil Vidmar, *The Performance of the American Civil Jury: An Empirical Perspective*, 40 Ariz. L. Rev. 849, 854 (1998).

35. Shari Seidman Diamond, *Truth, Justice, and the Jury*, 26 Harv. J. L. & Pub. Pol'y 143, 145 (2003) (showing that the focus on rare high jury awards is misplaced).

36. Hana Financial, Inc. v. Hana Bank, 135 S.Ct. 907, 912 (2015) (holding that the question of whether tacking is appropriate in a trademark case should be decided by a jury). On the epistemic point see Alex Stein, *An Essay on Uncertainty and Fact-Finding in Civil Litigation, with Special Reference to Contract Cases*, 48 U. Toronto L.J. 299, 299, 302 (1998).

37. Turner v. Rogers, 131 S. Ct. 2507, 2512–13 (2011). Elizabeth G. Patterson, *Civil Contempt and the Indigent Child Support Obligor: The Silent Return of Debtor's Prison*, 18 Cornell J.L. & Pub. Pol'y 95, 103 (2008). The history of the judicial contempt power gives little comfort to anyone concerned about judges *or* juries. Consider Martin Luther King Jr.'s state court contempt hearing for violation of an unconstitutional injunction imposed at the last minute, before judicial review of the injunction could be obtained, to prevent a march in Birmingham, Alabama in April 1963. *See* Walker v. City of Birmingham, 388 U.S. 307, 321 (1967) (holding that regardless of whether the injunction was unconstitutional or not, the protestors could be punished for its violation). A jury in that time and place would not have made a better decision than the state judge. David Luban, Legal Modernism 221–43 (1994) (providing an overview and analysis of *Walker*).

38. As G. K. Chesterton wrote: "And the horrible thing about all legal officials, even the best, about all judges, magistrates, barristers, detectives, and policemen, is not that they are wicked (some of them are good), not that they are stupid (several of them are quite intelligent), it is simply that they have got used to it. . . . Strictly they do not see the prisoner in the dock; all they see is the usual man in the usual place. They do not see the awful court of judgment; they only see their own workshop. Therefore the instinct of Christian civilization has most wisely declared that into their judgments there shall upon every occasion be infused fresh blood and fresh thoughts from the streets." G. K. Chesterton, Tremendous Trifles 67–68 (1920), *quoted and discussed in* Robert P. Burns, The Death of the American Trial 11 (2009).

39. Alexander Hamilton, The Federalist No. 83, *reprinted in* 5 The Founders' Constitution 358, 360 (Philip B. Kurland & Ralph Lerner, eds., 1987).

40. On the broader debate about expertise, objectivity, and popular sovereignty see Peter Novick, That Noble Dream: The 'Objectivity Question' and the American Historical Profession 1 (1988); Edward A. Purcell Jr., The Crisis of Democratic Theory: Scientific Naturalism and

THE PROBLEM OF VALUE 42–43 (1973); Richard B. Stewart, *The Reformation of American Administrative Law*, 88 HARV. L. REV. 1669, 1678–79 (1975).

41. On the difficulty of judges without economic training in deciding antitrust cases, see Michael R. Baye & Joshua D. Wright, *Is Antitrust Too Complicated for Generalist Judges? The Impact of Economic Complexity and Judicial Training on Appeals*, 54 J.L. & ECON. 1, 5 (2011). On juror training as a new method of assisting jurors with complex evidence, see N.J. Schweitzer & Michael J. Saks, *Jurors and Scientific Causation: What Don't They Know, and What Can Be Done about It?* 52 JURIMETRICS J. 433 (2012).

42. *See* Shari Seidman Diamond et al., *The "Kettleful of Law" in Real Jury Deliberations: Successes, Failures, and Next Steps*, 106 Nw. U. L. REV. 1537, 1552–57 (2012) (explaining studies demonstrating the importance jurors attribute to jury instruction).

43. The statute that permits individuals to sue for constitutional violations is 42 U.S.C. § 1983; City of Monterey v. Del Monte Dunes at Monterey, Ltd., 526 U.S. 687, 708–9 (1999) (holding that a § 1983 action is an "action at law" for Seventh Amendment purposes). One study demonstrates that lawsuits impact policies in some police departments, a subject discussed in chapter 2. *See* Joanna C. Schwartz, *What Police Learn from Lawsuits*, 33 CARDOZO L. REV. 841, 862 (2012).

44. For a summary of these restrictions and the reasons courts have given for not revealing this information to jurors, see Lahav, *The Jury and Participatory Democracy, supra* note 32 at 1052–54, nn. 117–27. These reasons basically come down to concern about juror bias or jurors subverting the process by reallocating damages to different categories. The problem is that studies show that reallocation of damages in reaction to damages caps happens anyway, and that jurors do consider questions like taxes, insurance, and attorneys' fees even when they are not instructed on them. See Seidman et al., *The "Kettleful of Law," supra* note 42 at 1575–84.

45. *See* Oscar G. Chase, *Helping Jurors Determine Pain and Suffering Awards*, 23 HOFSTRA L. REV. 763, 777–78 (1995) (proposing that courts provide jurors with a grid informing them of the range of awards made by other juries in their state in similar cases).

46. Catherine M. Sharkey, *Unintended Consequences of Medical Malpractice Damages Caps*, 80 N.Y.U. L. REV. 391 (2005).

47. U.S. v. Kahn, 325 F.Supp.2d 218, 220 (E.D.N.Y. 2004).

48. Benjamin Weiser & Joseph Goldstein, *Without Jury, Judge Warned that Stop-and-Frisk Ruling Would Be Disputed*, N.Y. TIMES, Jan. 3, 2014, at A15.

49. While that group would not have been a true stand-in for the heterogenous population of the City of New York, it might have introduced considerations that the judge herself might not be aware of.

50. As Milner Ball wrote: "If the advocate's presentation of his client's case is a form of theater which is played to the judge or jury and which contributes to judgment, there is also the theater of the courtroom itself—embracing all that goes on within—played to the public at large. It is the function of this drama to provide an image of legitimate society. In this sense, it is importantly an end in

itself." MILNER S. BALL, THE PROMISE OF AMERICAN LAW: A THEOLOGICAL, HUMANISTIC VIEW OF LEGAL PROCESS, 136–38 (1981). It may be that the reason for the practice of not requiring reasons from juries is that it may be more difficult for people to agree on a result when they must produce reasons. Or it may be that if the jury gives reasons, this will make its work reviewable by a judge, which would undermine their independence. Already juries sometimes give reasons informally after the fact in media interviews. To some extent, special verdict forms allow jurors to explain how they decided each question, although they do not require reasons for those decisions. For a discussion see Nancy S. Marder & Valerie P. Hans, *Introduction to Juries and Lay Participation: American Perspectives and Global Trends*, 90 CHI.-KENT L. REV. 789, 793–95 (2015).

51. For discussions of the courts as exemplars see GUTMANN & THOMPSON, Preface, note 4 at 45; RAWLS, POLITICAL LIBERALISM, Preface note 3 at 231–40 (discussing the Supreme Court as the exemplar of public reason).

CHAPTER 4

1. The judicial oath of office is found at 28 U.S.C. § 453. John Adams, "Novanglus Papers" no. 7. THE WORKS OF JOHN ADAMS, (Charles Francis Adams, ed.) vol. 4 at 106 (1851); MA CONST., ART. XXX ("to the end it may be a government of laws, and not of men"). The idea that equality requires that people be treated with equal concern and respect is from Ronald Dworkin's influential work. RONALD DWORKIN, TAKING RIGHTS SERIOUSLY 370 (1977). Debbie Elliot, NPR, *BP's Oil Slick Set to Spill into Courtroom* (Feb. 16, 2012), available at http://m.npr.org/news/front/146938630?page.

2. On the idea of the right to have rights, see HANNAH ARENDT, THE ORIGINS OF TOTALITARIANISM 298 (1966); SEYLA BENHABIB, THE RIGHTS OF OTHERS: ALIENS, CITIZENS AND RESIDENTS 49–69 (2004); Frank I. Michelman, *Parsing the Right to Have Rights*, 3 CONSTELLATIONS 200 (Oct. 1996). For an inquiry into the question of equality as part of democracy see Elizabeth S. Anderson, *What Is the Point of Equality?*, 109 ETHICS 287 (1999) (discussing the concept of democratic equality); David Miller, *Equality and Justice*, 10 RATIO 222, 230, 233 (1997). There are too many works on equality and justice to mention here. Those that I have found influential on my thinking include YARON EZRAHI, IMAGINED DEMOCRACIES: NECESSARY POLITICAL FICTIONS (2012); MICHAEL WALZER, SPHERES OF JUSTICE: A DEFENSE OF PLURALISM AND EQUALITY (1983); Kenneth L. Karst, *The Supreme Court, 1976 Term—Foreword: Equal Citizenship under the Fourteenth Amendment*, 91 HARV. L. REV. 1 (1977); Samuel R. Bagenstos, *Employment Law and Social Equality*, 112 MICH. L. REV. 225, 273 (2013); William B. Rubenstein, *The Concept of Equality in Civil Procedure*, 23 CARDOZO L. REV. 1865 (2002). Perhaps it is better not to speak of equality at all, but rather in minimum standards required to achieve access to justice. That is, A may have less than B, but what matters is not that they have the same amount, but rather that they each have enough to litigate adequately. For a discussion along these lines see Frank I. Michelman, *Foreword: On Protecting the Poor through the Fourteenth Amendment*, 83 Harv. L. Rev. 7, 17–18 (1969).

3. In *Richardson v. Ramirez*, 418 U.S. 24 (1974), the Supreme Court held that barring convicted felons from voting was constitutional under the penalty clause of the Fourteenth Amendment to the US Constitution. That clause allows states to disenfranchise persons convicted of "participation in rebellion, or other crime" without losing representation in Congress. As of 2012, approximately 5.85 million people were barred from voting due to felony disenfranchisement laws. See www.sentencingproject.org for statistics and pending cases challenging felony disenfranchisement. When in jail, inmates' rights to sue are limited by the Prison Litigation Reform Act, discussed later in this chapter. Once they are out of jail, however, individuals have the same rights to sue regardless of their previous conviction. John Hart Ely justified his influential theory of judicial review on the grounds that some segments of society were marginalized or excluded from the political system. JOHN HART ELY, DEMOCRACY AND DISTRUST (1981).

4. *See, e.g.,* Batson v. Kentucky, 476 U.S. 79(1986) (holding that a juror may not be dismissed based on race); Edmonson v. Leesville Concrete Co., 500 U.S. 614 (1991) (applying *Batson* to civil litigation); J.E.B. v. Alabama ex rel. T.B., 511 U.S. 127 (1994) (applying *Batson* to gender discrimination). The Supreme Court held that poll taxes violate the right to vote. Harper v. Virginia State Bd. of Elections, 383 U.S. 663 (1966) (holding the poll tax unconstitutional under the equal protection clause), but as we shall see it has not applied this same rational consistently to litigation.

5. Bridges v. Wixon, 326 U.S. 135, 166 (1945) (Murphy, J., concurring). In that case the Supreme Court overturned the deportation order of Harry Bridges, who was to be deported for affiliation with the Communist Party. The rules governing civil discovery, which treat plaintiffs and defendants equally, are FED. R. CIV. P. 26–37.

6. The Fugitive Slave Act of 1850, ch. 10, 9 Stat. 362. On the litigation surrounding this act see Burt Neuborne, *The Myth of Parity*, 90 HARV. L. REV. 1105, 1111–14 (1977). For some background on the history of suits for freedom and limitations see MARK TUSHNET, THE AMERICAN LAW OF SLAVERY (1981); ARIELA GROSS, WHAT BLOOD WON'T TELL: A HISTORY OF RACE ON TRIAL IN AMERICA (2008).

7. The theory is that repeat players and those with access to resources are more likely to succeed in litigation. Marc Galanter, *Why the "Haves" Come Out Ahead: Speculations on the Limits of Legal Change*, 9 LAW & SOC'Y REV. 95 (1974); Shauhin Talesh, *How the "Haves" Come Out Ahead in the Twenty-First Century*, 62 DEPAUL L. REV. 519 (2013).

8. Rubenstein, *The Concept of Equality in Civil Procedure, supra* note 2 at 1915; Alan Wertheimer, *The Equalization of Legal Resources*, 17 PHIL. & PUB. AFFAIRS 303 (1988). The last observation draws generally on Michael Walzer's political theory. *See* MICHAEL WALZER, SPHERES OF JUSTICE: A DEFENSE OF PLURALISM AND EQUALITY (1984). For a discussion of shrinking budgets for court systems, see Erwin Chemerinsky, *Symposium on State Court Funding: Keynote Address*, 100 KY. L.J. 743 (2012) and sources cited therein.

9. On the subject of formal equality, Anatole France famously quipped, "The law, in its majestic equality, forbids the rich as well as the poor to sleep under bridges,

to beg in the streets, and to steal bread." *Quoted in* Griffin v. Illinois, 351 U.S. 12, 23 (1956). For a discussion of alternative legal systems less dependent on equal adversaries, see John Langbein, *The German Advantage in Civil Procedure*, 52 U. CHI. L. REV. 823 (1985); Amalia D. Kessler, *Deciding Against Conciliation: The Nineteenth-Century Rejection of a European Transplant and the Rise of a Distinctively American Ideal of Adversarial Adjudication*, 10 THEORETICAL INQUIRIES IN L. 423 (2009).

10. *See, e.g.,* Galanter, *Why the "Haves" Come Out Ahead, supra* note 7; Robert G. Bone, *Settlement in American Civil Adjudication: The Role of Procedural Law and the Courts*, 36 COMP. L. REV. 1, 32–36 (2003). For a historical view of the same dynamics at work, see Samuel Issacharoff & John Fabian Witt, *The Inevitability of Aggregate Settlement: An Institutional Account of American Tort Law*, 57 VAND. L. REV. 1571, 1592 (2004). For an empirical study showing the difference between types of lawyering in results for clients, see Nora Freeman Engstrom, *Sunlight and Settlement Mills*, 86 N.Y.U. L. REV. 805, 840 (2011).

11. On the failure of lawyers to fight the "same actor" defense, see Scott Moss, *Bad Briefs, Bad Law, Bad Markets: Documenting Poor Quality of Plaintiffs' Briefs, Its Impact on the Law, and the Market Failure It Reflects*, 63 EMORY L. J. 59–125 (2013). Moss also discusses the reasons this defense has been criticized. For a more recent discussion of the Galanter thesis see IN LITIGATION, DO THE "HAVES" STILL COME OUT AHEAD? (Herbert M. Kritzer & Susan Silbey, eds.) (2003). The origin of the same actor inference was a law review article. John J. Donohue III & Peter Siegelman, *The Changing Nature of Employment Discrimination Litigation*, 43 STAN. L. REV. 983, 1017 (1991).

12. Boddie v. Connecticut, 401 U.S. 371 (1971). The Court in *Boddie* was careful to note that unlike other disputes which can be resolved through negotiation, a divorce can only be granted by the state. But the Court's narrow view of which disputes require substantive equality need not be the last word on the subject. In dissent Justice Brennan pointed out that the problem was one of equal protection of the laws for rich and poor. *Id.* at 388 ("The question that the Court treats exclusively as one of due process inevitably implicates considerations of both due process and equal protection. Certainly, there is at issue the denial of a hearing, a matter for analysis under the Due Process Clause. But Connecticut does not deny a hearing to everyone in these circumstances; it denies it only to people who fail to pay certain fees."). For a discussion of how to draw the line, see Frank I. Michelman, *The Supreme Court and Litigation Access Fees: The Right to Protect One's Rights—Part One*, 1973 DUKE L.J. 1153.

13. M.L.B. v. S.L.J., 519 U.S. 102 (1996) (striking down requirement that indigent parents pay transcript fees to appeal termination of parental rights); Mayer v. Chicago, 404 U.S. 189, 195–96 (1971) (striking down similar requirement for petty criminal offenders); Griffin v. Illinois, 351 U.S. 12 (1956) (striking down transcript requirement for indigent appeals of serious crimes).

14. Kenji Yoshino, *The New Equal Protection*, 124 HARV. L. REV. 747 (2011) (describing a doctrinal shift away from equal protection of groups). Immediately after the decision in *Boddie*, the Supreme Court limited that ruling. *See* United States v. Kras, 409 U.S. 434 (1973) (access fee to bankruptcy court does not violate

due process); Ortwein v. Schwab, 410 U.S. 656 (1973) (access fee for review of agency determination does not violate due process). The refusal of the Supreme Court to recognize the importance of material equality to due process lies in the negative conception of liberty applied in the due process cases. For a critical discussion see Susan Bandes, *The Negative Constitution: A Critique*, 88 MICH. L. REV. 2271 (1990); John C.P. Goldberg, *The Constitutional Status of Tort Law: Due Process and the Right to Law for the Redress of Wrongs*, 115 YALE L. J. 524, 593 (2005). For a defense of the limitation of constitutional protection to negative liberties see, e.g., David P. Currie, *Positive and Negative Constitutional Rights*, 53 U. CHI. L. REV. 864 (1986); DeShaney v. Winnebago County Dept. of Soc. Serv., 489 U.S. 189, 195 (1989).

15. Schroeder v. Weighall, 179 Wash.2d 566 (2014) (holding that a statute of limitations that does not toll for minority violates the state constitution); Zeier v. Zimmer, Inc., 152 P.3d 861 (2006) (holding that a certificate of merit requirement which raises the cost of bringing suit violates the state constitution). For states holding that damages caps violate equal protection, see *Arneson v. Olson*, 270 N.W.2d 125, (N.D. 1978) (striking down a statutory cap of $300,000 on equal protection grounds); Moore v. Mobile Infirmary Ass'n, 592 So.2d 156, 165–71 (1991); Brannigan v. Usitalo, 134 N.H. 50, 587 A.2d 1232, 1234–36 (1991), *aff'd* Carson v. Maurer, 120 N.H. 925, 424 A.2d 825 (1980); Ferdon ex rel. Petrucelli v. Wisconsin Patients Comp. Fund, 284 Wis. 2d 573, 590, 701 N.W.2d 440, 448 (2005). Some states applying equal protection doctrine in the context of barriers to suit have applied either strict or intermediate scrutiny to the legislation at issue, meaning that the burden is on the state to provide a compelling reason for its differential treatment of citizens. But other states, such as Wisconsin, have struck down these laws applying only rational basis review, meaning that the state was unable to convince the court that it had a rational basis for the legislation that singled out the vulnerable for lesser treatment.

16. 28 U.S.C. § 1915 (federal in forma pauperis statute); 42 U.S.C. § 1988 (providing for fee shifting in cases brought for constitutional violations). In the last twenty years numerous limitations have been placed on fee shifting. *See* Pamela S. Karlan, *Disarming the Private Attorney General*, 2003 U. ILL. L. REV. 183.

17. Carnegie v. Household Int'l., 376 F.3d 656, 661 (7th Cir. 2004).

18. Liberty and equality are often presented as being in tension with one another, but they are also intertwined. *See* Yoshino, *The New Equal Protection, supra* note 14, 124 HARV. L. REV. at 749–50 (noting the widespread understanding that "equality and liberty claims are often intertwined"). Articles that help in thinking through these problems include Pamela S. Karlan, *Equal Protection, Due Process, and the Stereoscopic Fourteenth Amendment*, 33 McGEORGE L. REV. 473 (2002); Kenneth L. Karst, *The Liberties of Equal Citizens: Groups and the Due Process Clause*, 55 UCLA L. REV. 99, 142 (2007); Kenneth L. Karst, *Foreword: Equal Citizenship under the Fourteenth Amendment*, 91 HARV. L. REV. 1 (1977); William N. Eskridge Jr., *Destabilizing Due Process and Evolutive Equal Protection*, 47 UCLA L. REV. 1183 (2000). For a discussion of the differences and distinctions between the two clauses, see Ira C. Lupu, *Untangling the Strands of the Fourteenth Amendment*, 77 MICH. L. REV. 981 (1979); Cass Sunstein, *Sexual*

Orientation and the Constitution: A Note on the Relationship between Due Process and Equal Protection, 55 U. CHI. L. REV. 1161 (1988).

19. On the portfolio approach to contingency fee cases, see HERBERT KRITZER, RISKS, REPUTATIONS AND REWARDS (2004). The courts' approach to class action fee awards is laid out in *Goldberger v. Integrated Res., Inc.*, 209 F.3d 43, 50 (2d Cir. 2000). Risk of losing is one of the factors the court will look at, along with the level of investment the lawyers have put into the case and other factors. For a very critical view of contingency fees, see LESTER BRICKMAN, LAWYER BARONS: WHAT THEIR CONTINGENCY FEES REALLY COST AMERICA (2011), and for a more nuanced view, although still critical, see JOHN C. COFFEE JR., ENTREPRENEURIAL LITIGATION: ITS RISE, FALL, AND FUTURE 28–29, 116–17 (2015).

20. Throughout this book I have endeavored to treat all types of litigation, from contract to civil rights, as contributing to democracy equally. I believe that this is true because, as noted earlier, the baseline belief that rights can be enforced is crucial to a government of laws, and this applies to all rights and obligations. *See, e.g.*, Shelly v. Kraemer, 334 U.S. 1 (1948) (prohibiting states from enforcing racially restrictive covenants). I think this is largely but not exclusively true. Large-scale private organizations can have a profound impact on people's lives on the order of governmental entities. In other words, the public/private distinction is difficult to maintain in thinking about the value of litigation. Yet nevertheless I express here a preference for equalization of civil rights cases because of the substantive principles at stake in those cases.

21. But there are people who are antiegalitarian; what raises ire, as the discussion in the text indicates, is the idea of *distributive* equality. *See* David Miller, *Equality and Justice*, 10 RATIO 222, 230, 233 (1997).

22. For critics making arguments that enabling litigation results in frivolous suits, the best statement is probably OLSON, THE LITIGATION EXPLOSION, Preface, note 1. For a thoughtful and nuanced criticism of mergers and acquisitions litigation and how plaintiffs do not in fact benefit, see COFFEE, ENTREPRENEURIAL LITIGATION, *supra* note 19 at 92–93, and for a trenchant critique of securities litigation, see 142–43. But as discussed in chapter 1, it is hard to agree on what constitutes a frivolous suit. Loss rates do not demonstrate the value of litigation because the idea that all cases in which the plaintiff ultimately loses should not have been brought in the first place fundamentally misunderstands the dynamics of litigation. In most cases, the outcome is uncertain, with no clear winner or loser at the start—after all, if all cases had clear winners and losers, either the plaintiff would drop the case or the defendant would agree to settle. There is some theoretical economic analysis of litigation which considers the effect of incentives to sue on what types of suits are brought. *See* Steven Shavell, *The Fundamental Divergence between the Private and the Social Motive to Use the Legal System*, 26 J. LEGAL STUD. 575 (1997). As Shavell points out, it is in the interests of lawyers to expand the use of legal services through litigation. *Id.* at 595. He is skeptical of the democratic or broader social values of litigation beyond dispute resolution. *Id.* at 606. *See also* Steven Shavell, *The Social versus the Private Incentive to Bring Suit in a Costly Legal System*, 11 J. LEGAL STUD. 333 (1982).

23. Prison Litigation Reform Act, Pub. L. No. 104–34, tit. 8, §§ 801–10, 110 Stat. 1321, 1321–66 to 77 (1996). 28 U.S.C. § 1915(b) excludes prisoners from ordinary in forma pauperis provisions. § 1914(a) sets the filing fee at $350, but some district courts include an additional $50 "administrative fee," bringing the filing fee up to $400. For an overview of the issues, see Margo Schlanger, *Inmate Litigation*, 116 HARV. L. REV. 1555 (2003).

24. 42 U.S.C. § 1997e(d)(3) caps defendants' liability for attorneys' fees in civil rights cases at 150 percent of the rate paid publicly appointed defense counsel, and § 1997e(d)(2) has been read to further cap defendants' liability for attorneys' fees in monetary civil rights cases at 150 percent of the judgment. *Robbins v. Chronister*, 435 F.3d 1238 (10th Cir. 2006) (en banc). The quote from the jail supervisor is from Schlanger, *Inmate Litigation*, 116 HARV. L. REV. at 1655. On the constitutionality of the law, Judge Tatel wrote in a concurring opinion arguing that the three-strikes provision ought to be ruled unconstitutional: "It is undoubtedly true that much prisoner litigation is not only frivolous and abusive, but also imposes substantial costs on the federal courts. That said, it is also undoubtedly true that some prisoners have legitimate constitutional claims." Thomas v. Holder, 750 F.3d 899, 909 (D.C. Cir. 2014). Decisions upholding prisoners' right to a library to enable them to sue to protect their fundamental rights include *Wolff v. McDonnell*, 418 U.S. 539 (1974) (affirming prisoner's right to bring civil rights suit) and *Bounds v. Smith*, 430 U.S. 817 (1977) (affirming prisoner's right to adequate law library).

25. For an analysis of the effects of the PLRA in recent times, see Margo Schlanger, *Trends in Prisoner Litigation, as the PLRA Enters Adulthood*, 5 U.C. IRVINE L. REV. 153, 178 (2015).

26. As Justice Blackmun observed, in a case overruled by the PLRA, "Because a prisoner ordinarily is divested of the privilege to vote, the right to file a court action might be said to be his remaining most fundamental political right, because preservative of all rights." McCarthy v. Madigan, 503 U.S. 140, 153 (1992) (quotation from *Yick Wo v. Hopkins*, 118 U.S. 356, 370 (1886) omitted), *superseded by statute* 42 USC § 1997e.

27. For a discussion of the erosion of class action doctrine, see Klonoff, *The Decline of the Class Action*, introduction, note 43. The argument that class actions "blackmail" defendants into settling meritless suits has been made by prominent judges. *See, e.g.,* HENRY J. FRIENDLY, FEDERAL JURISDICTION: A GENERAL VIEW 120 (1973); In re Rhone-Poulenc Rorer, Inc., 51 F.3d 1293, 1299–300 (7th Cir. 1995). There are many other cases which are cited in Charles Silver, *"We're Scared to Death": Class Certification and Blackmail*, 78 N.Y.U. L. REV. 1357, 1358 (2003). For a deconstruction and refutation of these arguments see Bruce Hay & David Rosenberg, *"Sweetheart" and "Blackmail" Settlements in Class Actions: Reality and Remedy*, 75 NOTRE DAME L. REV. 1377, 1379 (2000); Warren F. Schwartz, *Long-Shot Class Actions: Toward a Normative Theory of Uncertainty*, 8 LEGAL THEORY 297, 298 (2002); Silver, *"We're Scared to Death,"* id.

28. AT&T Mobility LLC v. Concepcion, 131 S. Ct. 1740 (2011). For academic discussion of these developments see Judith Resnik, *Fairness in Numbers: A*

Comment on AT&T v. Concepcion, Wal-Mart v. Dukes, *and* Turner v. Rogers, 125 HARV. L. REV. 78 (2011). For a counterpoint on arbitration's possibilities see Michael A. Helfland, *Arbitration's Counter-Narrative: The Religious Arbitration Paradigm*, 124 YALE L. J. 2994 (2015).

29. Judith Resnik, *Diffusing Disputes: The Public in the Private of Arbitration, the Private in the Courts and the Erasure of Rights*, 124 YALE L. J. 2680 (2015).

30. Am. Exp. Co. v. Italian Colors Rest., 133 S. Ct. 2304, 2311 (2013). Of course the law might be enforced by the Department of Justice filing an antitrust suit or a plaintiff with enough resources to bring a suit on his or her own, such as the retailer Walmart. I discussed the possibilities for enforcement beyond private litigation in chapter 1.

31. Bell Atlantic v. Twombly, 550 U.S. 544 (2007). *See also* Ashcroft v. Iqbal, 556 U.S. 662 (2009). In that case the Court's concern about high-ranking officials has special resonance for the idea of equality in the context of civil rights where special solicitude for the government can lead to what appears to be an antiplaintiff bias.

32. Twombly, 550 U.S. at 560. The Court cited no empirical evidence for the proposition that expensive discovery pushes defendants to settle nonmeritorious cases.

33. Ashcroft v. Iqbal, 556 U.S. 662, 686 (2009); U.S. CONST., ART. II, SEC. 3.

34. The issue of prioritization (with attention to the attendant complexities) is set out in I. Glenn Cohen, *Rationing Legal Services*, 5 J. LEGAL ANALYSIS 221, 254 (2013). For a proposal that would make fee shifting universal, see Issachar Rosen-Zvi, *Just Fee Shifting*, 37 FLORIDA STATE L. REV. 717 (2010).

35. For a learned volume on the barriers of access to justice with suggestions for reform, see DEBORAH L. RHODE, ACCESS TO JUSTICE (2004). For a description of the idea of unbundling legal services, see Deborah L. Rhode, *Access to Justice: A Roadmap for Reform*, 41 FORDHAM URBAN L. J. 1227, 1241–52 (2014). Molly M. Jennings & D. James Greiner, *The Evolution of Unbundling in Litigation Matters: Three Case Studies and a Literature Review*, 89 DENV. U. L. REV. 825 (2012). For a history of complaints about access to justice see Deborah L. Rhode, *Too Much Law, Too Little Justice: Too Much Rhetoric, Too Little Reform*, 11 GEO. J. LEGAL ETHICS 989 (1999). For a description of an experimental study currently under way see Dalié Jiménez et al., *Improving the Lives of Individuals in Financial Distress Using a Randomized Control Trial: A Research and Clinical Approach*, 20 GEO. J. ON POVERTY L. & POL'Y 449 (2013). Nearly half the states had created access to justice commissions as of 2012. Richard Zorza, Turner v. Rogers: *The Implications for Access to Justice Strategies*, 95 JUDICATURE 255, 265 (2012). For a policy description on how courts can be made more accessible for pro se litigants, see RICHARD ZORZA, THE NAT'L CENTER FOR STATE COURTS, THE SELF-HELP FRIENDLY COURT: DESIGNED FROM THE GROUND UP TO WORK FOR PEOPLE WITHOUT LAWYERS (2002). I should also note here that in some cases, such as those involving family law, people want a less adversarial proceeding and as a result may prefer not to have a lawyer who will change the dynamic. *See* Rebecca Aviel, *Why Civil Gideon Won't Fix Family Law*, 122 YALE L. J. 2016, 2117–18 (2013).

36. Martin v. Franklin Capital Corp., 546 U.S. 132, 139 (2005) ("Discretion is not whim, and limiting discretion according to legal standards helps promote the basic principle of justice that like cases should be decided alike"); Lahav, *The Case for "Trial by Formula,"* chapter 3, note 15, at 634; Rubenstein, *The Concept of Equality in Civil Procedure, supra* note 2 at 1893. For examples of the Supreme Court's concern about inconsistency in litigation see, e.g., *Exxon Shipping Co. v. Baker,* 554 U.S. 471, 499 (2008) (expressing concern about unpredictability in punitive damages awards), *Metro-North Commuter R. Co. v. Buckley,* 521 U.S. 424, 433 (1997) (expressing concern about threats of "unlimited and unpredictable liability"), and *Consolidated Rail Corp. v. Gottshall,* 512 U.S. 532 (1994) (same). *But see* Hana Financial, Inc. v. Hana Bank, 135 S. Ct. 907, 912 (2015) ("The fact that another jury, hearing the same case, might reach a different conclusion may make the system 'unpredictable', but it has never stopped us from employing juries in [the tort, contract, and criminal justice] contexts").

37. The variation in Vioxx verdicts is described in Alexandra D. Lahav, *Recovering the Social Value of Jurisdictional Redundancy,* 82 TULANE L. REV. 2369, 2380 (2008); Howard M. Erichson & Benjamin C. Zipursky, *Consent versus Closure,* 96 CORNELL L. REV. 265, 277–80 (2011) (describing the Vioxx litigation and settlement). For a more theoretical treatment of the idea of a lottery in adjudication, see Adam M. Samaha, *Randomization in Adjudication,* 51 WM. & MARY L. REV. 1 (2009). The quote is from *Hana Financial, Inc.,* 135 S. Ct. at 912.

38. For a proposal to equalize outcomes, see Edward K. Cheng, *When 10 Trials Are Better Than 1000: An Evidentiary Perspective on Trial Sampling,* 160 U. PA. L. REV. 955 (2012). On the philosophical debate about whether equality means anything more than applying the law to the facts of the case, see generally PETER WESTEN, SPEAKING OF EQUALITY: AN ANALYSIS OF THE RHETORICAL FORCE OF "EQUALITY" IN MORAL AND LEGAL DISCOURSE (1990) (focusing on the confusion created by resorting to principles of equality); Peter Westen, *The Empty Idea of Equality,* 95 HARV. L. REV. 537, 542 (1982). For some responses to these arguments, see generally Erwin Chemerinsky, *In Defense of Equality: A Reply to Professor Westen,* 81 MICH. L. REV. 575 (1983); Kent Greenawalt, *How Empty Is the Idea of Equality?,* 83 COLUM. L. REV. 1167 (1983); Kent Greenawalt, *"Prescriptive Equality": Two Steps Forward,* 110 HARV. L. REV. 1265 (1997); Kenneth W. Simons, *The Logic of Egalitarian Norms,* 80 B.U. L. REV. 693 (2000); Jeremy Waldron, *The Substance of Equality,* 89 MICH. L. REV. 1350 (1991).

39. These problems are discussed in greater detail in Lahav, *The Case for "Trial by Formula,"* chapter 3, note 15 at 624.

40. KENNETH R. FEINBERG, WHAT IS LIFE WORTH? THE UNPRECEDENTED EFFORT TO COMPENSATE THE VICTIMS OF 9/11, at 21–26, 182–83 (2005).

41. The historical development of wrongful-death damages tracks a recognition of value in persons who had previously not been valued (monetarily) by the legal system. John Fabian Witt, *From Loss of Services to Loss of Support: The Wrongful Death Statutes, the Origins of Modern Tort Law, and the Making of the Nineteenth-Century Family,* 25 LAW & SOC. INQUIRY 717 (2000); JOHN FABIAN WITT, THE

ACCIDENTAL REPUBLIC: CRIPPLED WORKINGMEN, DESTITUTE WIDOWS AND THE REMAKING OF AMERICAN LAW 22 (2006).

42. I don't mean to imply that on every legal issue state laws differ widely, but only that there are differences and these differences can matter.

43. For a general overview of juries and judges see Shari Seidman Diamond, *Juries* in INTERNATIONAL ENCYCLOPEDIA OF THE SOCIAL AND BEHAVIORAL SCIENCES 907–12 (2nd ed., 2015). For a discussion of the need for uniformity and whether it is as important a value as is often claimed (with a focus on the federal system) see Amanda Frost, *Overvaluing Uniformity*, 94 VA. L. REV. 1567, 1568 (2008).

44. Neil Vidmar & Jeffrey J. Rice, *Assessments of Noneconomic Damage Awards in Medical Negligence: A Comparison of Jurors with Legal Professionals*, 78 IOWA L. REV. 883, 890–91 (1993). Some studies show that deliberation increases jury verdicts. Shari Seidman Diamond & Jonathan D. Casper, *Blindfolding the Jury to Verdict Consequences: Damages, Experts, and the Civil Jury*, 26 LAW & SOC'Y REV. 513, 554–57 (1992) (conducting a study demonstrating an increase in jury awards after deliberation); David Schkade et al., *Deliberating about Dollars: The Severity Shift*, 100 COLUM. L. REV. 1139, 1140–41 (2000) (same). How we evaluate this finding depends on what one thinks of the amount jurors award absent deliberation—is it too low or just right?

45. Robert L. Rabin, *The Tobacco Litigation: A Tentative Assessment*, 51 DEPAUL L. REV. 331 (2001); PETER PRINGLE, CORNERED: BIG TOBACCO AT THE BAR OF JUSTICE (1998). For a sophisticated discussion of the relationship between past cases and present cases, see Kent Greenawalt, *How Empty Is the Idea of Equality?*, 83 COLUM. L. REV. 1167, 1173 (1983).

46. *See* Robert M. Cover, *The Uses of Jurisdictional Redundancy: Interest, Ideology, Innovation*, 22 WM. & MARY L. REV. 639 (1981); Alexandra D. Lahav, *Recovering the Social Value of Jurisdictional Redundancy*, 82 TUL. L. REV. 2369 (2008).

47. In the federal courts, judges may overturn jury verdicts only if the judge finds no reasonable juror could have reached the verdict and may remit an award only if it is so large that it "shock[s] the conscience." 11 CHARLES ALAN WRIGHT, ARTHUR R. MILLER & MARY KAY KANE, FEDERAL PRACTICE AND PROCEDURE § 2815 (2d ed., 1995); FED. R. CIV. P. 59 (announcing the standard for a new trial and altering a judgment). In some state courts the standard is lower. For example, in New York the standard is whether the verdict deviates materially from what would be reasonable compensation. N.Y. C.P.L.R. § 5501(c) (MCKINNEY 1995). On using comparable cases to calculate remittiturs, see Joseph B. Kadane, *Calculating Remittiturs*, 8 LAW PROB. & RISK 125, 125–26 (2009).

48. A *National Law Journal* survey of a sample of 348 state and 57 federal judges found that two-thirds of the judges said that jury awards are excessive in only a few or in "virtually no" cases. Neil Vidmar, *The Performance of the American Civil Jury: An Empirical Perspective*, 40 ARIZ. L. REV. 849, 854 (1998) (citing *The View from the Bench: A National Law Journal Poll*, NAT'L L.J., Aug. 10, 1987, at 1); Brian Ostrom et al., *A Step above Anecdote: A Profile of the Civil Jury in the 1990s*, 79 JUDICATURE 233 (1996) (finding low rates of reversal of jury verdicts). Yet jury verdicts in medical malpractice cases are often reduced. In medical malpractice cases, one study found that plaintiffs ultimately received an average of 60 to 70

percent of the jury's award. The larger the verdict, the greater the reduction in the compensation plaintiffs ultimately received. In a study of medical malpractice verdicts over one million dollars, plaintiffs received an average of 37 percent of the original verdict. Neil Vidmar et al., *Jury Awards in Medical Malpractice: A Profile of Awards, Proportions for General Damages, and Post-Verdict Adjustments*, 42 DePAUL L. REV. 265 (1998) (finding plaintiffs receive lower amounts than the jury awarded, a median of 73 percent less and a mean of 60 percent less); Neil Vidmar et al., *Million-Dollar Medical Malpractice Cases in Florida: Post-Verdict and Pre-Suit Settlements*, 59 VAND. L. REV. 1343 (2006) (finding that the largest verdicts have the largest reductions and that in large verdicts plaintiffs received an average of 37 percent of the jury verdict).

49. I have written elsewhere on how this approach could be improved using basic observations from statistics, including the use of random sampling of trials. *See* Lahav, *The Case for "Trial by Formula,"* chapter 3, note 15.

50. *See* Samuel Issacharoff & John Fabian Witt, *The Inevitability of Aggregate Settlement: An Institutional Account of American Tort Law*, 57 VAND. L. REV. 1571, 1585 (2004) (explaining that beginning in the 1880s, work injuries were often compensated by using standardized settlement practices); Nora Freeman Engstrom, *Run-of-the-Mill Justice*, 22 GEO. J. LEGAL ETHICS 1485, 1532–33 (2009) (explaining that settlement negotiators and insurance adjusters have a common understanding of certain injuries' values).

51. Elizabeth S. Anderson, *What Is the Point of Equality?* 109 ETHICS 287, 313 (1999). "This is the lively hope named by the word equality: no more bowing and scraping, fawning and toadying; no more fearful trembling; no more high-and-mightiness; no more masters, no more slaves." MICHAEL WALZER, SPHERES OF JUSTICE xiii (1989); Jason M. Solomon, *Civil Recourse as Social Equality*, 39 FLA. ST. U. L. REV. 243, 255 (2011).

EPILOGUE

1. DIRECTV, Inc. v. Imburgia, 136 S. Ct. 463, 471 (2015).

2. For example, a significant part of Robert Kagan's argument against litigation in his book is that the results of litigation are inconsistent. ROBERT A. KAGAN, ADVERSARIAL LEGALISM: THE AMERICAN WAY OF LAW 141 (2003). In chapter 3 we saw the reasons for this inconsistency, many of which are embedded into our federal form of government. There is indeed evidence, as Kagan claims, that Americans prefer adversarial systems to nonadversarial ones, including the turn against no-fault regimes that would seem to be beneficial. For an incisive analysis, Nora Freeman Engstrom, *Exit, Adversarialism, and the Stubborn Persistence of Tort*, 6 J. TORT L. 75 (2013) (noting that no-fault regimes suffer from lower payouts as compared to the tort system, as well as increased adversarialism over time); Nora Freeman Engstrom, *An Alternative Explanation for No-Fault's "Demise,"* 61 DePAUL L. REV. 303 (2012) (tracing the convergence of no-fault and fault systems). However, as we saw in the introduction, there is also evidence that the adversarialism expressed by the creation of private rights of action in the US system can also be explained as a structural phenomenon. The argument is

well made by Sean Farhang in his book THE LITIGATION STATE, introduction, note 18.

3. On the colonial period see BRUCE H. MANN, NEIGHBORS AND STRANGERS: LAW AND COMMUNITY IN EARLY CONNECTICUT 68 (1987). On the 1850s see Stephen N. Subrin, *David Dudley Field and the Field Code: A Historical Analysis of an Earlier Procedural Vision*, 6 LAW & HIST. REV. 311 (1988). The 1906 speech, which had a significant effect, is found at Roscoe Pound, *The Causes of Popular Dissatisfaction with the Administration of Justice*, 40 AM. L. REV. 729 (1906). Still, many were excluded. For a history of the courts from the perspective of how they have not helped those most in need in society, see JEROLD S. AUERBACH, UNEQUAL JUSTICE (1973). For a description of the reaction to the rights revolution in the 1960s, see Galanter, *The Turn Against Law*, introduction, note 3; Galanter, *The Vanishing Trial*, introduction, note 23 at 489, Figure 19 (2004) (showing a rise in filings from 1962 to 1986 and a decline thereafter). On the role of the Second World War in this decline, see James R. Maxeiner, *The Federal Rules at 75: Dispute Resolution, Private Enforcement or Decisions According to Law?*, 30 GA. ST. U. L. REV. 983, 1003 (2014) (quoting Judge Alfred P. Murrah). Marc S. Galanter, *Real-World Torts: An Antidote to Anecdote*, 55 MD. L. REV. 1093, 1103 (1996) ("it should be noted that per capita litigation rates were higher at some points in nineteenth and early twentieth century America—and higher still, from the few studies we have, in colonial America"); Marc S. Galanter, *Reading the Landscape of Disputes: What We Know and Don't Know (and Think We Know) about Our Allegedly Contentious and Litigious Society*, 31 UCLA L. REV. 4, 39 (1983) (discussing evidence of nineteenth-century filing rates). For a judicial expression of the view that litigation rates were too high, see *Lepucki v. Van Wormer*, 765 F.2d 86, 87 (7th Cir. 1985) (per curiam) ("Relatively low barriers to entry have . . . generated an undesirable result—a deluge of frivolous or vexatious claims filed by the uninformed, the misinformed, and the unscrupulous").

4. Galanter, *The Turn Against Law*, introduction, note 3; SARA STASZAK, NO DAY IN COURT: ACCESS TO JUSTICE AND THE POLITICS OF JUDICIAL RETRENCHMENT (2015).

5. The law requiring the publication of these statistics is the Civil Justice Reform Act of 1990, 28 U.S.C. § 476. A study has found that motions decided increased right before the deadline for measuring productivity, indicating that judges are deciding motions in response to the threat of publicity. INSTITUTE FOR THE ADVANCEMENT OF THE AMERICAN LEGAL SYSTEM, CIVIL CASE PROCESSING IN THE FEDERAL DISTRICT COURTS: A 21ST-CENTURY ANALYSIS 78–79 (2009).

6. Hon. William G. Young & Jordan M. Singer, *Bench Presence: Toward a More Complete Model of Federal District Court Productivity*, 118 PENN ST. L. REV. 55, 258, 273 (2013); Jordan M. Singer & Hon. William G. Young, *Measuring Bench Presence: Federal District Judges in the Courtroom, 2008–2012*, 118 PENN ST. L. REV. 243, 258, 273 (2013) (describing data of the decline in courtroom hours and that there is no correlation between bench presence and speed of case resolution); Steven S. Gensler & Hon. Lee H. Rosenthal, *Pretrial Bench Presence*, 48 NEW ENG. L. REV. 475, 483 (2014); Steven S. Gensler & Lee H. Rosenthal, *The Reappearing Judge*, 61 KAN. L. REV. 849, 853 (2013); Mark R. Kravitz, *Written*

and Oral Persuasion in the United States Courts: A District Judge's Perspective on Their History, Function, and Tenure, 10 J. APP. PRAC. & PROCESS 247, 263 (2009). Whether the finding regarding speed is robust is a separate question, and there may well be judges for whom additional bench presence would cut into the speed of case resolution. For a discussion of other options, including fast tracking some cases, see Stephen B. Burbank & Stephen N. Subrin, *Litigation and Democracy: Restoring a Realistic Prospect of Trial,* 46 HARV. C.R.–C.L. L. REV. 399 (2011). One important criticism of the fast-track approach is that the rules of procedure already permit such broad discretion for judges that they could bring cases to trial without a formal rule system that sets a certain class of cases apart for a different, perhaps lesser, process. The relationship between speed and accuracy in adjudication is addressed in A. A. Zuckerman, *Quality and Economy in Civil Procedure—The Case for Commuting Correct Judgments for Timely Judgments,* 14 OXFORD J. LEGAL STUD. 353 (1994).

7. Oscar G. Chase & Jonathan Thong, *Judging Judges: The Effect of Courtroom Ceremony on Participant Evaluation of Process Fairness-Related Factors,* 24 YALE J.L. & HUMAN. 221, 232 (2012).

8. One of the core features of the current system is that it is supposed to apply the same procedures to cases about very different disputes—civil rights and anti-trust, accidents and contracts. There have been some suggestions that cases about different subject matter should have different rules, and already legislation has carved out some cases for different treatment in an attempt to curb controversial types of suits, such as the Private Securities Litigation Reform Act, for example; see Pub. L. No. 104–67, 109 Stat. 737 (1995) (codified in scattered sections of 15 U.S.C.). The benefit of giving all suits the same procedures, and binding both sides to the same requirements, is that it gives more powerful parties an incentive to fight for fair rules for both sides because they know that the same rules will be applied to them. But where some types of litigants frequently find themselves on one side of a lawsuit, they will have every incentive to shape the litigation process to increase their own chances of success at the expense of the opposing side. *See* Marc Galanter, *Planet of the APs: Reflections on the Scale of Law and Its Users,* 53 BUFF. L. REV. 1369 (2006). Tightened pleading standards in federal court benefit organizational defendants who hold information over individual plaintiffs who do not, and constraints on class actions operate similarly. *See* Alexandra D. Lahav, *Symmetry and Class Action Litigation,* 60 UCLA L. REV. 1494 (2013). Perhaps a better way to shift the conversation to what is really at stake—our ability to promote democratic deliberation through litigation—is to address the specific power dynamics and constraints in discrete areas of law and to fashion a procedure consistent with democratic values for each. For support of the idea of special rules for different cases, see Stephen N. Subrin, *The Limitations of Transubstantive Procedure: An Essay in Adjusting the "One Size Fits All" Assumption,* 87 DENV. U. L. REV. 377, 387 (2010).

INDEX

abstention, 171n29, 180n41, 181n4
access to courts. *See* equality
access to information. *See* information, access to; transparency
accountability, 8, 32–34, 47, 54, 161n37 of government representatives, 84, 86 overlap with answerability and deterrence, 87, 166n2
activism and civil rights, 41–46
ADA. *See* Americans with Disabilities Act
adoption, 64
administrative agencies
expertise, 35–36, 167n6
regulation by, 35–37
adversarialism, 85, 95, 110, 117, 198n2
adverse impact, 160n31
Affordable Care Act litigation, 160n29
Agent Orange litigation. *See* Vietnam veterans
Air Force, 73–75
Alien Tort Claims Act, 68, 177n19
alternative dispute resolution, 14. *See* arbitration; settlement

American Express Co. v. Italian Colors Restaurant (2013), 127–28, 164–165n48, 168n10, 178n27, 195n30
American Law Institute, 94, 184n22
American Society of Anesthesiologists, 61–62
Americans with Disabilities Act of 1990 (ADA), 31, 33, 40
Anderson, Elizabeth, 140, 189n2, 198n51
answerability, 32–34, 47, 54, 175n7 overlap with accountability and deterrence, 87, 166n2
antidiscrimination. *See* Civil Rights Act; civil rights cases; discrimination
antitrust cases, 33, 37, 104, 128, 130, 168n10, 188n41
appeals, 136, 138
Apple and Samsung patent litigation, 71
arbitration. *See also* arbitration agreements/clauses
benefits of using, 25–26, 164n45

arbitration (*Cont.*)
  change from "folklore" to
    "litigation"-like process, 164n46
  as constraint on litigation, 25–27
  preference over settlement, 185n23
  as privatization, 73, 163n45, 178n27
  small claims and, 163n43
  transparency lost due to, 73, 178n27
  unconscionability and, 26
  vindication of rights doctrine and, 26
arbitration agreements/clauses
  business-to-business transactions
    and, 158n17
  class actions prohibited in, 27,
    126–128, 164–165n48, 168n10
  in consumer contracts, 11, 25, 73,
    144, 164n47
Ashcroft, John, 72, 129, 143
Ashcroft v. Iqbal (2009), 1, 72, 129,
  151n1, 162n42, 177–178n22,
  178n26, 195n31, 195n33
asymmetry of parties in litigation,
  5, 161n36. *See also* information
  asymmetry
AT&T Mobility LLC v. Concepcion
  (2011), 127, 151n1, 164n48,
  178n27, 195n28
attorney-client relationship,
  183n12, 195n35
  incompetent representation,
    distortion of law resulting from, 118
attorneys' fees, 27–28, 165n50
  as bar to bringing suit, 131–132, 144
  in civil rights cases, 124–125, 194n24
  contingency fees, 193n19
  in private litigation, 39
automobile accidents, settlement of
  damages in, 139
automobile manufacturers
  damages caps limiting suits
    against, 47–49
  private venues chosen to resolve
    warranty complaints, 25, 164n45

backlash, 40, 42–43, 155n11,
  169n15, 169n17

Balkin, Jack M., 18, 160n29, 181n1
Batson v. Kentucky (1986), 190n4
Bell Atl. Corp. v. Twombly (2007),
  128–129, 162n42, 175n5, 178n22,
  195nn31–32
"bellwether" trials, 93, 97, 139,
  148, 184n19
Blakely v. Washington (2004),
  181n2, 185n28
Boddie v. Connecticut (1971), 119, 154n6,
  191n12, 191–192n14
Boies, David, 66
*Brown v. Board of Education of
  Topeka, Kan.* (1954), 18, 24,
  42–45, 163n44, 169–170nn17–18,
  170n21, 171n24
Bush, George W., 81
business
  arbitration agreements not used in
    business-to-business transactions,
    11, 26, 158n17
  commercial cases, 11, 157n15
  effect of litigation on, vii, 33, 126,
    152n2, 153n3

Carnegie v. Household Int'l (2004),
  121, 192n17
Casale v. Kelly (2010), 86, 116,
  121, 182n5
Catholic Church sexual abuse scandal,
  76, 179n31, 179n34
cell phones
  traffic accidents linked to use
    of, 62–63
Center for Auto Safety, 62,
  174–175n4, 176n10
Chaplin v. Du Pont Advance Fiber Sys.
  (2005), 18, 160n31
chokeholds, police use of, 21–22,
  161–162n40
city of. *See name of specific city*
civil case filings, 13–14, 156n12,
  157n15. *See also* federal courts;
  state courts; *specific types of cases*
Civil Justice Reform Act
  (1990), 199n5

Civil Rights Act (1964), 39, 42, 170n18
  Title VI, 34, 167n5
  Title VII, 64–65
civil rights cases, 41–46, 157n15,
    158n18, 163n42, 165n50, 193n20
  attorneys' fees and, 27–28,
    124–125, 194n24
  class actions, 94
  controversial nature of, 33
  criticisms of, 42, 71–72
  effectiveness of, 41
  fee shifting in, 131
  heightened pleading requirement
    in, 129
  number of claims filed, 11, 145
  number of trials, 13
  of prisoners, 124–125, 194n24
  pro se plaintiffs, 12. *See also*
    self-representation
  solicitude for government officials vs.
    civil rights of plaintiffs in, 72, 129,
    177–178n22, 195n31
civil rights movement, 43–44, 184n21
class actions, 151n1, 152n3, 161n37,
    163n43. *See also* mass tort claims
  accessibility for the disabled in Taco
    Bell case, 31–33, 166n1
  arbitration clauses prohibiting, 27,
    126–128, 164–165n48
  Brown v. Board of Education.
    See Brown v. Board of Education
    of Topeka, Kan.
  certification, 163n44
  considered "blackmail," xvii, 129,
    163n43, 194n27
  constraints on bringing of, 23–24,
    68–69, 126–128, 144, 163n43,
    177n21, 194n27, 200n8
  contingency fees and, 193n19
  developing alternative forms of
    participation in, 92
  foster care case in Texas, 24–25
  9/11 terror attacks, first responders'
    litigation, 95–97
  opportunities to participate
    in, 90–98

reasoned dialogue provided by
    litigation in, 84, 92, 94–95
  structuring aggregate settlement in,
    183–184n16
  trial participation of individual
    plaintiffs in, 92
  against unscrupulous debt collectors,
    54–55, 174n42
  vicarious participation, 93
  Vietnam veterans and Agent Orange,
    93, 184n20
Colgrove v. Battin (1973), 100, 186n31
commercial cases, 157n15
confidentiality agreements in settlements,
    75–78, 144. *See also* settlements,
    lack of transparency and
conservative impact litigation,
    8, 156n11
conspiracy claims, 128, 129
Constitution, U.S. *See also specific*
    Amendments
  Article II, sec. 3, 195n33
  Article III, 98
constraints on litigation, viii, 5–6,
    21–29, 143
  arbitration as, 25–27. *See also*
    arbitration agreements/clauses
  attorneys' fees limits as, 27–28.
    See also attorneys' fees
  class actions, limitations on, 23–24,
    27. *See also* class actions
  damages caps as, 28–29, 48–49.
    See also damages
  dangers of, 144–145
  discovery costs as. *See* discovery
  economic analysis and, 193n22
  litigation costs as. *See* costs of
    litigation
  personal jurisdiction as, 22, 143
  plausibility pleading as, 23, 162–163n42
  rules of procedure creating, 21, 59,
    143, 171n29
  settlements as, 27. *See also* settlements
  standing doctrine as, 21, 22,
    143, 162n40
  tort reform as, 28

Consumer Finance Protection Bureau, 35, 167n6
consumer law, 11, 145, 164nn45–47. *See also* arbitration agreements; automobile manufacturers; products liability cases
contempt proceedings, 102–103, 187n37
contracts cases
  jury awards, 14
  filings, 10–11, 33, 182n8
  number of trials, 13–14
  punitive damages, 159n24
copyright infringement, 19–20, 64, 161n34
corporate plaintiffs, 12, 158n21
corruption, 102–103
costs of litigation, vii, 20, 152n2, 153n3
  discovery, 60, 69–71, 128–129, 175n5, 195n32
  equality issues and, 123, 127, 131, 192nn14–15
  expert reports increasing, 28, 120
  fee shifting regimes, 123–124, 131, 192n16, 195n34
  government-driven litigation, 38
  insurance premium costs, 159n27
  medical malpractice suits, 53–54
  prisoner cases. *See* prisoner suits
COX-2 inhibitors, 36–37
criminal sentencing, 181n2
  advisory juries, use of, 108

Daimler AG v. Bauman (2014), 177n21
Daimler Benz, 68, 177n21
damages. *See also* jury verdicts and awards; punitive damages
  caps, 28–29, 48–49, 52, 106–108, 120–121, 144, 165n52, 173n39, 188n44, 192n15
  compensation matrix used to determine amount for settlements, 139–140
  equality and, 120–121, 135
  median jury awards, 14, 172n30
  pain and suffering damages, 136
  predictability of, 102, 196n36

  reasons for limitations on damages, 165n51–52
  wrongful death, 196n41
debt collection, unfair practices, 54–55, 174n42
decentralization of adjudication, 39, 134, 137–139, 141
Deepwater Horizon (2010), 91, 152n1, 183n15
default judgments, 13, 15–16
deliberative democracy, ix, 5, 15, 64, 84, 93–95, 98, 100, 105, 110, 148–149, 155n7, 156n13, 180n1, 200n8. *See also* reasoned dialogue
democracy. *See also* deliberative democracy
  equality as part of, 189n2
  individuals having day in court and, 160n27
  litigation's promotion of, vii, 1–2, 4, 6–9, 29–30, 82–83, 88, 110, 146, 193n20
  litigation's role in, under attack, 143
  self-government and, 6
deregulation, 19
deterrence effect of litigation, 32–34
  medical malpractice suits, 51–52
  overlap with answerability and accountability, 87, 166n2
  tort cases, 32, 47–49, 87, 162n41, 166n2
dignity, litigation as affirmation of, 32, 112–113, 147, 189n1
DIRECTV, Inc. v. Imburgia (2015), 144, 198n1
discovery, 8, 23, 56–57, 58–69
  Apple and Samsung patent litigation, 71
  costs of, 60, 69–71, 128–129, 175n5, 195n32
  critique of, 69–72, 143
  defendants learning of pattern of problems and able to fix by learning from, 61–62
  in medical malpractice cases, 61–62, 77–78
  protective orders, 75–76, 179n35

state secrets privilege and, 73–75,
181n26, 179n29
time and effort expended in, 71–72,
177–178n22
discrimination, 7. *See also* civil rights
cases; racial discrimination; sex
discrimination
prohibited in juror selection, 85, 114,
181n3, 190n3
distributive equality, 123, 193n21
"downhill" vs. "uphill" cases, 7, 155n10
due process, 88, 191n12,
192–193n18, 192n14
Dworkin, Ronald, 113, 189n1

E. coli
Jack in the Box fast food chain and,
49–50, 86–87, 182nn6–7
lax government regulation
and, 49–50
Odwalla apple juice and,
56–57, 174n1
education and schools
desegregation cases, 94. *See also
Brown v. Board of Educ. of
Topeka, Kan.*
playgrounds and liability issues, 16,
19, 159–160n27
religion and, 8
elections and voting
felons' disenfranchisement,
114, 190n3
jury service compared to voting, 98,
185–186n28
poll taxes, 190n4
right to sue vs. right to vote, 114
voter identification law, 6
Electronic Communications Privacy
Act, 74–75, 179n30
Ellsberg, Daniel, 3–5
employment discrimination, 12, 18,
160n31, 161n36, 169n16
enforcement of law, vii, 2, 4, 31–55, 144.
See also regulation
activism and case of civil rights, 41–46.
See also civil rights cases
in civil society, 54–55, 154n6

E. coli outbreak, 49–50. *See also E. coli*
effectiveness of litigation, 41, 87
government lawsuits, regulation
by, 37–38
limits on recovery curtailing, 47–49
medical malpractice litigation, 51–54.
See also medical malpractice cases
private lawsuits, regulation by,
38–41, 145
tort law, 47. *See also* tort cases
weak role of litigation in, 33
environmental cases, 33, 145
equality, vii, 2, 3, 4, 112–141
access to the courts, 7–8, 113–114,
145, 195n35
attorneys' fees as bar to filing suit,
131–132
of case outcomes, 114,
132–140, 196n36
class action limits and, 126–128
costs of litigation and, 123, 127, 131,
192nn14–15
criticisms of laws constraining,
123–132
distributive equality, 123, 193n21
formal equality distinguished
from material equality, 116–117,
130–131
formal inequality, examples of,
115–116
France (Anatole) on formal
equality, 191n9
individualized attention to cases and,
138–139
legislation limiting access to courts,
124–126, 192n15
liberty interest and, 143, 192n18
likelihood of repeat litigants gaining
success and, 118, 190n7
"litigation lottery" charges, 133,
138, 196n37
material inequality, 130–131,
135–136, 192n14
meaning of equality before the law,
140–141
need to lower bar to bringing suit for
weaker litigants, 130

equality (*Cont.*)
  pain and suffering damages in tort
    cases and, 136
  participation in self-government
    and, 6–7
  protection of, 119–123
  social inequality reflected in court
    system, 7, 114, 117–118
  societal change's effect on, ix, 137–138
equal protection, 42, 45, 120, 136,
    190n4, 191n12, 191n14, 192n15,
    192–193n18. *See also* Fourteenth
    Amendment
Exxon Valdez oil spill (1989), 152n1

fairness. *See also* justice
  consistent outcomes and, 132–134, 140
  like cases treated alike and, 115
  procedural fairness and perceptions
    of fairness, 185n23
  proposal to settle mass tort claims by
    plaintiff vote and, 94–95
  sanctions for frivolous actions
    and, 160n30
Fairness in Class Action Litigation Act,
    vii, 151n1
Farhang, Sean, 39, 153n3, 155n8,
    158n18, 171n29, 198n2
fast tracking of cases, 200n6
federal agencies, 35–36
Federal Arbitration Act, 73, 164n47
federal courts
  evaluation of judges in, 97–98,
    146–148, 199n5
  number of claims filed in, 13–14, 39,
    145, 157n15
  settlement rates, 158–159n22
Federal Judicial Center, 70
Federal Rules of Civil Procedure
  creating constraints on
    litigation, 21
  Rule 11, 160n30. *See also* frivolous
    litigation
  Rule 16, 165n49
  Rules 26–37, 174n3, 190n5. *See also*
    discovery

Rule 56, 165n49. *See also* summary
    judgment
fee shifting regimes, 123–124, 131,
    192n16, 195n34
Feinberg, Kenneth, 80, 135
felon disenfranchisement laws, 114, 190n3
Ferguson, Missouri police
    department, 38
filing rates, 10–12, 39, 51, 157n15
  historical perspective, 145
  arbitration, effect on, 163n43
Firestone tires litigation, 76–77
First Amendment, 4–5, 81–82, 86,
    116, 176n14
Floyd v. City of New York (2013), 63, 65,
    92–93, 108–109, 176nn11–12,
    176n16, 184nn17–18
Floyd v. Cosi, Inc. (2015), 89, 183n10
Food and Drug Administration (FDA),
    35–37, 93, 167n7
food safety. *See E. coli*
forbearance of courts to decide cases,
    38, 81–82, 168–169n14
Foreign Intelligence Surveillance Act,
    74–75, 179n30
foster care class action, 24–25
Fourteenth Amendment, 42, 75,
    190nn3–4
Fourth Amendment, 75, 92, 99–100, 109
Freedom of Information Act, 56, 62
freedom of speech, 4, 81–82, 86, 181n1.
    See also First Amendment
freedom of the press, 5
frivolous lawsuits
  business costs of, 152n2, 153n3
  class actions and, 126
  courts, effect on, 161n38, 199n3
  determining what constitutes,
    18–19, 193n22
  legislation to counter, vii–viii,
    151n1, 153n3
  medical malpractice and, 52–53, 174n41
  prisoner suits and, 124,
    125–126, 194n24
  sanctions to curtail, 160nn30–32
Fugitive Slave Act, 115–116, 190n6

Galanter, Marc S., 14, 153n3, 155n10,
    161nn37-38, 181n3, 182n8, 190n7,
    191nn10-11, 199n3, 200n8
General Motors faulty ignition cases,
    47–49, 58, 62, 179n35
Ginsburg, Ruth Bader, 144
government lawsuits, regulation by,
    37–38, 167n5
Guantánamo Bay prisoners, 60
Gutmann, Amy, ix, 152n4, 155n7,
    180n1, 181n4, 189n51

Hamilton, Alexander, 103, 187n39
Hana Financial, Inc. v. Hana Bank
    (2015), 102, 134, 187n36,
    196nn36-37
Hand, Learned, viii, 151–152n2
Harvard study on medical malpractice
    suits, 52–53, 173–174nn40–41
Hellerstein, Alvin, 95–96, 185n24
Holocaust Victim Assets Litigation,
    67–68, 177n18
homeless persons, loitering statute
    enforced against, 85–86, 116
hospitals. *See* medical malpractice cases
Howard, Philip K., viii, 151n1, 153n3
Hugo Boss, 68

incompetent representation, distortion
    of law resulting from, 118
inconsistency. *See* unpredictability
indigent persons, 85, 191n13
    fee waiver, 85
    right to counsel for, 85, 103, 148
individualism, 40, 132, 134, 138–140
individual rights, 5, 143
individual suits
    class actions vs. *See* class actions
    settlement rates, 158–159n22
inequality. *See* equality
information, access to, 8–9, 56–83,
    140, 144. *See also* discovery;
    transparency
information asymmetry between parties,
    23, 60, 69, 79, 175n5, 178n22
In re. See name of party

insurance companies, pricing of
    settlements by, 139, 198n50
insurance premium costs,
    159n27, 165n52
integration, 42. *See Brown v. Board of
    Education of Topeka, Kan.*
intelligent design case, 8
interest groups and regulatory
    agencies, 36

Jack in the Box fast food chain, 49–50,
    86–87, 182nn6-7
Jim Crow laws, 44, 171n25
J. McIntyre Mach., Ltd. v. Nicastro
    (2011), 22–23, 162n41
judges. *See also* judicial system reform
    attitudes toward litigants,
        102–103, 146
    compared to juries in terms of
        awards, 102, 137
    compared to juries in terms of
        fairness, 100–102, 109–110
    elected vs. appointed, 9, 156n13
    Founders' view of, 102
    incentives, 146–47
    pretrial role of, 161n38
    as strategic and political actors,
        181n1, 182n4
judicial process, defense of, 9
judicial review, 9, 138, 156n13,
    180n40, 190n3
judicial system reform, 8
    measurement of judicial performance,
        27, 97–98, 146–148, 199n5
juries and jury service, 6,
    84–85, 98–105
    advisory juries, use of, 108–109
    bench trial compared to jury trial,
        100–102, 109–110
    bias against certain litigants or
        defendants, 181n2, 186n32, 188n44
    as check to judicial and governmental
        action, 103–104, 186nn30–31
    compared to voting, 98, 185–186n28
    criticism of jury trial system,
        100–110, 186n32

juries and jury service (*Cont.*)
  deciding law as well as fact, 185n27
  discrimination prohibited in juror
    selection, 85, 114, 181n3
  inability to understand complex
    litigation, 104, 186n32
  jury instructions, use of,
    105–107, 188n42
  lack of commitment on part of jurors,
    allegations of, 105
  need to educate jurors, 106–107, 139,
    188n41, 188n45
  number of jury trials, 85, 100,
    144, 181n3
  pluralist society, fair consensus
    reached in, 101, 186n34
  reforms to improve, 110
  right to jury trial, 85, 98
  six-member vs. twelve-member civil
    juries, 186n31
  unavailability of jury reasoning,
    109–110, 189n50
  unpredictability of, 101–102,
    106, 136, 186n32,
    186n34, 196n36
jury verdicts and awards, 14
  compared to judge-awarded
    compensation, 102, 137
  damages caps and, 107–108,
    188n44
  deliberation's effect on, 197n44
  judges considering as
    reasonable, 197n48
  media reporting of, 10, 14, 16, 19, 47,
    172n30, 187n35
  in medical malpractice cases,
    197–198n48
  remittitur by judge or appellate
    review, 138, 197n47
  special verdict forms, use of, 189n50
justice, 4. *See also* fairness
  equal justice. *See* equality
  looking beyond constraints of trial
    for, 184n21
  minimum standards to
    achieve, 189n2

participation in litigation producing
  sense of, 96–97, 143
just society, 155n7

Kennedy, Anthony M., 129,
  177n22
Kennedy, Randall, 45, 171n23, 171n28
King, Martin Luther, Jr., 44,
  170n21, 187n37
Kiobel v. Royal Dutch Petroleum Co.
  (2013), 177n21
Klarman, Michael J., 43, 169n17,
  170n18, 170n20, 171nn24–25

Lane v. Franks (2014), 64, 176n14
Lassiter, Abby Gail, 89–90, 102, 146
*Lassiter v. Dep't of Soc. Serv. of Durham
  County, N.C.* (1981), 103,
  146, 183n11
Law, Bernard F. (cardinal), 76
law enforcement. *See*
  enforcement of law
lawsuit. *See* litigation
Lawsuit Abuse Reduction Act (2013),
  vii, 151n1
Ledbetter, Lilly, 64–65, 152n1
Ledbetter v. Goodyear Tire & Rubber Co.
  (2007), 65, 152n1, 176n15
legal process school, viii–ix, 154n7
lemon laws, 164n45
libel actions, 16–17, 160n28
liberty interest
  in due process cases, 192n14
  promotion of, 58
  tension with equality, 143, 192n18
Lilly Ledbetter Fair Pay Act (2009), 65,
  152n1, 176n15
litigation
  affirming human dignity, 32
  asymmetry of parties in, 5, 161n36
  constraints on, 5–6, 21–29. *See also*
    constraints on litigation
  costs of. *See* costs of litigation
  criticism of litigious society, vii, 5,
    151n1, 153n3, 156–157n14
  definition of, 6, 142

democratic value of, vii, 1–2, 4,
6–9, 29–30, 82–83, 88, 110,
146, 193n20
distracting government officials from
other work, 178n26, 195n31
effectiveness of, 33, 41, 148
enforcement of values through, 4, 148
filing rates, drivers of, 10–12,
123, 199n3
good vs. bad, 16–20, 123
individual plaintiffs vs.
organizational plaintiffs, 12
overview of, 10–16
"public-life conception" of, 181n1
rarity of trials, 13–14
reality vs. media reporting of, 10
reform. *See* reform proposals
silence of useful speech due to
intimidation of, 78
as social good, 142
solicitude for government officials vs.
civil rights of plaintiffs in, 72, 129,
177–178n22, 195n31
Los Angeles, City of v. Lyons (1983),
21–22, 161–162nn39–40
losing party and losses in litigation
publicity for, 8, 64, 155–156n11
spurring legislation, 65, 90
value of litigation compared to loss
rates of plaintiffs, 193n22
lottery, litigation as, 133, 138, 196n37
Lyons, Adolph, 21–22

marriage equality, 66, 110, 177n17
Massachusetts Constitution, Article
XXX, 112, 189n1
mass tort claims, 88, 91, 93–94, 153n3,
158n18. *See also* Vioxx litigation
ethical issues raised in, 184n16
proposal to settle by plaintiff
vote, 94–95
media reporting
juror revealing reasoning in
interview, 189n50
perception of large verdicts and, 10,
14, 16, 19, 47, 172n30, 187n35

mediation, 14
medical malpractice cases, 28, 47,
51–54, 153n3, 156n14
American Society of
Anesthesiologists (ASA)
and, 61–62
confidentiality agreement as part of
settlement, 77–78
dropping suit after discovery, 61
hospital use of litigation data to
assess risk and change procedures,
61–62, 172–173n37, 175n7
jury verdicts in, 197–198n48
statute of limitations and, 28,
165n51
Merck pharmaceutical company, 91,
93, 133, 183n15. *See also* Vioxx
litigation
mergers and acquisitions
litigation, 193n22
M.L.B. v. S.L.J. (1996), 119, 191n13
Model Rules of Professional
Conduct, 179n32
Moeller v. Taco Bell Corp. (2014),
31–33, 166n1
*Montgomery, City of v. Montgomery
Improvement Ass'n* (1957),
45, 171n28
Montgomery bus boycott (1955),
44–45
motion practice, 147
motions to dismiss, 12, 13
Mueller, Robert, 129, 143
Murphy, Frank, 115
music downloading. *See* copyright
infringement

narratives
historians construct of, 177n19
litigation as test of narratives, 66
litigation's production of explanatory
narratives, 57–58, 61, 65–67, 82,
144, 184n21
National Highway Traffic Safety
Administration, 62
National Security Agency (NSA), 74

national security concerns, 3, 5,
154nn4-5
state secrets privilege and, 73–75,
178n26, 179n29
New York City Police Department, 9,
63, 65, 85–86, 156n12,
176n12
New York Legal Aid Society, 38
New York State study of medical
malpractice, 51
New York Times, 3–5, 154nn4–5
New York Times Co. v. United States
(1971), 154n4
9/11 terror attacks, tort litigation from,
95–97, 110, 135, 185nn24–25
no-fault regimes, 198n2
nonenforcement norm, 161n37
nonlawyers' role in litigation, 132
North Carolina voter
identification law, 6

Odwalla, 56–57, 174n1
Oil spills, 1, 91, 113, 152n1
*Oil Spill by the Oil Rig "Deepwater
Horizon" in the Gulf of Mexico, on
April 20, In re* (2012), 113, 183n15

parental activism, 159–160n27
*Parents Involved in Community Schools
v. Seattle District No. 1* (2007),
43, 170n19
participation in self-government, vii, 2,
3, 6–7, 84–111, 144, 155n9
collective litigation, participation in,
90–98. *See also* class actions
individual bringing constitutional
violation to court as form of, 156n13
jury service as, 84–85, 98–105.
See also juries and jury service
litigant as participant, 84–88
9/11 terror attacks, litigation
over, 95–97
self-representation and, 88–90
vicarious participation, 93
voting system proposal to settle mass
tort cases, flaws in, 94–95

patent cases
Apple and Samsung, 71
controversial nature of, 33
penalties. *See also* punitive damages
copyright infringement, 161n34
Pentagon Papers, 3–5
personal jurisdiction, 22, 143
plausibility pleading, 23, 162–163n42
pleading standards, 143, 158n20,
162–163n42, 200n8
PLRA. *See* Prison Litigation Reform Act
pluralist society and reaching a fair consensus, 101–102, 149
police officers
chokeholds, use of, 21–22,
161–162n40
Ferguson, Missouri police
department, 38
learning from lawsuits to improve
performance, 169n16, 188n43
New York City police department, 9,
63, 65, 156n12, 176n12
Portland, Oregon police
department, 41–42
reasonable conduct of, jury
determination of, 99, 105
stop and frisk and racial profiling, 9,
63, 65, 92–93, 156n12, 176n12,
184nn17–18
political participation. *See* participation
in self-government
poll taxes, 190n4
popular sovereignty, 187n40
Portland, Oregon police
department, 41–42
Posner, Richard, 121, 167n5, 178n22
Pound, Roscoe, 29, 145, 199n3
powerless groups. *See also* indigent
persons
ideal of equal status for, 140–141
limited court access of, 124
material equality created for, 131
practice of law, changes in areas of
specialization, 12–13
preclusion doctrine, 171n29
preemption, 167n7

pretrial motions, 14, 159n22. *See also* motions to dismiss
prior restraint, 4
prisoner suits, viii, 38, 124–126, 141, 157n15, 194n23
excessive force, 38
Prison Litigation Reform Act (PLRA), 124–126, 151n1, 190n3, 194n23, 194nn25–26
privacy rights vs. government electronic surveillance for national security purposes, 74–75
private lawsuits, regulation by, 38–41, 145
Private Securities Litigation Reform Act (1995), 151n1, 200n8
procedural limits on litigation, 5, 144–145, 155n8, 171n29
products liability cases, 28, 162n41
jury awards, 14
media reporting of verdicts, 172n30
pro-se litigants. *See* self-representation
protective orders, 75–76, 179n35
Public Citizen, 62
public/private distinction and value of litigation, 193n20
punitive damages, 14, 47, 49, 159n24, 196n36

qualified immunity doctrine, 81–82, 180n39

racial discrimination, 160n31
education, 94
fugitive slaves, treatment of, 115–116
juror prejudice against black defendants, 181n2
police department using racial profiling, 9, 63, 65, 92–93, 108–109, 110, 176n12, 184nn17–18
prohibited in juror selection, 85, 114, 181n3, 190n3
racially restrictive covenants, 193n20
transportation, 44
Rakoff, Jed S., 38
rational basis review, 192n15

rationality of adjudication, 155n7
Rawls, John, viii, 152n3, 189n51
reasonableness standard, 99–100, 181n4, 186n30
reasoned dialogue provided by litigation, viii–ix, 3, 5, 29, 84, 92, 94–95, 110, 142
reform proposals, x, 29–30, 147–149, 153n3
"bellwether" trials, use of, 93, 97, 139, 148, 184n19
database creation to capture settlement information, 79–80, 148
judicial productivity measures, 147–148
juries and jury service, 110, 148
motion practice, 147
right to counsel for indigent persons, 148
separate procedures for separate types of cases, 200n8
settlements, limitations on, 148
regulation, 34–41. *See also* enforcement of law
by agency, 35–37
debates over, 20
deregulation, 19, 167n3
by government lawsuits, 37–38, 167n5
litigation and, 34
by private lawsuits, 38–41
types of, 34–35
regulatory capture, 36–37, 38
religion and education, 8
resistance and oppression narratives, 155–156n11
Reynolds, United States v. (1953), 73–75, 178n28, 179n29
right to counsel, 90, 103, 182n10, 183n12
for indigent persons, 85, 103
termination of parental rights cases, 89–90, 183n12
right to have rights, 113, 126, 189n2
right to jury trial, 85. *See also* Seventh Amendment

risk management, 41, 51, 57, 61–62, 172n37
rule of law, 1, 4, 154n6, 155n9
    costs of litigation and, 131
    democracy and, 6
    enforcement as crucial to, 55, 87, 127
    equality before the law and, 115, 124
    future of, 33
    prisoner cases and, 125
rules of procedure. *See also* Federal Rules of Civil Procedure
    creating constraints on litigation, 21, 59, 143, 171n29
    equal access to the courts and, 115

Safety, 51–52, 62–63, 65, 87
    trade-off with expense, 159n27
    trade-off with secrecy needs, 78–79
"same actor" defense, 118, 191n11
same-sex marriage, 66, 110, 177n17
Sapir, Estelle, 67–68
Scalia, Antonin, 85, 128
Scheindlin, Shira, 108–109
schools. *See* education and schools
Schroeder v. Weighall (2014), 120, 192n15
Scott v. Harris (2007), 99–101, 105, 108, 186n29
search and seizure, 64, 75, 92, 186n30. *See also* Fourth Amendment; stop and frisk
Second Amendment, 156n11
Secret Service and qualified immunity, 81–82
Section 1983 actions, 188n43
Securities and Exchange Commission, 37
securities litigation, viii, 193n22
    Private Securities Litigation Reform Act (1995), 151n1, 200n8
self-defense, 6
self-government, 2, 3, 6–7, 84–111, 144. *See also* participation in self-government
self-representation, 12, 88–90, 125, 183n10, 195n35

September 11th Victim Compensation Fund, 96–97, 135
settlements
    access to information about previously settled cases, 140
    attorney pressure to accept, 27, 184n22
    cherry-picking settlement strategy, 118
    compensation matrix used to determine amount of damages, 139–140, 198n50
    database creation to capture settlement information, proposal for, 79–80, 148
    judicial power and, 27, 185n24
    lack of transparency and, 27, 56–58, 69, 75–79, 144, 178n26
    rates of, 13, 27, 158–159n22, 163n43
Seventh Amendment, 98, 108, 188n43. *See also* juries and jury service
sex discrimination, 64–65, 177n19, 181n3, 190n4
slavery, treatment of fugitive slaves, 115–116, 190n6
small claims, 10, 157n15, 163n43
Snowden, Edward, 4, 75, 154n5
social policy
    jury trials and, 98
    relationship with litigation, 19–20, 78–79, 87–88, 182n9
societal change. *See also* values
    information provided in litigation leading to, 58, 64–65
    jury service and, 84–85
    litigation as motivating, 8, 90
    outcomes of cases affected by, 137–138
    tort litigation and, 158n18
Sotomayor, Sonia, 102
standing, 21, 22, 143, 162n40
State v. See name of opposing party
state agencies, 35–36
state courts
    justice commissions, 195n35
    median jury awards in, 172n30

number of claims filed in, 10, 13,
157nn15–16
remittur by judge or appellate review,
197–198nn47–48
settlement rates, 158n22
variations in outcomes from state to
state, 133, 136, 197n42
state secrets privilege, 73–75,
178n26, 179n29
statute of limitations, 120, 153n3, 192n15
medical malpractice, 28, 165n51
Title VII of Civil Rights Act, 64–65
Stevens, John Paul, 99
stigma on the plaintiff, 20
stop and frisk and racial profiling, 9, 63,
65, 92–93, 108–109, 110, 156n12,
176n12, 184nn17–18
strict scrutiny, 192n15
summary judgments, 12, 144,
158n20, 165n49
sunshine litigation acts, 78, 179n35
Supreme Court, U.S.
avoiding making waves while striking
down Jim Crow laws, 171n25
on discovery costs, 175n5
as exemplar of public reason, 189n51
law declaration model and, 180n41
limiting substantive rights through
procedure, 171n29
moral deliberation in, 180n1
Swiss banks litigation, 67–68, 177n18
Sykes v. Mel S. Harris & Assocs., LLC
(2015), 54–55, 174n42

Taco Bell and accessibility for the
disabled, 31–33, 40, 166n1
termination of parental rights, 89–90,
183n12, 191n13
Thompson, Dennis, ix, 152n4, 155n7,
180n1, 181n4
tobacco litigation, 137–138
Tocqueville, Alexis de, 98, 185n27
tort cases, 10, 47, 157n15, 158n18.
See also damages; medical
malpractice cases
compensation principle in, 135–136
consumer safety cases, 47–50

controversial nature of, 33, 167n3
definition of tort, 165n51
deterrence effect of litigation, 32,
47–49, 87, 162n41, 166n2
effectiveness of, 41, 169n15
jury awards, 14
no-fault regimes, 198n2
number of claims filed, 11, 47
number of trials, 13–14
pain and suffering damages, 136
punitive damages, 159n24
relationship with agency rulemaking,
168–169nn14–15
societal change and, 158n18
tort reform to limit suits, 28, 173n39
trademark cases, 187n36
traffic accidents and cell phone use, 62–63
transactional cases, 157n15
transparency, vii, 1–2, 3, 56–83.
See also discovery
access to information about
previously settled cases, 140
administrative agencies and,
62–63, 56–57
arbitration's effect on, 73, 178n27
argument that it contravenes the
inherent private dispute aspect of
litigation, 175n4
Catholic Church sexual abuse
scandal, 76, 179n31, 179n34
discovery, 8, 23, 56–57, 58–69
Firestone tires litigation, 76–77
increasing number of lawsuits, 80,
156n12, 157n15
information asymmetry and, 23, 60,
69, 79, 175n5, 178n22
in jury trials, 107
legislation and, 58, 87, 174n1
public value of, 62–63, 82–83
qualified immunity doctrine
and, 81–82
risk management and, 61–62
settlement and, 27, 56–58, 75–80,
148, 178n26
as social good, 57
state secrets privilege and, 73–75,
178n26, 179n29

transparency (*Cont.*)
  threats to, 72–82, 178n27
  trials enabling, 66–67
trials. *See also* juries and jury service
  "bellwether" trials, 93, 97, 139,
    148, 184n19
  class actions, participation of
    individual plaintiffs in, 92.
    See also class actions
  judge and jury role, 138, 144
  rate of, 13–15, 100, 144, 181n4
  relation to settlements, 185n23
  transparency achieved
    through, 66–67
Turner v. Rogers (2011), 102–103,
    146, 187n37

unconscionability, doctrine of, 26
*United States v. See name of
    opposing party*
unbundling legal services,
    132, 195n35
unpredictability
  of case outcomes, 132,
    196n36, 198n2
  of juries, 101–102, 106, 136, 186n32,
    186n34, 196n36
  of punitive damages, 196n36
"uphill" vs. "downhill" cases, 7,
    130, 155n10
US Army inspection of Odwalla juice
    plant, 56–57
US Chamber of Commerce, 152nn2–3

V.L. v. E.L.(2016), 64, 176n14.

values
  American value of adversarial
    system, 198n2
  American value of
    decentralization, 39
  contesting of, 155n7
  transparency and, 62–63, 82–83
verdicts. *See* jury verdicts
Vietnam veterans and Agent Orange,
    93, 184n20
vindication of rights doctrine, 26
Vioxx litigation, 11, 36–37, 91, 93, 133,
    139, 183n15, 184n19, 196n37
Volkswagen, 68
Voltaire, 20
voting. *See* elections and voting

Warner/Chappell and "Happy
    Birthday" song, 64
Washington Post, 3–4
Weigel, Natasha, 48, 58
Weinstein, Jack, 88–89, 93, 183n10,
    183n14, 184n16
whistleblowers, 64, 75, 176n14
Wood v. Moss (2014), 81–82, 180n39
wrongful death, 73–75, 196n41

Yeazell, Stephen, 80, 179n37
  Yoshino, Kenji, 66, 177n17,
    191n14, 192n18
Young, William G., 147, 185n27, 199n6

Zeier v. Zimmer, Inc. (2006),
    120–121, 192n15
Zyprexa (drug) litigation, 91, 183n14